The Incredible Years

A Trouble-Shooting Guide for Parents of Children Aged 2-8 Years

Carolyn Webster-Stratton, Ph.D.

The Incredible Years
A Trouble-Shooting Guide for Parents of Children Aged 2-8

Original copyright © 1992 by Carolyn Webster-Stratton *The Incredible Years A Trouble-Shooting Guide for Parents of Children Aged 3-8*, reprinted 1994, 1996, 1997, 1998, 1999, 2000, 2001, 2002, 2003, 2004, 2005, 2006.

Illustrations by David Mostyn
Book design by Janice St. Marie

Webster-Stratton, Carolyn
The Incredible Years

Includes bibliographical references and index.
ISBN 978-1-892222-04-6

Publisher:

Incredible Years
1411 8th Avenue West
Seattle, WA 98119 USA
206-285-7565
www.incredibleyears.com

Printed in USA

For Mary and Len, my parents
Seth and Anna, my children
John, my husband

Acknowledgments

I owe a great deal to the many families with whom I've worked over the past 25 years. They have taught me so much about parenting and children—without them this book would not have been written. Next, I am indebted to the staff of the Parenting Clinic at the University of Washington—not only did these colleagues provide quality data to evaluate these concepts and principles, but they also contributed invaluable insights into family interactions and common problems.

Next, I am indebted to several researchers for their outstanding research on family and child interactions. In particular, the chapter on Play evolved from the clinical writings of Dr. Connie Hanf at the Oregon School of Medicine; the chapters on Ignore, Time Out, and Commands grew out of the pioneering research on childhood aggression conducted by Dr. Jerry Patterson and Dr. John Reid and their colleagues at the Oregon Social Learning Center; the chapter on Communication and Problem Solving emerged from the critical theoretical and intervention research by Dr. John Gottman and Dr. Neil Jacobsen at the University of Washington; the chapter on Self-Control came from the research regarding depression by Dr. Aron Beck at the University of Pennsylvania; and finally the chapter on Problem Solving with Children evolved from the early research of Myrna Shure and G. Spivak. These researchers have provided the theoretical bases and rationale for the context discussed in this book.

Special thanks to Dr. Jamila Reid for her careful review and input regarding the new chapters in this book and to Lisa St. George for her copy editing and production managing.

Last but not least, thank you to my daughter Anna and my son Seth for teaching me so much about myself as a parent.

Contents

Introduction   17

    Promoting Responsive and Sensitive Parenting   18
    The Attention Rule   18
    Children Will Live Up To or Down To Parent's Expectations   18
    Nonviolent Discipline   19
    Accept Each Child's Unique Temperament   19
    Use Parental Power Responsibly   20
    Practice Makes Perfect   20
    All Children Have Behavior Problems   21
    All Parents Make Mistakes   21
    Enjoy Parenting   21
    Background for the Book   22
    How the Guide is Organized   23
    To Sum Up...   25

PART ONE: Foundations for Successful Parenting

Chapter One: How to Play with Your Child   29

    Follow Your Child's Lead   30
    Pace the Play to Suit Your Child   30
    Be Sensitive to Your Child's Cues   31
    Avoid Power Struggles   31
    Praise and Encourage Your Child's Ideas and Creativity   32
    Encourage Emotional Understanding Through Fantasy or Pretend Play   33
    Be an Appreciative Audience   34
    Use Descriptive Commenting   34
    Use Academic Coaching to Promote School Readiness Skills   35
    Use Emotion Coaching to Promote Emotional Literacy   36
    Coaching Positive Peer Play   37
    Encourage Your Child's Independent Problem Solving   37
    Give Attention to Play   38
    A Word of Caution   39
    To Sum Up...   40

Chapter Two: Positive Attention, Encouragement and Praise   41

    Does praise spoil children?   42
    Should children know how to behave?   42
    Is praise manipulative and phony?   42
    Should praise be saved for outstanding performances?   43
    Does behavior have to change before praise is given?   44
    What about the child who rejects praise?   44
    Do some parents find it harder than others to praise their children?   44
    Is there a difference between encouragement and praise?   46
    Making Praise More Effective   46
    Be Specific   47

Praise Appropriately   47

Show Enthusiasm   47

Avoid Combining Praise with Put-Downs   48

Praise Immediately   49

Target Specific Behaviors You Want to Encourage According to Your Child's Individual Needs   50

Behavior Doesn't Have to Be Perfect to Deserve Recognition   50

Encourage Children to Praise Themselves and Others   50

Doubling the Impact   51

To Sum Up...   51

Chapter Three: Tangible Rewards, Incentives and Celebrations   52

Examples of Tangible Rewards   54

Establishing Objectives   56

Be Specific about Appropriate Behaviors   56

Make the Steps Small and Work Up to Bigger Goals   56

Pace the Steps Correctly   57

Choose the Number of Behaviors Carefully   58

Focus on Positive Behaviors   59

Choosing Rewards   60

Choose Inexpensive Rewards   60

Calculate Daily and Weekly Rewards   61

Involve Children in the Program   62

Appropriate Behavior, Then the Reward   63

Use Tangible Rewards for Everyday Achievements   63

Replace Tangible Rewards with Social Approval   64

Have Clear and Specific Reward Menus   65

Have a Varied Menu   66

Be Sure Your Incentives are Age Appropriate   67

Be Positive   67

Keep Reward Programs and Discipline Separate   67

Keep Control of your Program   68

Working with Teachers   69

To Sum Up...   69

Chapter Four: Limit Setting   70

Reduce Commands   70

One Command at a Time   72

Give Realistic Commands   72

Give Clear Commands   73

Give "Do" Commands   74

Polite Commands   75

Use Start Commands   75

Allow Time to Comply   76

Give Warnings and Reminders   76

"When—Then" Commands   77

Give Options   77
Give Short Commands   77
Supportive Commands   78
Follow Through with Praise or Consequences   78
To Sum Up...   79

Chapter Five: Ignore   81

Avoid Discussion and Eye Contact   81
Use Consistent Ignoring—Be Prepared for Misbehavior to Get Worse at First   82
Ignore and Distract   83
Move Away from your Child but Stay in the Room   84
Ignoring Teaches Self-control   84
Teach Others to Ignore   84
Limit the Number of Behaviors to Ignore   85
Certain Behaviors Should not be Ignored   85
Examples of Behaviors That Can Be Effectively Ignored in Preschool Children   86
Pay Attention to Positive Behaviors   86
Give Back Your Attention as Soon as Possible   87
Use Subtle Ignores   87
Stay in Charge   87
To Sum Up...   88

Chapter Six: Time Out to Calm Down   90

Steps to Setting Up Time Out   91
Time Out location   92
Describe the challenging behaviors that will result in Time Out   92
Time Out length   93
Keys to initiating Time Out   93
Set a timer   94
End of Time Out: calm for two minutes   94
Follow Through: repeat the command for noncompliance   94
Responding to Children Who Refuse to Go to Time Out   95
Refusing to Stay in Time Out   96
Initially Misbehavior will Get Worse   97
Be Positive   97
Teach Your Child How to Take a Time Out   97
Pitfalls to Implementing Time Out   97
Edit Criticisms and Nagging   97
Identify Problems Early   98
Expecting Remorse   99
Five-Minute Time Out with Two Minutes of Quiet   99
Overuse of Time Out   100
Don't Wait to Explode   101
Freedom within Limits   101
"If—Then" Warnings and Follow-Through   102
Avoid Interaction During Time Out   102
Avoid Physical Restraint   103

Refusals to Come Out of Time Out   103
No Time Out Room Available   104
Other Power Struggles   104
Other Principles of Time Out   105
Hold Children Responsible   105
Expect Persistence   105
Time Out in Public   106
Pace Yourself   107
Support Each Other   107
There is No Instant Solution   108
Build Up Your Account with Love and Support   108
Time Out for Parents   109
Moving Beyond Discipline   110
To Sum Up...   110

Chapter Seven: Natural and Logical Consequences   111

Examples of Natural Consequences   111
Examples of Logical Consequences   111
Be Sure Your Expectations are Age Appropriate   112
Be Sure You Can Live with the Choices   113
Consequences Should Be Fairly Immediate   113
Give Your Child Choices Ahead of Time   114
Consequences Should Be Natural or Logical and Nonpunitive   115
Involve Your Child Whenever Possible   115
Be Straightforward and Friendly   116
Consequences Should Be Appropriate   116
To Sum Up...   117

Chapter Eight: Teaching Children to Problem Solve   118

Parent as Model   119
STEP ONE: Discuss Hypothetical Problems   120
STEP TWO: Brainstorm Solutions   121
STEP THREE: Think Through Consequences   122
STEP FOUR: What Is The Best Solution or Choice?   122
STEP FIVE: Implementation of Problem-solving Skills   123
STEP SIX: Evaluating Outcome   123
Discover Your Child's View of the Problem First   124
Encourage Your Child to Come Up with Multiple Solutions   124
Guided Problem Solving   125
Be Positive and Fun   125
Ask about Feelings   126
Encourage Many Solutions   127
Use Open-Ended Questioning and Paraphrasing   127
Think about Positive and Negative Consequences   127
Model Your Thinking Out Loud   128
Focus on Thinking and Self-Management   128
Praise and More Praise   131
To Sum Up...   131

Chapter Nine: Helping Children Learn to Regulate Their Emotions 133

What Is Emotional Regulation? 134
How Quickly Do Children Learn Emotional Regulation? 135
Here Are Some Ways You Can Help 136
Provide Stability and Consistency 136
Accept Your Child's Emotions and Emotional Responses 136
Talk About Your Own Feelings 136
Encourage Children to Talk Freely About Feelings 137
Model Emotional Regulation 137
Teach Positive Self-Talk 138
Identify Tough Situations and Use Them as Springboards to Teach
    Problem Solving 139
Teach the "Turtle Technique" 140
Help Children Recognize Stages in the Build Up of Tension 141
Use Time Out for Inappropriate Emotional Angry Outbursts 142
Teach Appropriate Expression of Negative Feelings 143
Avoid Letting It All Hang Out 144
Praise Children's Efforts to Regulate Their Emotions 144
Alter Child's Self-Image and Paint a Positive Future 145
To Sum Up... 145

Chapter Ten: Teaching Children Friendship Skills and Ways To Cope with Peer Problems 146

Why Are Children's Friendships Important? 147
Why Do Some Children Have More Difficulty Making Friends? 147
What Can Parents Do? 148
Teach Children How to Initiate an Interaction and Enter a Group 148
Play Daily with your Child to Model and Encourage Social Skills 149
Help Your Child Learn How to Talk with Friends 150
Set up Play Dates at Home—and Provide Careful Monitoring 150
Coach and Praise Social Skills During Peer Play at Home 151
Teaching Problem Solving/Conflict Resolution 153
Teach Your Child to Use Positive Self-talk 154
Helping Your Child Control Anger 154
Encourage Positive Peer Contacts in the Community 155
Collaborating with Teachers 155
Empathy Training 157
To Sum Up... 157

PART TWO: Communicating and Problem Solving

Chapter Eleven: Controlling Upsetting Thoughts 161

Step One: Be Aware of Your Negative and Positive Thoughts 163
Step Two: Decrease Your Negative Thoughts 163
Step Three: Increasing Positive Thoughts 165

Refute Negative Labels and Focus on Specific Positive Behaviors   167
Avoid Speculations about Intentions   168
Think Positively   168
Thought-Stop and Substitute Coping Thoughts   169
Normalize and Dispute Negative Self-Talk   170
Think about Long-Term Goals   171
Objectify and Normalize   171
Focus on Being Calm and Using "I" Messages to Receive Support   173
Focus on Coping   174
Modeling Coping Self-Talk   174
To Sum Up...   175

Chapter Twelve: Time Out From Stress and Anger   176

Time Out for a Breather   177
Time Out on the Go   178
Time Out for Visualizing and Imagining   178
Time Out to Control Anger   178
Self-Talk about Stress   180
Personal Time Out   180
To Sum Up...   181

Chapter Thirteen: Effective Communication Skills   182

Active Listening   182
Speaking Up   185
Feeling-Talk   187
Stop Action and Refocus   189
Be Polite and Positive and Edit Your Complaints   189
Focus on Fixing the Problem, Not the Blame   192
A Problem is Always Legitimate   193
Focus on Realistic Changes   194
Ask What the Other Person Is Thinking and Feeling   194
Be Calm and Stop Action   194
Announce Your Filter and Get Feedback   195
Edit Complaints and Make Positive Recommendations   196
Strive for Consistent Messages   197
Give Positive Requests and Commands   197
To Sum Up...   198

Chapter Fourteen: Problem Solving Between Adults   199

Six Steps to Effective Problem Solving   200
STEP ONE: Set aside a time and place and decide on an agenda   200
STEP TWO: State and define the problem   200
STEP THREE: Summarize goals and expectations   201
STEP FOUR: Brainstorm solutions   201
STEP FIVE: Make a plan   202
STEP SIX: Evaluation of outcome   203
Defining the Problem   203
Collaboration   203

Be Positive   204
Be Specific and Clear   204
Express Your Feelings   204
Be Future-oriented   205
Be Brief and Keep to One Problem at a Time   205
Goals and Expectations   206
Reflect and Summarize   206
State the Goal and Desired Behaviors   206
Brainstorming Solutions   207
Be Open   207
Postpone Details   207
Be Creative and Innovative   207
Making a Plan   208
Review Your List   208
Evaluating Ideas   208
Identify Barriers and Possible Ways to Overcome Them   209
Write the Plan Down   209
Schedule the Next Meeting   209
Praise Your Efforts   210
To Sum Up...   211

Chapter Fifteen: Working With Teachers To Prevent Problems   212

Why Should You Form a Partnership with Your Child's Teacher?   212
Start Connections with Teachers Right Away   213
Work to Maintain Regular Communication   214
Have a Parent Involvement Plan   214
Set Up a Study Routine at Home   214
Join Parent Education Groups   215
Recognize the Value of a Teacher-Parent Partnership Model   215
Having A Successful School Conference Meeting   216
Some Communication Guidelines for Conferencing About a Problem
    in the Classroom   219
Address Problems Early On – They are Easier to Solve   219
Speaking Up About Your Concerns   219
Obtaining Teacher Input   221
Be Polite and Positive and Edit Your Complaints   222
Focus on Fixing the Problem   222
Continue to Advocate for Your Child   223
Express Hope   223
Agree on Mutual Goals and Brainstorm Solutions   223
Express Confidence in Teacher   224
Plan Follow Up   224
When to Involve School Counselor or Principal   226
Adopt a Unified, Productive Approach In Front of Children   226
Take a Long Term Perspective   226
To Sum Up...   227

PART THREE: Coping with Common Behavior Problems

Problem One: Taking Control of Your Child's
  "Screen Time"   231
Problem Two: Behavior in Public Places   240
Problem Three: Dawdling   244
Problem Four: Sibling Rivalry and Fights
  Between Children   248
Problem Five: Child Disobedience   256
Problem Six: Resistance to Going to Bed   261
Problem Seven: Nighttime Wakenings   265
Problem Eight: Stealing   268
Problem Nine: Lying   271
Problem Ten: Mealtime Problems   275
Problem Eleven: Bed Wetting   281
Problem Twelve: Hyperactivity, Impulsivity and Short
  Attention Span   285
Problem Thirteen: Helping Your Children with Divorce   293
Problem Fourteen: Fears   300
Problem Fifteen: "Reading with Care" to Promote Your Child's
  Reading Skills   308

Selected Readings   313
Index   317

Author's Comments About the Revision
Responsive and Nurturing Parenting
Sets the Stage for Children's Social, Emotional and Academic Development

I wrote *The Incredible Years* book almost 15 years ago in order to help parents feel more confident in coping with behavior problems that occur all too frequently in young children. Since then we have used this book at the University of Washington Parenting Clinic as the text for those enrolled in our parenting groups. Our own research, as well as that of other professionals working to support positive parenting throughout the world have indicated that the principles of managing children's behavior and establishing positive relationships with them are pretty universal. While parents' goals for their children may differ, with some parents wanting to encourage their children's obedience and commitment to community while others want to promote creativity or independence, there is also remarkable similarity which transcends culture. Most parents want their children to do well in school, to respect their parents, to be happy and healthy and to have close and supportive friends. The book has been translated into 7 languages—Spanish, Vietnamese, Cambodian, Norwegian, Swedish, Dutch, and Danish and has received positive evaluations from diverse, multi-ethnic populations.

I have decided to publish a revision at this time, not because the material in the prior edition is outdated or erroneous, but rather to broaden the focus of the book to include an emphasis on promoting children's social, emotional and academic competence as well as strategies for reducing behavior problems. Consequently, in Part One, a new Chapter Nine discusses parenting strategies that will help your children learn how to regulate their emotions and a new Chapter Ten details strategies for helping your children learn social skills and make lasting friendships. In Part Two, Chapter Fifteen, you will find new information about how you can partner with your child's teacher to promote his or her school success. Other minor changes have been made throughout the book, but you might note in particular a new section in Part Three regarding ways to respond to children's fears and anxieties as well as strategies that will help your child learn to read. I hope you will continue to enjoy learning about parenting and playing every day with your children, for these opportunities offer the next generation the necessary nurturing and hope to equip them for the future.

Introduction

Parenting children ages three to eight years can be a difficult time for both parents and children. For children it is a period of major transitions when they are moving from a world where fantasy and reality are often confused to a more concrete world where rules and ideas become permanent. One minute they need security and affection, and the next they need to be independent and prove they can do things by themselves. It is a time when they test the limits of their environment, finding out what will or will not be tolerated. When they move out of the home to preschool and kindergarten, they discover there are new rules and responses from other adults and children. And as children experience these conflicting needs and pressures, they may throw tantrums, whine or become destructive when they don't get their own way; or they may lie or steal in order to get what they want or to get attention; or they may withdraw and avoid feared situations. Did you know that one out of four social interactions with another child in preschool is aggressive? Or, that approximately 70% of toddlers have at least one temper tantrum a day?

For parents, these reactions and behaviors are often surprising, and sometimes difficult to handle. As your children grow from infants to preschoolers, you may feel a sense of loss of control over their experiences, and anger when they refuse to cooperate. You will probably feel anxiety about their vulnerability and concern that they do well in school and make friends. Often you may wonder how much discipline or control they need versus how much freedom. You may frequently feel guilty about not having handled a problem more effectively or about having perhaps expected too much from them. And you may not realize just how much stress is created when children misbehave. In fact, parenting is probably one of the hardest jobs an adult will undertake, but probably also the one for which the least amount of training and preparation is provided.

I have written this guide to help parents sort out, or troubleshoot, the issues they face with young children and to set the stage for sensitive, nurturing and competent parenting that fosters positive social behaviors in children as well as enhanced self-esteem. It is my belief that by learning the most effective parenting approaches, parents can reduce their children's behavior problems before they get out of control and can strengthen their social, emotional and academic competence. While this book provides specific and detailed strategies, there are a number of themes that run through the chapters.

Promoting Responsive and Sensitive Parenting

This guide is based on psychological principles of how behavior is learned and changed. Rather than seeing behavior problems as the fault of a child for being bad or of parents for being inept, I believe the most competent parents are those who are sensitive to the interaction between themselves and their children. That is, they learn how to be responsive to the temperaments of their children and the cues that their children give them they are ready to learn and they use these cues to guide their parenting responses. For example, the parent who notices when their child is getting frustrated and offers just enough support and guidance (without taking over) to give their child a sense of accomplishment. Or, the parent of a hyperactive and impulsive child who adjusts his or her expectations to understand that their child is socially and emotionally younger than other children the same age and needs additional monitoring and support to learn social skills and to follow through with instructions.

In a sense the parent is a kind of "coach" for their children, understanding what children are capable of learning (according to their development and temperament), cheering them on for their small steps towards mastering something new, and guiding them to achieve appropriate goals with support and nurturing.

The Attention Rule

The "attention rule" is the basic principle behind much of what is discussed in the following pages. Simply stated, it is that children will work for attention from others, especially parents, whether it is positive (praise) or negative (criticism) in nature. If children do not receive positive attention, then they will strive for negative attention through misbehavior since that is better than none at all. Therefore, if you want to promote more prosocial behaviors you need to give your child attention when he is exhibiting some of these behaviors.

Children Will Live Up To or Down To Parents' Expectations

Children recognize their parents' expectations for them much quicker than most people realize. If parents label their children negatively by telling them how bad or incapable they are, the youngsters may come to believe this image of themselves. Therefore, parents need to think positively about their children and project positive images of their future and their ability to successfully cope with situations. Statements such as, "Let's try again" and "You'll do better next time" and "You stayed calm and patient and that was frustrating" give children confidence to learn from their mistakes.

Nonviolent Discipline

Parents need to develop an ethical approach to discipline that teaches their children that there are consequences for misbehaving, while at the same time letting them know they are loved and expected to do better next time. The position taken here is that there are serious disadvantages to spanking and physical punishment as a discipline strategy and many alternative nonviolent approaches that provide better long-term results for the child's emotional and social development as well as for the parents' ongoing relationship with the child.

Accept Each Child's Unique Temperament

The key to using this book successfully is for parents to understand, appreciate, accept and adapt to the unique temperament and development of each individual child and to highlight their strengths as well as accept their limitations. By temperament, I'm referring to a person's natural, innate style of behaving and traits such as activity level, mood, intensity, adaptability, impulsivity and persistence. Think about your children—are they slowpokes and dreamers, or moody and hypersensitive, or perhaps they are social butterflies, flibbertigibbets, and chatty, or on the other hand, reserved, somewhat withdrawn and quiet? Perhaps one of your children is even-keeled, malleable and cooperative and the other the opposite—stubborn, resistant to change and inattentive.

There is a wide range of normal in regard to temperament traits. Studies have shown that 10-20 percent of normal children have temperaments which would be considered "difficult." These are children who are highly active or impulsive with a short attention span and they are much harder for parents to manage. Such personality traits are not related to intelligence, they are associated with uneven neurological development. Therefore, it is important if you are the parent of one of these children to remember that these behaviors are not intentional, nor are they deliberate attempts to thwart your efforts. And while you can help temperamentally difficult children manage behaviors and channel their energy in a positive direction, you can't fundamentally change these traits—nor would you want to. No one can make hyperactive, energetic, boisterous youngsters into quiet, reserved ones. Such an attempt will not only be frustrating for parents, but harmful to children. These children will each have their own kind of adjustments to make to the real world and parents can help best by being tolerant, patient, accepting, and understanding of their children's temperaments—in order for them to reach their full potential.

Use Parental Power Responsibly

One of the most basic areas of confusion among parents is whether or not a family is a democracy. If parents feel it is one, composed of equals, then they usually avoid leadership and back off from discipline. But a family is not a democracy—neither power nor responsibility are equally distributed between children and adults. In order to feel secure children need their parents to provide behavior control and decision making in the early years because they can't solve problems alone. They need to be taught to share, wait, respect others and accept responsibility for their behavior. Although limit setting may make children feel frustrated and resentful, it helps them learn self-control and to balance their wishes against those or others.

Parents must learn to use their power responsibly however. They need to determine which problems need firm discipline and close monitoring (such as destructive behaviors and not complying) and which can be left up to their children (such as what they eat or wear). The key is to strive for a workable balance of power. So as long as children behave appropriately, they may be given some control; when they behave inappropriately, their parents have to assume control. If children are never given any control in family relationships, power struggles will occur and they will strive to get control in inappropriate ways (such as refusing to get dressed). In order to foster cooperative relationships in a family and promote children's self-confidence and eventual independence parents must avoid being too permissive or authoritarian. Necessary commands and discipline should be balanced by warmth, praise and sensitivity to children's special needs.

Practice Makes Perfect

As parents try out strategies outlined here with their children, they may feel artificial or even phony, especially if it is the first time they have used a particular technique. This awkwardness is a normal reaction whenever people are learning anything new. Don't be discouraged by the apparent complexity and don't expect to feel comfortable immediately. With practice, these parenting skills become more natural until you will use them automatically.

Keep your radar antennae turned on at all times.

All Children Have Behavior Problems

It is important to remember that it is normal for children to have behavior problems and they are likely to be controlled if they are managed appropriately. Although such problems can't be stamped out, being creative and trying out strategies will make a big difference. Parents should not be alarmed if after an initial period of progress with managing a particular behavior problem, children revert. Progress is marked by spurts, regressions, consolidation and further growth.

All Parents Make Mistakes

Just as all children have behavior problems so do all parents feel angry, guilty, frustrated, helpless or incompetent at times. Parents, like children, learn, experiment, and make mistakes all the time. There is no permanent harm done to children when parents make mistakes since they are remarkably flexible and resilient. The important thing is that children see their parents continuing to learn and cope in more effective ways. The purpose of this guide is to stimulate new ideas, warn of pitfalls, recognize learning opportunities and help parents find what will work best for them and their children.

Enjoy Parenting

Since this guide presents many do's and don'ts, things to remember and things to avoid, parents may mistakenly believe there is a perfect solution that can be followed consistently. Or they may worry there is no room for spontaneity or fun. This is not true. If parents are confident and ready for inevitable problems and pitfalls, there will be room for flexibility, whimsy, and creativity. For instance, if a reserved child finally opens up five minutes before bedtime, a confident and sensitive parent will realize that this is a good time to make an exception to a rule and let the child stay up later. Consistency is a virtue but not when it becomes an inflexible policy. Once parents understand the temperament and developmental stage of their children, as well as the basic behavioral principles discussed in this guide, then they can try out different strategies, adapt the advice to suit their priorities and enjoy the creative process of parenting. Indeed, there is no magic blueprint or pat formula for parenting. Every situation is different and parents must invent their own parenting style that will work best for them. They need to have faith in their children and in their own common sense and imagination as they and their children learn together.

Background for the Book

The Incredible Years is based on research at the Parenting Clinic at the University of Washington. Over the past 25 years we have collaborated with, studied, and conducted parenting programs with over 3000 parents

Promoting parents' problem-solving and effective coping strategies.

who have children between the ages of three and eight with behavior problems. The primary purpose of this research has been to design effective treatment programs to help families whose young children are highly unmanageable. As a result we have studied youngsters with relatively minor problems, such as whining and throwing tantrums, and those with more severe problems, such as lying and stealing. We have also worked with all kinds of families: two-parent families, single-parent families, step-families, adoptive and foster families. We have worked with families from many different cultures including Asian, Hispanic, African American and East African families. Not only have we observed them a minimum of eight times in their homes, we have also observed them playing with their children. These families have shared their parenting styles, experiences and problems with us. In addition, we have obtained information from the teachers of these children. As a result of these studies plus additional work with families who have children who exhibit few behavior problems, we have been able to determine the most effective parenting techniques. This information has provided the basis for this book.

Data from our studies indicate that parents who have taken our courses have been able to reduce their children's inappropriate behaviors and increase their children's social and emotional competence. They have learned to be nurturing and sensitive parents. Moreover, parents report that they feel confident and comfortable with their discipline strategies. It is our hope that by creating this guide, we will be able to reach more parents and help them manage their preschool and school-age children with confidence, joy, respect and a spirit of cooperation. If a family's problems are relatively mild, this guide may help smooth out rough edges. Families involved in long-standing struggles may not be able to change what is going on simply by reading the guide. In such cases, they should seek out the support of a therapist to help make some of the necessary changes.

How the Guide is Organized

It is important to read through the chapters in the order in which they are presented as each one builds on the knowledge presented in the previous one. Of course, it is likely that parents will be tempted to turn first to the chapter that interests them the most, or the situation they are struggling with. However, parents are still encouraged to start at the beginning of the book and read the entire guide. As can be seen in the picture of the pyramid below, the first three chapters focus on building

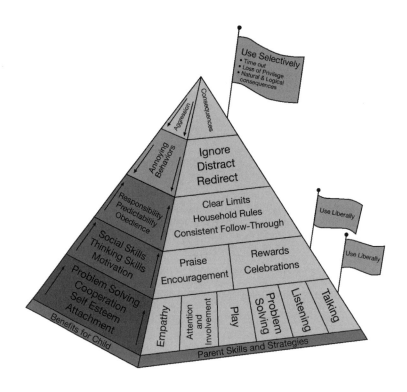

Parenting Pyramid

the pyramid's foundation by learning parenting approaches that will create a strong bond or attachment between you and your child. This positive relationship will give you opportunities to encourage positive behaviors and build your child's self-esteem and social competence. Many parents find that when they focus on the material covered in these chapters, they have less of a need for discipline or that discipline goes much more smoothly. As we progress up the pyramid, Chapters Four and Five focus on how you limit set with children and how to respond when children do not obey. The next two chapters discuss other non-violent approaches that will help parents to avoid confrontations and to reduce negative behaviors. The eighth chapter focuses on teaching children how to problem solve, so that they can learn to cope with conflicts and come up with their own solutions to problems. Chapter Nine focuses on emotional regulation and Chapter Ten friendship skills. At the end of Part One, parents will have the basics of what we feel are the most effective parent management strategies. Notice that the skills learned on the lower levels of the pyramid are the parenting strategies that are used the most often with children.

Part Two of the guide focuses on issues related more to parents' interpersonal skills than parenting skills per se. The first two chapters cover personal self-control strategies and help parents understand how to cope with depressing, angry, frustrating and hopeless thoughts about their skills on their children. Chapter Eleven emphasizes self-control in terms of challenging and changing thought processes while Chapter Twelve emphasizes physical control through relaxation exercises and ways to manage life stress. The next chapter discusses effective communication strategies to use with children and adults. The following chapter focuses on adult relationships so parents can learn how to discuss family problems together in a noncritical and cooperative way, and how to come up with solutions. The final chapter in Part Two discusses how you can use the communication and problem solving strategies to develop collaborative partnerships with your children's teachers. Developing these partnerships will help promote consistency in approaches and goals from home to school as well as provide support for both yourself and your child's teacher.

Part Three applies the principles learned in the first two sections to common problems, including dawdling, resistance to going to bed, hyperactivity, mealtime problems, sibling fights, fears of separating from parents or particular situations and learning to read. In these chapters, possible reasons for each problem are presented followed by practical suggestions about what to do.

To Sum Up...

The social, emotional and academic development of children is an incredible process—as is the growth and development of parents! Give yourself permission to enjoy this process by trusting your instincts, learning from your blunders, laughing at your mistakes and imperfections, getting support from others, taking time for yourself, and by having fun with your children. It is the incredible years—with all its tears, guilt, anger, laughter, joy and love.

PART ONE

Foundations for Successful Parenting

CHAPTER ONE

How To Play With Your Child

There is a widespread belief in our society that the time parents and children spend playing together is frivolous and unproductive. The deep conviction that play is trivial is reflected in comments such as, "She's only playing," "Stop playing around," and "Why bother to send them to preschool? All they do is play." It is also reflected in the tendency for parents to try to teach their children a variety of skills rather than to *just* play with them. In a society that places a tremendous emphasis on achievement in school, economic success and the importance of work, it is difficult to break loose from the idea that play is a waste of time.

But we should break loose from this idea because play benefits children in many ways by providing opportunities for them to learn who they are, what they can do and how to relate to the world around them. Sometimes parents realize the benefits of play but see no need to get personally involved in it. They mistakenly assume that play is instinctive—the one thing that children can do for themselves without adult help. It is true that very young children engage in a certain amount of spontaneous play, but it is also true that the instinct toward creative play gradually disappears without adult intervention to stimulate its development.

For these reasons and many more, it's important for you to play with your children. Play helps to build a warm relationship and strong attachments between family members and to create a bank of positive feelings and experiences that can be drawn upon in times of conflict. Through play, you can help your children to solve problems, test out ideas and explore their imaginations. As well, playtime with adults encourages the development of vocabulary so that children learn to communicate their thoughts, feelings and needs. It also helps them to interact socially by teaching them how to take turns, share and be sensitive to the feelings of others. Moreover, play is a time when you can respond to your children in ways that promote feelings of self-worth and competence. Studies have shown that children tend to be more creative and have fewer behavior problems if their parents engage in make-believe and fantasy with them when they are young.

Unfortunately, the fact remains that most parents do not play with their children, and all too often the reason is simply that they don't know how. The following pages therefore offer some pointers on how to play with your children and how to avoid the most common pitfalls parents encounter when playing with their children.

Follow Your Child's Lead

Some parents try to structure their child's play by giving lessons on what to do—how to build the castle the *right* way, to make the perfect valentine or complete a puzzle correctly. Possibly they believe this will make play a worthwhile activity. Unfortunately, the result of this undue emphasis on the product of play is a string of commands and corrections that usually make the experience unrewarding for both children and adults.

Consider for instance, what happens when Lisa and her mother settle down to play with Lisa's new doll house. Mom says, "First let's put the fridge and stove in the kitchen." Lisa suggests a place for the kitchen, and her mother responds, "Okay, and now all these other kitchen things must go over there too." She then goes on to say, "And the living room furniture must go here." As Lisa begins to put some of the furniture in the living room, her mother shows her where to put the bathroom items. Soon Lisa stops playing, sits back, and watches her mother organize everything in the *correct* rooms. By now, Lisa's mother is doing all the playing and has no idea what Lisa might have wanted to do with the doll house. If she had waited she might have found that Lisa's play was highly imaginative, with beds that could fly and living room furniture in every room.

The first step in playing with your children is to follow their lead, ideas and imagination rather than imposing your own. Don't structure or organize activities for them by giving commands or instructions. Don't try to teach them anything. Instead, imitate their actions and do what they ask you to do. You'll soon discover that when you sit back and give them a chance to exercise their imagination, they become more involved and interested in playing, as well as more creative. This approach will also foster the development of your children's ability to play and think independently.

Pace the Play to Suit Your Child

When young children are playing, they tend to repeat the same activity over and over again. How often have you seen a toddler repeatedly fill and empty a box? How often have you groaned inwardly when asked to read the same story yet again? Certainly, repetitive play soon bores most parents, and it's tempting to quicken the pace by introducing some new idea or a more sophisticated way of using a toy. The problem is that children need to rehearse and practice an activity in order to master it and feel confident about their abilities. If they are pushed into a new activity, they may feel incompetent. Or they may get frustrated and give up playing with their parents because they feel the challenge is too great. In the end, they feel they're not able to meet their parents' expectations.

Be sure to pace the play according to your child's tempo. Allow plenty of time for him to use his imagination. Don't push him simply because you are bored—wait until he decides on his own to do something different. Remember, children move much more slowly from one idea to another than adults. Pacing slowly will help to expand your child's attention span and encourage him to concentrate on one activity for a period of time.

Be Sensitive to Your Child's Cues

Sometimes parents present play ideas or toys that are too advanced for a child's developmental level. For instance, a father may think his three-year-old daughter is ready to learn to play tic-tac-toe or to put together a puzzle. As he tries to teach her, he may find that she resists. Very likely, this resistance occurs because she is not developmentally ready for the activity and feels frustrated at being asked to do something that she doesn't understand.

When playing with your child, watch for the clues she gives you. If she's not interested in playing with a puzzle or learning a game, move on to something she does want to do. You can offer new activities periodically, and when she shows interest, you can respond supportively. No matter what play involves, the important thing is for you to give your child time to think, explore and experience. Don't worry if tic-tac-toe or a card game is transformed into something altogether different, such as tickets to a movie, a spinning game or a creative design.

Avoid Power Struggles

Have you ever found yourself in a power struggle with your preschooler over who won a game, what the rules are, or which picture is best? If so, you're not alone. Many parents unwittingly set up a competitive relationship with their children. When playing board games for instance, they may feel it is necessary to teach them to play by the rules and to be good losers, or they may simply do their part of an activity so well that their children can't help feel incompetent. Consider a mother and son who are playing with building blocks. For a few minutes Billy is happily absorbed in getting the first wall of his house to stay up. When it finally does, he looks to Mom for approval only to find that she has a whole house finished. Billy feels inadequate and he also feels he is somehow involved in a competition with his mom—one, moreover, that he isn't equipped to win. At this point, Billy may give up playing or resort to other ways of getting control of the situation, such as having a tantrum.

Avoid Unnecessary struggles.

The basic importance of play is to foster children's feelings of competence and independence and provide them with opportunities for legitimate control and power. Young children, in fact, are permitted few chances for this in their interactions with adults. Play is the one activity where they can have legitimate control and can, to some extent, set their own rules.

Toddlers and preschoolers don't really understand the rules and sequences of board and card games. Not until they are seven or eight do they begin to show signs of cooperative interaction and even then, their understanding of rules may be somewhat vague. Nonetheless, they can enjoy playing at a game with adults as long as excessive competition and rules are avoided. If they come up with rules that allow them to win, this should be permitted. You don't need to worry about your children not learning to lose—many other aspects of their lives will teach them that and if you cooperate with their rules and model acceptance, then they are more likely to go along with your rules in other situations.

Praise and Encourage Your Child's Ideas and Creativity

It is easy to fall into the trap of correcting your children when they are playing. How often have you heard yourself say, "No, that doesn't go there," or "That's not the right way to do it"? These kinds of criticisms and corrections eventually make children wary of exploring their ideas or experimenting with toys. They also tend to foster helplessness in youngsters because their parents' attention is focused on what is being done wrong rather than on appropriate behavior. Instead of encouraging the creative process, this type of parental emphasis communicates that perfection is the goal of play.

Don't judge, correct or contradict your children while playing with them. Creating and experimenting are what's important, not the finished product. Keep in mind that children's play does not have to make sense to you. Cars can fly and horses can talk. During play, focus on the socially appropriate things that your children are doing. For instance, you might say, "That's great. Your giraffe is a nice red color," or "You've come up with your very own game. How exciting!" Think of ways to praise your children's ideas, thinking and behavior. You can reinforce a variety of skills, such as concentration, persistence, problem solving efforts, inventiveness, expression of feelings, cooperation, motivation and self-confidence. As an exercise in learning how to do this, try to praise something your children do every two to three minutes.

Encourage Emotional Understanding Through Fantasy or Pretend Play
Some adults are reluctant to engage in imaginative play—to crawl on the floor making train noises or to act out fairy tales. They feel silly and embarrassed. Fathers in particular seem to feel uncomfortable playing dolls or dress up games with their children. Other parents tell us that they consider make-believe and fantasy play to be a sign of emotional disturbance.

Encouraging children's pretend play is important not only because it builds children's imaginary worlds, creative thinking and story telling but

Encourage make-believe.

also because it helps children learn about regulating emotions and sharing feelings. When children play make-believe, they are learning to manipulate representations of things rather than the concrete objects themselves. Most healthy youngsters are doing this by the age of three, and some as early as 18 months. Imaginary companions are common among four-year-olds. Play that involves fantasy steadily increases into middle childhood and then begins to disappear. It is important for you to encourage this kind of play because it helps your children to develop a variety of cognitive, emotional and social skills. Allow boxes and chairs to become houses and palaces, and doll figures to turn into relatives, friends or favorite cartoon characters. Fantasy helps children to think symbolically and gives them a better idea of what is real and what isn't. Role-play allows them to experience the feelings of someone else, which helps them to understand and be sensitive to the emotions of others. Encourage the use of puppets, dress up clothes, pretend telephones, play money or discussions about imaginary creatures. Children may be more likely to share painful or scary feelings with their parents in the context of puppet or fantasy play.

Be an Appreciative Audience

It is important to be a good audience when you play with your children. Some parents become so involved in playing that they ignore their children or take over what they are doing. The youngsters end up watching while the parents play. Remember Lisa's mom? And Billy, who ended up feeling inadequate and frustrated because he couldn't do as good a building job as his mom did?

When you play with your children try to focus on them instead of getting involved in what you are doing. Playtime is one of the few situations that children can control as long as they behave appropriately. It is also one of the few times when they can have you applaud what they are doing without a lot of rules and restrictions getting in the way. Try to think of yourself as an appreciative audience. Sit back and watch whatever your children create and praise their efforts with enthusiasm. (And if you really want to make your own fantastic Lego castle or create an artistic masterpiece with that 48-piece set of colored pencils, there's nothing to stop you from doing it once the children are in bed!)

Use Descriptive Commenting

Occasionally parents have a tendency to ask a string of questions while playing: "What animal is that?" "How many spots does it have?" "What shape is that?" "Where does it go?" "What are you making?" By asking many questions, parents usually intend to help their children learn. All too often it has the reverse effect, causing them to become defensive, silent and reluctant to talk freely. In fact, question-asking, especially when parents know the answer, is really a type of command since it requires children to perform. Queries that ask children to define what they are making often occur before they have even thought about the final product or had a chance to explore their ideas. The emphasis ends up being on the product rather than the process of play. And when questions are answered, often parents do not respond with feedback or reinforcement. Such an omission can communicate a lack of interest and enthusiasm.

You can show interest in your children's play by simply describing and providing supportive comments about what they are doing. This approach actively encourages language development. For instance, you might say, "You're putting the car in the garage. Now it's getting gas," and so forth. Soon you will find that your children spontaneously imitate your commenting. You can then praise their learning efforts and they will feel excited about their accomplishments. Descriptive commenting is a running commentary on your children's activities and often sounds like a sports announcer's play-by-play description of a game. Because it is a novel way of communicating, you may feel uncomfortable when you first try to speak this way. The discomfort will diminish as you practice in a variety of situations. And if you are persistent, you will find that your children come to love this kind of attention and that this communication style enhances their vocabulary as well. (Please note that noises such as frog croaks, dog barking and pig grunting also constitute a type of descriptive commenting!)

If you do ask questions, be sure to limit the number and to complete the teaching loop. This means that when you ask a question, you follow a response with positive and noncritical feedback and encouragement. Children should be praised for independent actions and given a chance to respond without interference. For example, if you ask, "What animal is that?" and your child responds, "It's a giraffe," you might add, "Oh, a giraffe. You really do know your animals. And not only that, it's a purple giraffe." Your positive feedback encourages efforts to answer the question and expands on the answer by adding information.

Use Academic Coaching to Promote School Readiness Skills

In addition to describing what your children are doing in their play, you can also describe attributes of the objects they are playing with such as their colors, shapes, numbers, sizes (long, short, tall, smaller than), and

Think of yourself as a sportscaster giving a play-by-play.

positions (up, down, beside, next to, behind). For example, you might say, "You are putting the blue block next to the yellow square, and the purple triangle is on top of the long red rectangle." This kind of language will help your children understand academic concepts and build the vocabulary they need for school-related activities. In addition, you can encourage your children's "on task" behavior by commenting on their ability to think hard, listen carefully, work independently, persist with a difficult task and follow directions. This can be especially helpful for expanding children's ability to sustain their attention or focus on an activity for longer periods of time.

Use Emotion Coaching to Promote Emotional Literacy

The coaching strategies used for teaching children emotions parallel the strategies for teaching them about academic concepts. First of all, identify, name and describe your children's feelings when you play with them. Notice and comment on times when they seem calm, happy, curious, relaxed, excited, confident, proud, frustrated, or tense. This is a very useful way to help children associate their feeling state with the word and will be helpful in promoting their vocabulary for feelings. Eventually they will be able to independently express feelings to others. For children who have one dominant feeling (such as anger or fear or sadness) it can be helpful to expand their repertoire of feelings by helping them to become more aware of times when they are calm and having more joyous or positive feelings. It is also helpful to pair comments about negative feelings with positive coping statements. For example "You look frustrated that your blocks fell over, but I see that you're staying calm and trying again."

Parents can also share their own feelings of enjoyment with their children. This will strengthen the bond between you and your children. Moreover, this emotional sharing on your part is modeling appropriate expression of feelings for children to learn.

Coaching Positive Peer Play

While adult play one-on-one with a single child is immensely valuable in strengthening the bond between you and your child, there are also benefits to your play with two or three children. If your child has siblings or friends who have come for a "play date" you can use this opportunity to coach your children's social skills. This time you will describe their social behaviors such as sharing, waiting, taking turns, helping another, saying thank you, asking before taking another's toy, and giving a friendly suggestion. This approach will strengthen your children's friendships. For example, you can say, "That's so friendly. You are sharing your blocks and waiting your turn." Or, "You listened to your friend's suggestion. That is so friendly." You can also prompt certain behaviors such as saying thank you, giving a compliment or apologizing. For example, "Look at what your friend has made. Do you think you can give him a compliment?" and then if your child gives a compliment, you can praise him/her.

Encourage Your Child's Independent Problem Solving

Sometimes when parents are trying to be helpful, they make it difficult for their children to learn how to problem-solve and play independently. Suppose a little boy is fretting because he's having difficulty putting the lid on a box. His mother responds, "Here, I'll do it for you." The child then gets upset because he didn't really want his mother to take over and do it for him. The same thing will likely happen to a father who does a puzzle for his child because he finds it hard to watch her become frustrated as she attempts to complete it. Giving too much help or taking over an activity decreases a child's sense of accomplishment and self-esteem, and fosters dependence on adults. Since youngsters are struggling between independence and dependence, they often give conflicting messages to their parents because they aren't sure of what they want. On the one hand, children may be asking for help and, on the other, they resent it when it is given. This makes it difficult for parents to know how to respond.

During play you can encourage your children's ability to think, solve problems and play independently. Instead of telling them that you'll put a puzzle together for them, suggest doing it together. Provide just enough support, praise and encouragement to keep them working on the puzzle, but not so much that they end up feeling no sense of accomplishment. You may also prompt them or offer guidance that helps them to accomplish a task. If your child is having trouble screwing bolts on with a wrench, you might say, "How about if I hold this part while you screw it on." In this way, the child can still feel a sense of accomplishment. The key is to help without taking over and to encourage independent problem solving. Remember, sometimes your children ask for help when that's not what they really want. They just want your attention. Often, all you need to do is sit back and give them the message that you are confident in their ability to find a solution on their own.

Give Attention to Play

When children are playing quietly, most parents naturally seize the opportunity to take care of their own business—make dinner, read or write a letter. In so doing, they may fail to let their children know how much they appreciate quiet play. The result is that youngsters feel ignored when they play quietly, appropriately and independently, and only get attention when they are noisy or deliberately do something to attract attention. If this happens, they will learn to misbehave in order to get noticed. A child will work for attention from others, especially parents, whether it is positive (praise) or negative (scolding or criticism). If your children don't receive positive attention for appropriate behavior, then they will work to gain negative attention by misbehaving. This is the basic principle behind the development of many common behavior problems.

You should value appropriate play and actively participate in play activities with your children. If you pay attention to play, they will have less need to devise inappropriate ways to force you to respond to them. In fact, many parents have told us that when they tried giving their children a regular half-hour dose of play each day, they found they were later able to take some personal time for themselves. If children are assured of regular parental attention, they don't need to invent inappropriate ways of attracting it.

Giving positive attention to your child's play builds self-esteem.

A Word of Caution

Be prepared for times when your child plays inappropriately or misbehaves by whining, yelling, throwing toys, or being destructive in other ways. If the behavior can be ignored, turn away and begin to play with another toy as if it were very interesting. Once the child behaves appropriately, you can turn back. However, if the behavior is destructive, the play period should be stopped with a simple explanation such as, "When you throw the blocks, we have to stop playing."

Sometimes parents are reluctant to play with their children because they fear that there will be a big fuss when they want to stop. The solution is to prepare a child for the end of a play session. Five minutes before the end of a play period you could say, "In a few minutes it will be time for me to stop playing with you." It's important to ignore any protests or arguments, and to do your best to distract your child by focusing on something else. When five minutes have passed simply state, "Now it's time for me to stop playing. I enjoyed this time with you." Walk away and ignore any pleading. Once your children learn that they can't manipulate you into playing longer, the protests will subside. And when they realize that there's a regular play period every day, they'll have less need to protest, knowing that there will be another opportunity to play with you tomorrow. Remember, playful adults help develop playful children.

To Sum Up...

It is important for you to value play and set aside playtime with your children. In addition, you can learn to play in ways that foster their self-esteem as well as their social, emotional and cognitive development. By following the suggestions for effective play in this chapter, you will provide a supportive environment that allows your children to try out their imaginations, explore the impossible and the absurd, test new ideas, make mistakes, express feelings, make friends, solve problems, and gradually gain confidence in their own thoughts and ideas. An atmosphere of support and approval provides children with opportunities to communicate their hopes as well as their frustrations. They live in a world where they have little power and few acceptable ways to express their feelings. Good play with you can give your children the chance to reduce their feelings of anger, fear and inadequacy, and provide experiences that enhance feelings of control, success and pleasure. A flexible approach to play reduces pressure in your interactions with your children and fosters each child's development into a unique, creative and self-confident individual.

Remember:
- Follow your child's lead.
- Pace at your child's level.
- Don't expect too much—give your child time.
- Don't compete with your child.
- Praise and encourage your child's ideas and creativity; don't criticize.
- Engage in role play and make-believe with your child (e.g., puppets, playing house).
- Be an attentive and appreciative audience.
- Use descriptive comments instead of asking questions.
- Use academic coaching to promote your child's school readiness (e.g., colors, shapes, numbers, positions, names of objects).
- Be a social skills coach by prompting, describing and praising children's friendly behaviors (e.g., sharing, helping, taking turns, being polite).
- Use emotion coaching and provide positive support for children's emotional regulation skills (e.g., being calm, waiting, solving a problem).
- Curb your desire to give too much help; encourage children's problem solving.
- Laugh, have fun and share your feelings of joy.

CHAPTER TWO

Positive Attention, Encouragement and Praise

Parents often overlook the importance of using praise and other social rewards such as positive attention, smiles and hugs with their children. They believe children should behave appropriately without adult intervention, and that praise should be reserved for exceptionally good behavior or outstanding performances. In many cases, parents don't praise their children when they play quietly or do chores without complaining. Research indicates, however, that a lack of praise and attention for appropriate behaviors can lead to an increase in misbehavior. In fact, praise and encouragement can be used to guide children through the many small steps it takes to master new skills, to help them develop a positive self-image, and to provide the motivation they need to stay with a difficult task. Unlike tangible rewards such as money or privileges, there can be an almost endless supply of praise and other social rewards. It takes very little time to encourage positive behaviors in children. A simple statement like, "I like the way you're playing quietly—what a big girl!" or a well-timed hug is all that's required.

While some parents believe they should not praise their children, many others simply do not know *how* or *when* to give praise and encouragement. Perhaps they received little praise when they were young and the words seem awkward and artificial, or they don't know what behaviors to praise. Yet, parents and other adults can learn praise and encouragement skills, and when they do, they find that using social rewards and providing positive attention often has a dramatic impact on their children's behavior.

In the first part of this chapter, we will discuss some of the erroneous objections parents raise to praising children, and in the second part we will discuss effective and ineffective ways to praise.

Does praise spoil children?

"Isn't there a danger of spoiling my child with praise? Won't he learn to cooperate only for the sake of some external reward or adult approval?"

The truth is that children are *not* spoiled by praise, nor do they learn to work only for external rewards. In fact, the opposite is true: children who will work only for external rewards tend to be those who receive little praise or reinforcement from adults. As a result, they need it so badly that they learn to demand it before complying with their parents' requests.

Children who receive a lot of praise from their parents develop increased self-esteem. They are also more likely to praise others, and this can have far-reaching effects. The principle that operates here is "you get what you give." Research indicates that children who give many positive statements to others in school are popular and get many positive statements from others. So remember: children imitate what they see and hear. If they receive frequent positive messages from their parents, they are more likely to internalize this form of thinking and use it to bolster their own confidence and with the people around them. Of course, the opposite it also true. If parents are negative and critical, their children will model this behavior and negative self-talk as well.

Should children know how to behave?

"My child should know how to behave. Surely I don't need to praise her for everyday things like doing chores or sharing toys?"

Expecting a child to function without praise or rewards is unrealistic. The only way a child learns to engage in a particular behavior is by having that behavior reinforced. If it is noticed and given attention by the parent, it is more likely to occur again. If it is ignored, it is less likely to occur in the future. Consequently, no good behavior should be taken for granted or it will soon disappear.

Is praise manipulative and phony?

"Isn't it rather manipulative to use praise to bring about a particular behavior in my child?" *"If I make a conscious effort to praise him, I just end up feeling phony."*

The word *manipulative* implies that a parent is contriving secretly to bring about some desired behavior against the child's wishes. In fact, the purpose of praise is to enhance and increase positive behavior *with* the child's knowledge. Praise and rewards that are planned for with children bring out the best behavior in them. This is not unlike employers who offer a bonus to employees who do especially well in their jobs. Praise may seem "phony" when it is first used—any new behavior feels awkward in the beginning. This is a natural reaction and is to be expected. But remember, the more you use praise, the more natural it will feel.

Should praise be saved for outstanding performances?

"I prefer to save my praise for something that's really worth praising—an A in math, a perfectly made bed, or a really good drawing. Doesn't this help a child reach for the top?"

The problem with this approach is that no one achieves perfection without completing many steps along the way. A parent's focus should be on the process of *trying* to create a drawing, make a bed or do math problems. Otherwise, the opportunity to praise may never come: children of parents who save praise for perfection usually give up trying before they have reached it.

Therefore, instead of hoarding praises, practice catching your child being good. Notice when he shares, talks nicely in a quiet voice, complies with a request, goes to bed when told, does chores... Don't take these everyday behaviors for granted, praise them. If you focus on the fact that your child is trying to make the bed or do the dishes, you will be shaping his behavior in the desired direction. In other words, remember to *praise the process of trying to achieve,* not just the achievement.

Catch your child being good.

Does behavior have to change before praise is given?
"My child can be very naughty and unhelpful. I can't start to praise her until she changes her ways."
The danger here is that you could become involved in a stalemate situation. It is unlikely that the child is going to be able to initiate a behavior change. But someone has to stop the negative interactions, and so this must be the parents.

Sam Jeffries provides a good example of the wrong approach. Sam is constantly irritated by the fact that his son Steve never tidies his room or puts away his toys or his outdoor clothes until Sam gets really cross. As a result, Sam is never in a mood to notice that Steve regularly and cheerfully sets the table. If this were pointed out to him, Sam would likely say "So what?" because he has become totally focused on the tidying up issue.

Parents have to learn to focus on the positive things their children are doing and to praise them for their efforts. Then children will likely repeat and expand these positive behaviors. In other words, only if adults take the responsibility for changing first is there the likelihood of positive changes in the relationship. This same principle is true of any relationship—with spouses, older children, or working colleagues. If one becomes obstinate and refuses to make a positive change in one's own behavior, the status quo is maintained and the relationship is unlikely to improve.

What about the child who rejects praise?
"Whenever I try to praise my child, he throws it back in my face. He never seems to believe what I say. It's almost as if he doesn't want me to praise him."
Temperamentally difficult and aggressive children can be hard to praise. Their behavior often makes parents angry and undermines their desire to be positive. To make matters more difficult, they may reject praise when it is given to them. They seem to have internalized a negative self-concept and, when parents present them with an alternative, positive view of themselves, the children find this difficult to accept and cling to their negative self-image. While "difficult" children are hard to praise and reward, they need it *even more* than other children. Their parents must constantly look for positive behaviors that they can reinforce until the children begin to internalize some positive self-concepts. At that point they will no longer have a need to reject in order to maintain their poor self-image.

Do some parents find it harder than others to praise their children?
"It's not that I have any real objection to praising my child, it just isn't something that comes naturally to me and so I don't do it."

Extra effort must be made for children who reject praise.

Very often parents who don't praise their children are people who don't praise themselves. They are often very critical of themselves for their mistakes, conflicts, and difficulties. They may tell their children about problems they have, but rarely do they mention their successes at work or in the home.

Such parents do not model self-praise. If they listened to their internal self-talk, they would find that they are not saying things like, "You're doing a good job of disciplining Johnny," or "You handled that conflict calmly and rationally," or "You've been very patient in this situation." Instead, they are quick to criticize themselves for every flaw. They must learn to speak to themselves in positive statements and to create positive experiences for themselves as incentives or rewards. They will then be more likely to do the same for their children. (See Chapter Controlling Upsetting Thoughts)

It is important for children to see their parents modeling self-praise statements. A mother might say out loud to herself, "I did a good job on my assignment at work," or "That was a tough situation but I think we handled it well," or "That casserole I made tonight tasted good." By modeling self-praise for our children, we teach them how to internalize positive self-talk to themselves. This is important because they are learning how to self-evaluate and internalize their own self-motivation strategies.

Remember to model self-praise in front of your children.

Is there a difference between encouragement and praise?

"I make a point of encouraging my child, isn't that enough?"

Some parents believe that they should *encourage* their children but not *praise* them. Often these are the same parents who worry about spoiling or ending up with children who work only for external rewards. They make supportive comments, but avoid any statements that sound like praise. This causes them to continually edit what they say, out of concern that their encouragement is really praise, and it creates an unnecessary complication since children aren't likely to notice the difference.

If there are any examples of children who have developed behavior problems as a result of receiving too much praise, they are rare indeed. In fact, the problem is usually the opposite—that the children are receiving a great number of commands and criticisms and few praise statements. Don't worry about how you are giving a positive statement, simply give encouragement and praise as frequently as you see the positive behaviors.

Making Praise More Effective

It sometimes happens that parents who praise their children do so in ineffective ways. Here are some ways to maximize your effectiveness in praising children.

Be Specific

Vague praise is often given quickly in a chain, with one comment following another. It is nonspecific and unlabeled. For example, you might say, "Good job...good boy...great... good...fine...." Unfortunately, these statements do not describe the behavior you are trying to praise.

It is more effective to give praises that are labeled. Labeled praise describes the particular behavior that you like. Instead of saying "Good girl," or "Good job," you would say, "You're sitting so quietly in your chair," or "I'm pleased that you said thank you," or "Good boy for picking up those blocks when I asked." This description of the positive behaviors will help your child understand exactly what prosocial behaviors are important.

Praise Appropriately

It is critical that praise be contingent on the child's appropriate behavior. Praise for sharing should occur at the time when the child is actually sharing a toy with her little brother. However, if the children are behaving inappropriately it is better to ignore whatever positive aspect there might be to their behavior rather than try to give some form of praise. It would not be appropriate to praise Sarah for sharing her crayons with Danny when they have been using them to scribble all over the wall. Giving phony praise when a child is behaving inappropriately is misleading and confusing. Wait for the child to do something more constructive and then praise that positive behavior.

Show Enthusiasm

Some praise is ineffective because it is boring, offered in dull tones, with no smiles or eye contact. The same words may be repeated over and over again in a flat, unenthusiastic voice. Such praise is not reinforcing to children.

The impact of a praise statement can be increased by using nonverbal methods of conveying enthusiasm. Smile at the child, greeting her with warmth in your eyes or giving him a pat on the back. The praise should be stated with energy, care and sincerity. Words thrown over the shoulder in a careless fashion will be lost on the child.

Show enthusiasm.

Remember children who are inattentive, impulsive, and distracted will be most likely to miss praise that is delivered in a neutral voice or a vague way. These children, in particular, need praise that is underscored by means of an enthusiastic tone of voice, clear descriptions (labeling) of the positive behaviors, clear positive facial expressions and positive touch.

One important caution: if giving praise is difficult for you and you are not used to it, it will sound somewhat artificial or boring in the beginning. This is to be expected. The genuine positive feeling will come as you use praise more and more often.

A few phrases to help you get started...
- I like it when you...
- You're putting away the blocks just like Mommy asked you to do. You are such a great helper.
- Good idea for...
- You are listening and minding Daddy so well.
- You've done a good job of...
- Mommy's very proud of you for...
- Look how well he/she did at...
- Beautiful! Fine! Great! Gorgeous! Tremendous!
- That's a perfect way of...
- Wow, what a wonderful job you've done of...
- It really pleases me when you...
- You're such a good friend for...
- Good boy for...
- Thank you for...
- What a nice job of...
- Hey, you are really sharp, you...
- Pat yourself on the back for...
- You must feel proud of yourself for...

Avoid Combining Praise with Put-Downs
Some people give praise and, without realizing it, they contradict it by being sarcastic or combining it with a punisher. This is one of the most disruptive things a parent can do in the reinforcement process. In particular, seeing their children do something they haven't done before seems to tempt some parents to make a sarcastic or critical remark about the new behavior. For example, a father may say to his children, "Tony and Angie, you both came to the table the first time I asked you. That's great. But next time how about washing your face and hands first." Or a mother may say, "Lee, I'm glad you're making your bed, but why can't you do it every morning?"

Avoid combining praise with put-downs.

It is important to be positive about new behavior. If you seem discouraged or discouraging, as did the parents above, your child will stop trying. When you give a child praise, it should be clear and unequivocal without reminders of prior failures or less than perfect performance.

Praise Immediately
Sometimes praise is given hours or even days after the positive behavior has occurred. For instance, a mother may mention that she appreciated her daughter cleaning up the kitchen or putting out the garbage a week after it happened. Unfortunately, praise loses its reinforcing value with time and tends to sound more artificial.

While delayed praise is better than no praise, the most effective praise is that which is given within five seconds of the positive behavior. This means that if you're trying to encourage a new behavior, you should watch for every time your children share, comply with a command, or try to put on their clothes. Don't wait for the clothes to be put on perfectly or the toys all put away before praising. Praise your children as soon as they begin to perform the desired behavior. The praise should be frequent and consistent in the beginning, and then gradually it can be replaced by more intermittent praise.

Target Specific Behaviors You Want to Encourage According to Your Child's Individual Needs

It can be very effective to target the particular behaviors you want to strengthen in your child. For example, if your child is quiet, withdrawn or fearful you can plan to praise her every time she takes a risk, speaks up, is brave or tries something new. On the other hand, if your child is inattentive and impulsive you can plan to praise him for being able to listen to your instructions, or for waiting a turn, or letting someone else go first. For the highly oppositional child, the single most important behavior to target for praise is the child's compliance to your requests. The same goes for strengthening academic skills. If your child has difficulty writing and spelling, you can praise your child's efforts in order to encourage her persistence and continued interest.

It can be helpful to make a list of behaviors you want to see more of and then select a couple to systematically watch for and praise. This plan can be shared with others in your family.

Behavior Doesn't Have to Be Perfect to Deserve Recognition

Behavior doesn't have to be perfect to deserve your praise or positive attention. In fact, when children are first attempting a new behavior, they need to be reinforced for each small step toward the goal. Otherwise, if they have to wait until they have mastered the new behavior before being praised, they may give up altogether. Praising a child at every step along the way reinforces the child for her efforts and learning. This process, known as "shaping", sets the child up for success.

Encourage Children to Praise Themselves and Others

Ultimately, we want children to learn to praise others, for this is a skill that will help them build positive relationships with other children. We also want them to learn to praise themselves, for this will help them attempt and persist with difficult tasks. Parents can help their children learn how to recognize their own feelings of accomplishment by the way they phrase the praise. For example, a statement such as, "You must feel proud of yourself for reading that entire chapter all by yourself. Give yourself a pat on the back" focuses on the child's own positive recognition of his work. Parents can also prompt their children to give compliments to others and then praise them for this friendly behavior. For example, "Lizzie, look at the great castle your friend has built. Can you give her a compliment?"

Doubling the Impact

Regardless of whether the reinforcer is attention, a hug, a smile, or verbal praise, the task of teaching a child a new behavior is long and difficult, and often very slow. It involves trying to reinforce the positive behavior every time it occurs. If there are two adults in the family, they should discuss which behavior they want to improve and how they will try to reinforce that behavior. With both participating, things should go more quickly. In addition, adults can double the impact of praise by praising children in front of other adults and by modeling self-praise.

To Sum Up...

- Catch your child being good—don't save praise for perfect behavior.
- Don't worry about spoiling your children with praise.
- Increase praise for difficult children.
- Model self-praise.
- Give labeled and specific praise.
- Make praise contingent on behavior.
- Praise with smiles, eye contact and enthusiasm.
- Give positive praise and attention to behaviors you want to encourage.
- Praise immediately.
- Give pats and hugs and kisses along with praise.
- Use praise consistently.
- Praise in front of other people.
- Express your belief in your children.

CHAPTER THREE

Tangible Rewards, Incentives and Celebrations

In the previous chapter we discussed parental attention, praise and encouragement. Tangible rewards are another important type of reinforcer that can be used as an incentive to motivate children to learn a particularly difficult behavior. A tangible reward is something concrete: a special treat, additional privileges, stickers, a celebration, or time spent with someone special. These rewards should be used less frequently than social rewards. They are generally reserved for encouraging children to accomplish a difficult task such as toilet training, playing cooperatively with siblings, doing homework without complaining, or getting dressed independently. When using tangible rewards to motivate children to learn something new, it is important to continue providing social rewards as well. The impact is much greater when both types of rewards are combined because each serves a different purpose. Social rewards are used to reinforce the small steps and efforts children make to master a new skill or behavior. Tangible rewards are usually used to reinforce the achievement of a specific goal.

There are two general ways of using tangible rewards. The first is as a surprise or spontaneous reward whenever you notice your child behaving in some desired way, such as sharing or sitting still in the car. For example, you might say, "Johnny, you did so well helping me in the store we'll go for a special treat." This approach works if your child already exhibits the appropriate behaviors fairly regularly and you wish to increase the frequency with which they occur. This is an especially valuable strategy for preschool children. The second approach is to *plan in advance* with your child which behaviors will result in a reward. This type of program, which is like a contract, is recommended when you wish to increase a rare behavior. Let's look at a concrete example.

Maria was concerned that seven-year-old Anna and five-year-old Karl often argued and fought over toys. Her goal was to reduce their fighting and increase sharing and quiet play between them. To achieve this, she planned a tangible reward program with both children. It motivated them through rewards for sharing and quiet behavior. Maria started the program by saying: "We're going to start a sticker chart to help you share with each other. Right now, you're having some trouble sharing and when you play together you argue a lot. I end up getting mad at you a lot when you're playing together. That's no fun for any of us. From now on, from the time you get home from school until dinner time, I'll be noticing how you're playing together. We'll set the kitchen timer each 15 minutes and every time it rings, I'll give you a sticker if you've been friendly, sharing, and helping each other. After dinner you can trade your stickers in for a prize. Now, I want you to help me make a list of some things you'd like to work for."

The list of incentives and special privileges was discussed, agreed upon and written down—a kind of reward menu. When it was finished Maria said, "You both came up with a great list. You've got Matthew coming overnight, an extra story at bedtime, going to the park with Dad, choosing your favorite cereal at the grocery store, going to a movie, and picking something from a surprise grab bag. We can add to this list if either of you thinks of something else you'd like to work towards. Now, let's figure out how many stickers each of these is worth." Once the number of stickers for each item was determined, the children drew a chart, which was placed on the refrigerator door.

For older children (6-8 years), it's a good idea to make the reward menu fairly long with small, inexpensive items as well as slightly bigger items. On Anna and Karl's list, an extra bedtime story might be worth five stickers, going to a movie, 30 stickers. This list can be altered as children come up with new suggestions. Children will vary in how long they are able to wait for their rewards. Five to six year olds may need to trade in stickers for something each day while older children can often wait a few days before trading in stickers or points for a reward. However, children vary in their developmental maturity and ability to wait. Some 5-year-olds may be able to delay gratification for a few days, while a very impulsive 8-year-old may need a daily prize. Preschool children between the ages of three and four will be confused by a complex system of trading in stickers for prizes. At this age, a special sticker, handstamp, or small prize (extra story, grab bag prize), given as soon as the desired behavior occurs, will be rewarding all by itself.

Examples of Tangible Rewards

Inexpensive Items
- markers, paints, crayons and paper, pencils, coloring books
- money [penny or nickel depending on child's age]
- baseball cards
- surprise "grab bag" with inexpensive objects [little car, marbles, erasers, jellybeans, balloons]
- new toy [specific cost limit]
- choosing favorite cereal at store
- choice of fruit to eat
- rent a child's video tape [make sure it is nonviolent]
- special snack after school
- special treat in lunch box
- new parts added to a toy or collection
- favorite drink
- section to train set
- new tool for tool box
- clothing item for a doll, etc.

Special Privileges at Home
- choosing the dessert for the family
- choice of TV or video program
- using telephone
- dressing up in parents' clothes
- having a friend overnight
- setting table
- sitting in father or mother's chair at dinner
- playing on the computer
- having a friend over to play
- making play dough

Special Outside Activities
- going to a baseball game
- going to a movie
- riding bicycle at school ground
- trip to park
- staying overnight at grandparents
- go for a picnic
- ride the escalator at store 3-4 times
- go swimming

A good reward program incorporates the small steps required by children to achieve a goal. First, observe how often the misbehaviors occur for several days. This baseline will be the key to establishing the right steps for your child. If you notice that she can sometimes go up one aisle in the grocery store without running or yelling, this would be the first step to reinforce. The program would involve giving her a sticker after walking quietly up each aisle. (You might find it useful to begin with a few practice trips in which you don't intend to do a big shopping. This keeps the time in the store at a minimum—5 to 10 minutes—and avoids the stress of trying to accomplish two major tasks at once: doing the week's shopping and teaching your child better behavior). With this approach, your child has a good chance of being successful and earning some stickers. Once she can go up and down several aisles without a problem, you can make the reward contingent on walking quietly down two aisles and gradually increase your time in the store. Remember, the idea is to plan your training and progress with small steps towards the desired goal.

Pace the Steps Correctly

The opposite problem occurs when parents make the steps too easy. In this situation, children are not motivated to work for the reward or they undervalue it because they get it so often. This is rarely a problem in the beginning since most parents make the steps too big. However, it can become a problem as the program continues. For instance, after a few weeks the three-year-old in the grocery store will consistently be getting a sticker at the end of each aisle. Unless the parent makes the program more challenging by asking the child to complete three aisles before receiving a sticker, the stickers will lose their reinforcing value.

A good rule of thumb is to make it fairly easy to earn a reward when children are first learning a new behavior. Initially, they need repeated successes to appreciate the rewards, and the parental approval, and to understand that they are capable of the desired behaviors. Then you can make it a little harder. Gradually, the rewards are spaced farther and farther apart until they are not needed at all. Ultimately, parental approval can maintain the behaviors. Be careful, however. Sometimes parents who are feeling successful with their program step it up too quickly and their children then regress in frustration at their inability to succeed. Constant monitoring of the correct pacing of the steps is one of the keys to a successful tangible reward program.

Keep your reward system simple.

Choose the Number of Behaviors Carefully

Programs sometimes fail because too many negative and difficult behaviors are tackled at once. We have seen highly motivated parents start reward programs involving stickers for compliance to parental requests, not teasing siblings and peers, going to bed without an argument, and getting dressed on time in the mornings. Such programs are too complex. The pressure to succeed in many different areas of life may seem so overwhelming that children give up before starting. Another drawback of this approach is that it requires constant monitoring by the parents all day long. Simply observing a child's compliance to parental requests throughout a day will require a tremendous amount of effort because these situations occur frequently. Remember, if you cannot realistically monitor your child's behavior and follow through with consequences, the best-designed program is bound to fail.

There are three main things to consider when deciding how many behaviors to help children learn at one time: the frequency with which each behavior occurs; your child's developmental stage; and what is realistic for you to carry out. In regard to frequency, remember that behaviors such as noncompliance, whining, teasing or arguing may occur often and therefore will require much parental supervision. This means that realistically you will not be able to focus on more than one such behavior at a time. On the other hand, behavior such as dressing, brushing teeth, or wearing a seat belt in the car, occurs relatively infrequently and three or four of these could be included on a chart at the same time.

The second important point to consider is the developmental stage of your child. Young children require easily understandable programs that focus on one or two simple behaviors at a time. Learning to be compliant to parental requests or staying in bed at night are major developmental tasks for a young child. Each will require many repeated learning trials, time and much patience on the part of the parents. However, as children get older (school age and adolescent), tangible reward programs can become more complex because they can understand and remember them better. As well, the problem behaviors at this stage usually occur less frequently and are easier to monitor. For a school age child, therefore, it would not be unrealistic to establish a program that included stickers for brushing teeth, hanging up clothes, doing homework and helping with the dishes.

Evaluation of how much monitoring you can realistically expect of yourself is the third factor in deciding which child behaviors to focus on. Even if she has no outside job, the mother of several preschoolers is unlikely to be able to monitor child compliance throughout the day. Therefore, she may want to choose a period of the day when she can focus on problem behaviors. For instance, two hours in the late afternoon when the baby naps or in the morning when the oldest child is in playschool may be good options. On the other hand, a parent who is rushed to get ready for work in the morning and exhausted by evening may only have the energy to monitor behavior problems every morning for half an hour.

Focus on Positive Behaviors

Another problem involves focusing exclusively on negative behaviors. Parents may clearly identify a negative behavior they want to eliminate, such as fighting. Their program outlines the rewards that their children will receive for going an hour without fighting. So far, so good; but the program hasn't gone far enough. While it tells children clearly what they should not do, it neither describes nor rewards the appropriate replacement behavior. Thus, inappropriate behavior receives more parental attention than appropriate behavior.

It is important to identify the positive behaviors that are to replace the negative behaviors and to include them in the tangible reward program. Children should be rewarded for sharing and playing quietly together, as well as for going 15 minutes without getting into an argument with brothers and sisters. It is critical that the positive behaviors be spelled out as clearly as the behaviors that are to be eliminated.

Choosing Rewards

Once you have chosen which behaviors you want to increase or decrease and have decided on the appropriate stages in which to do this, the next task is to choose tangible rewards with your child's assistance.

Choose Inexpensive Rewards

Believe it or not, we have seen reward programs that almost bankrupted their planners. All children will want to include expensive items such as a bicycle, or a trip to Disneyland on their reward menu. Some parents may give in and place such items on the list, either because they think their children will never earn enough points to get them or because they feel guilty and would like to be able to give them these things. Still others include expensive items because they have trouble setting limits with their children. Even if parental motives are good, inclusion of expensive rewards is destructive to the program. All too often children do earn the required number of stickers or points. Parents then find themselves in the awkward position of either being unable to afford the reward, or of giving their children the reward but resenting it. In this case, children receive a mixed message about their parents' pleasure in the achievement of the goal. This defeats the purpose of a reward program and undermines the parents' credibility for future efforts to promote positive behaviors. Even when families can afford more expensive rewards, exclusive use of these teaches children to learn to expect big rewards for their successes. The emphasis is placed on the magnitude of the reward, rather than on the satisfaction and pride felt by both parent and child at the child's success.

Beware of rewards which can bankrupt parents.

The best rewards often cost nothing.

Generally it is a good idea to set a limit on the expense of any one item on a list, such as one dollar or less, depending on what your family can afford. Your children can be told this at the beginning. Although they will ask for expensive items and test the rules around this, in general inexpensive things are more powerful reinforcers. Young children often like to earn time with parents, such as extra story time, going to the park, and playing ball. Small food items such as raisins, candy, choosing their favorite cereal or dessert can also be appealing. Older children like to earn money and special privileges such as extra television, having a friend overnight, using the telephone, planting flowers and so forth. Remember, it is much easier to scale up a reward system than to scale one down.

Calculate Daily and Weekly Rewards

Sometimes parents not only make the rewards too big and expensive, but they also make the time interval until their children can earn them too long. Suppose Tom's father says, "When you get 400 stickers, you can have a bicycle," or "With 100 points you can go to the baseball game." Depending on how many stickers or points can be earned in a given day, it may take Tom a month or longer to earn the reward. Most young children (3-4 years) will give up if they don't receive a reward on a daily basis. Older children (6-8 years) should earn something every week.

To set a realistic value on your rewards, first determine how many stickers, points or tokens could be earned in a day if your child was 100 percent compliant with the program. For instance, if Tom, 7 years old, earned stickers for brushing his teeth (two, for twice a day), putting on his seat belt (two car rides per day), playing independently from 5:00 to 5:30 (one a day), and for going to bed when asked (one), then the total number he could earn per day would be six stickers. Tom's reinforcement menu should therefore include small items worth four stickers, so that when he was on target with two-thirds of the positive behaviors in one day, he could choose something from the list. It would also be a good idea to have other items ranging in value from four to 25 points so that he could choose to wait two to three days before cashing in his stickers to get favorite dessert, worth 10 points. Waiting for Tom to get 100 points for a baseball game would take 16 days if he was perfect every day. If he was successful two-thirds of the time, 100 points would take 25 days. The key to setting up effective reinforcement menus is not only a creative list of items for your child to earn, but also a realistic price for each item, based on the child's usual daily salary of points. Parents who use points or stickers for compliance to parental requests may find that their children can earn as many as 30 points a day. The price of items for their children would therefore be higher than for a child who can only earn six a day.

Involve Children in the Program
Occasionally parents choose tangible rewards that are more reinforcing for themselves than for their children. They include items such as going out for pizza or to a concert, which are activities they want to do. A related problem is parents who take too much control over the program. We have seen elaborate charts with pictures pasted on them and fancy stickers chosen by the parents, not the children. Unless children are given some control, the program is likely to fail. The goal of a tangible reward program should be to teach your children to take more responsibility for their own behavior. If they sense that you are unwilling to delegate some control, they may dig in their heels for a fight, in which case their focus is shifted from the pleasure of cooperation and good behavior to the satisfaction of winning a power struggle by escalating their bids for negative attention.

Find out what is most rewarding for each of your children. You can do this by priming yourself with lots of ideas for rewards, just in case they don't have any to start with. However, try hard to get your children to come up with their own suggestions. You might say to a reluctant child, "You like having Julia over. How about putting that on your list?" And remember that a reinforcement menu does not need to be completed in one discussion but can be added to over time as your children think of other things to work for. If you use stickers, allow your children to pick them out in the store, and involve them in drawing up charts and deciding how many stickers particular items are worth. Get your children involved in the fun of the game and excited about how to earn the items.

Appropriate Behavior, Then the Reward
What is the difference between a bribe and a reward? Consider a father in a bank who says to his screaming child, "Eliza, you can have this chocolate bar if you'll stop screaming." Or a father whose child has been getting out of bed at night who says, "Sunjay, I'll give you this snack if you go back to bed afterwards." In these examples, the chocolate and the snack are bribes because they are given before the desired behavior occurs and are prompted by inappropriate behaviors. The parents are teaching their children that if they behave badly, they will be rewarded.

Rewards should be given for positive behaviors after they have occurred. It is helpful to remember the "first—then" principle. That is, first you get the behavior you want and then your child gets a reward. In the bank example, Eliza's father could have said before going to the bank, "Eliza if you stay by my side quietly in the bank, I will take you to the park when we are finished." The parent first gets the desired behaviors and then gives the reward. In the bedtime example, Sunjay's father might have said, "If you stay in your bed all night, you can choose a game to play with me in the morning."

Use Tangible Rewards for Everyday Achievements
Some parents save tangible rewards for their children's special achievements such as getting A's on a report card, cleaning up the entire house or being quiet during a two-day car trip. This is actually an instance of making the steps towards the final goal too big. Not only do the parents wait too long to give the rewards, but they save the rewards for perfection. This gives their children the message that everyday behaviors, such as compliance, sharing or completing chores, don't really count.

Think about giving small, frequent rewards. For example, parents who want a quieter car trip might prepare a surprise bag (crayons, books, puzzles, games) to be opened every 80 to 100 miles if their children have been quiet and there have been no fights. Such rewards can help satisfy the children's need for stimulation during a long car ride. Certainly you can plan rewards for special achievements, but you should also use them for smaller steps along the way, such as doing math homework, putting

First you get the appropriate behavior, then you reward it.

away toys, sharing, sleeping all night, and going to the bathroom. Only by rewarding the steps can the larger goals of good grades, consistent compliance, or good relationships with friends be accomplished.

Replace Tangible Rewards with Social Approval

Parents often worry about using too many tangible rewards. They are concerned that their children will learn to behave correctly only for a payoff instead of developing internal controls. This is a legitimate concern and it could possibly happen in two kinds of situations. The first involves the parent who is "sticker dependent," giving stickers or points for everything the child does but forgetting to provide social approval and praise. In essence, this parent is teaching the child to perform for payoffs rather than for the pleasure both parent and child feel about the accomplishments. The second situation arises when the parent does not plan to phase out the tangible rewards and maintain the behaviors with social approval. In other words, the children are not given the message that the parent expects they will eventually be able to behave on their own without rewards.

The use of tangible rewards should be seen as a temporary measure to help children learn new and more difficult behaviors. They must be accompanied by social rewards. Once you have taught the new behaviors, you can gradually phase out the tangible rewards and maintain them with your social reinforcers. For instance, Sonja's mother might say, "Now that you are going pee in the toilet almost all the time, and earning lots of stickers, let's make the game more fun. Now you have to have dry pants for two days before earning a sticker." Once Sonja is successful on a regular basis for two days, the interval can be extended to four days, and so forth, until stickers are no longer necessary. At that point, her mother may want to use stickers to help her with a different behavior. She could say, "You remember how well you did learning to go pee with the sticker game we played? Well, let's help you learn to get dressed in the mornings using stickers." Thus, reward programs can be phased out and begun again for different behaviors.

Sticker dependence.

An important aspect of a reward program is the message that accompanies the reward. Parents must clearly communicate that not only do they approve of their child's success, but they also recognize that the child's effort—not the payoff, per se—is responsible for the success. In this way, parents help the child to internalize successes and take credit for them. For example, Mark's dad might say, "I'm proud of you for learning to stay in your bedroom at night. You've worked hard and you must feel good about it. You are certainly growing up." Here Mark's father gives his son the credit for his accomplishments.

Have Clear and Specific Reward Menus

Another common difficulty in reward programs is that the rewards are too vague. Victor says to his daughter, "When you do what I ask you to do and earn lots of points, you can buy something. What would you like?" Tina responds, "Garfield the Cat." And Victor says, "Well, maybe we could buy that or something else. If you get lots of points we'll see." In this example, the father is vague about the reward and about how many points it will take to earn it. The result is that Tina will not be very motivated to earn points.

Effective reward programs are clear and precise. You and your children should write down the chart that includes the rewards you have agreed upon and the value of each item. This menu should be posted in a place where everyone can see it. It might look like this:

No Teasing—Playing Together Nicely							
	M	T	W	T	F	S	S
4:30-4:45							
4:45-5:00							
5:00-5:15							
5:15-5:30							
Total							

A sticker means no teasing and playing together nicely for 15 minutes.
3 stickers = extra story read by Mom or Dad
6 stickers = go to park with Dad
3 stickers = pick favorite dessert
6 stickers = take bike to school
3 stickers = pick from grab bag
12 stickers = have friend overnight
12 stickers = go to movies with friend

_____

Parent's Name

_____

Child's Name

The above chart resembles a contract. If you have older children, you may want to sign it with them to signify that everyone understands it. It's also a good idea to let them know you'll look at the program after one week to see if there is a need for revisions, changes, or new items to be added.

Have a Varied Menu
Some reward programs rely on a fixed menu. That is, the parents and children set up a menu during one discussion and do not revise it for the next three months. The problem with this approach is that, at the beginning, children often aren't sure what they want to work for. They may think of more interesting items later on.

Make your reward menus flexible and varied. Encourage your children to include a variety of items, such as time with you, special privileges, inexpensive toys, outside activities and treats. Of course, the key is to discover what will be most motivating for them. Usually, appealing and varied menus give children options as their interests and moods change from day to day. Moreover, it is important to evaluate menus every few weeks and permit them to add new things to the list as this will help keep them interested in the program after the initial novelty wears off.

Be Sure Your Incentives are Age Appropriate

For 3- to 5-year-old children your incentive program should be clear, simple and playful. Children of this age love to collect different stamps and stickers or perhaps even earn a little prize from a surprise grab bag. There is no need to complicate the system for young children with reward menus or trading things in for bigger prizes. Just receiving the sticker coupled with your encouragement and seeing their sticker book fill up is all the reward they need.

Once children have learned the concept of numbers and understand the notion of days in a week and of time passing (6 years and older), they like to participate in programs where they collect things and trade in things. This is the age when "collections" start—remember all those collections of football or baseball cards, rocks, coins and stamps. At this age children can be offered the chance to collect stickers and trade them in for a bigger prize.

Be Positive

What happens if you put a lot of effort into setting up a reward program but your children fail to earn points? You may be tempted to respond by criticizing or lecturing them on why they should try harder. Unfortunately, not only would this give them a discouraging message about their ability (which could become a self-fulfilling prophesy), but the negative attention and ensuing power struggle could inadvertently reinforce misbehavior or noncompliance with the program. In other words, they would get more pay-off for not doing the program than for doing it.

If your child fails to earn points or stickers it is best to calmly say, "You didn't get one this time but I'm sure you'll earn some next time." If you're going to predict the future, it's helpful to convey a positive expectation. However, if your child continues to have difficulties earning points, make sure that you have not made the steps too big.

Keep Reward Programs and Discipline Separate

Some parents create tangible reward programs and then mix in punishment. For instance, a child may receive stickers for sharing and have them taken away for fighting. The stickers then take on negative rather than positive associations. This approach can be even more problematic if the child is left with a negative balance. If the only prospect is to earn stickers to get out of debt, all the positive incentive for good behavior is gone. The natural outcome is for the child to become discouraged and abandon all efforts to change.

Keep your reward program separate from your discipline program. Do not remove earned points or rewards as punishment because this will defeat the purpose of the program, which is to give attention to appropriate behaviors. If you want to use privilege removal as a discipline technique, keep any privileges you foresee withdrawing (TV time, use of bicycle, for instance) off your reward menu.

Keep Control of your Program

There are several ways you can lose control of your reward program. The first is by paying for "almost" performance; that is, giving rewards to your children when they haven't earned the required points. This usually happens because they argue for them, claiming they've done everything required. Unfortunately, it undermines the rules of the contract as well as your authority. It is also likely to result in your children escalating their begging and debating with you over the attainment of points. Instead of a behavior problem being solved, a new one is created. A second difficulty occurs if you leave the stickers and rewards around the house so your children have access to them. Lack of follow-through can be a third problem. This happens when your children have behaved according to the program but you fail to notice the behaviors or you forget to give them the stickers. If the rewards are given very late or in an inconsistent manner, their reinforcing value is minimal.

Tangible reward programs require a lot of work on the part of parents in order to be effective. You must consistently monitor your children's behavior in order to determine whether they have earned stickers or points. Only give stickers to children who claim they shared or went to the bathroom if you have observed these behaviors. If you and your children are working on high frequency problems such as noncompliance to requests or no teasing or whining for 15 minutes, then a great deal of vigilance will be required. Rewards are most effective if they are given *immediately* after the desired behavior is performed. Also, in order for these programs to work, you must be a consistent limit-setter. All children will test the limits and try to see if they can get rewards for less work. That's natural, but it means that you must prepared for this testing, stay committed to the menu, and ignore arguments, debates or pleading when your children have not earned enough points. Finally, you need to keep control of the rewards. Prizes and stickers should be hidden and awarding points and stickers determined by you, not your children.

Working with Teachers

If you are working on a behavior problem that also occurs in the classroom, it is wise to coordinate your plans with your child's teacher. For instance if your child's oppositional behavior and aggression are also problems at school, you and the teacher can plan an incentive system that occurs in both settings. The teacher might give your child hand stamps or stickers whenever she notices your child sharing or following directions. At the end of the day this report card goes home informing you of how many stickers your child earned that day. You can then double the impact by offering your child bonus stickers on his chart at home for achieving an agreed upon number of stickers at school. Then you continue your home behavior chart whereby your child again earns stickers for following your directions and sharing with others. When children receive the same behavior management program across settings, the misbehavior improves much more quickly.

To Sum Up...

- Define appropriate child behavior clearly.
- Make the steps small.
- Gradually increase the challenge.
- Don't make programs too complex—choose one or two behaviors to start.
- Focus on positive behaviors.
- Choose inexpensive rewards.
- Have daily rewards.
- Involve your child in choosing rewards.
- Get the appropriate behavior first, then reward.
- Reward everyday achievements.
- Gradually replace rewards with social approval.
- Be clear and specific about rewards.
- Have a varied menu.
- Show your child you expect success.
- Don't mix rewards with punishment.
- Consistently monitor the reward program.
- Co-ordinate your program with your child's teacher.

CHAPTER FOUR

Limit-Setting

As important as it is (and it is important) to praise and reward children when they are good, there are also times when it is necessary for parents to control and set limits on inappropriate behavior. Indeed, families that have few clearly communicated standards or rules are more likely to have children who misbehave. Consistent limit-setting helps children feel calm and safe.

However, it is also important to remember that all children will test their parents' rules and commands. This is especially true if parents have been inconsistent in the past and not enforced their rules. Be prepared for such testing, as only by breaking a rule can children come to learn that it is really in effect. Only consistent consequences for misbehavior will teach them that good behavior is expected. *Research shows that normal children fail to comply with their parents' requests about one-third of the time.* Young children will argue, scream or throw temper tantrums when a toy is taken away or a desired activity prohibited. School-age children, too, will argue and protest when an activity or object is denied. This is normal behavior, and a healthy expression of a child's need for independence and autonomy. When such protests happen, don't take them as an attack on you personally. Remember, your children are simply testing your rules to see if you are going to be consistent. If you aren't they will probably test even harder the next time. Try to think about your children's protests as learning experiences, ways that they can explore the limits of their environment and learn what behaviors are appropriate and inappropriate.

On the following pages, you will find some of the problems parents frequently encounter when setting limits with their children as well as some effective ways to give commands.

Reduce Commands

Few parents are aware of the actual number of commands they give their children. Would it surprise you to hear that the average parent gives 17 commands in half an hour? And in families where children have more

Child in a command storm.

behavior problems, the number rises to an average of 40 commands in half an hour. Moreover, research has shown that the children of parents who give an excessive number of commands develop more behavior problems. Frequent commands, then, do not improve a child's behavior. Therefore, it is essential for you to evaluate both the number and type of commands that you give your children and to reduce them to those that are most necessary.

Some parents tend to repeat a command when their children are already doing as requested. For example, Joy's dad says, "Put away the toys" a second time when Joy has already begun to put them away. If her father had been paying attention, he would have realized that it was unnecessary to give the command again but that praising Joy was important. Other parents give commands about issues that are not important. They might say, "Color that frog green," "Wear your blue shirt," or "Finish your dessert." These orders are unnecessary. Children should be allowed to decide such matters for themselves rather than become involved in a battle of wills with their parents. It's important to remember that if parents are giving 20 to 40 commands in half an hour, it is impossible for them to follow through. The result is that confusing messages are given to children about the importance of commands.

Before giving a command, think about whether or not this is an important issue, and whether you are willing to follow through with the consequences if your child doesn't comply. One exercise that can be helpful is to write down the important rules for your family. You will probably find that you have five or ten that are "unbreakable." These should be posted on the fridge or in some other place where all the family can see them. In this way, everyone, including baby sitters, will know what the rules are. Such a list might include:

• Seat belts must be worn in the car at all times.
• Hitting is not allowed.
• Throwing is not allowed indoors.
• TV must be off until 7 o'clock.
• Food must stay in the kitchen.

Once you have clarified the important rules, you will find not only that you are more precise when you state them but also that you are able to reduce other, unnecessary commands. The result is that your children will learn that your commands are important and compliance is expected.

One Command at a Time

Sometimes parents string commands together in a chain, without giving their child time to comply with the first command before going on to several more. For young children, this can result in information overload. For example, Eva tells her four-year-old, "It's time for bed. I want you to put your markers away, pick up your papers, go upstairs and get your pajamas on, and then brush your teeth." A series of commands such as this is difficult for youngsters to remember. Most can retain only one or two things at a time. Another problem with rapid commands is that the parent is not able to praise the child for complying with any of the individual commands. Eventually, this usually results in noncompliance partly because the child simply can't comply with everything, partly because there is no reinforcement for compliance.

Another type of chain command involves the parent saying the same thing over and over again as if the child has not heard it. Many parents repeat the same order four or five times, and their children quickly learn that there is no real need to comply until the fifth time. Moreover, chain commands reinforce noncompliant behavior by the amount of attention constant repetition provided.

Instead of repeating commands as if you expect your child to ignore them, state your command once. Say it slowly and then wait to see whether or not your child will comply. If it helps you to wait, you might want to count silently as you watch to see how your child will respond. This will help you resist nagging.

Give Realistic Commands

Occasionally parents give commands that are unrealistic or not appropriate for the age of their children. For instance, Tim's mom asks her three-year-old son to make his bed or share his favorite toy with his one-year-old sister. These requests will fail because they're not realistic for Tim's age. Other examples of unrealistic or inappropriate commands include expecting a four-year-old to keep the bathroom clean, a three-year-old to be quiet while parents have a long discussion, or children of any age to eat everything on their plate all the time.

Give commands that you believe your children are capable of carrying out successfully. Don't set them up for failure and yourself for frustration.

Avoid chain commands.

And if you have a child who is inattentive, hyperactive and impulsive, it is especially important to give commands that are realistic. You shouldn't expect such a child to sit for long periods at dinner, or to stay still for a long while. More realistic expectations would be staying at the table for five or ten minutes.

Give Clear Commands

While some parents have too many rules and commands, others dislike establishing any rules at all. They feel guilty when they tell their children to do something that might be unpleasant. Often these parents are vague and indirect about rules, disguising their commands in order to ease their guilt. Some examples of common vague or nonspecific commands are, "Watch out," "Be careful," "Be nice," "Be good," "Knock it off," and "Just a minute." These statements are confusing because they do not specify the behavior that is expected of the child.

Another type of unclear command is the one that is stated as a descriptive comment. For instance, Delia says to her daughter, "Oh Denise, you're spilling your milk. You'd better watch out!" Or Derek's father looks out the window and says, "Derek, your bike is still in the yard!" In addition to lacking clarity, these statements contain an implied criticism. Not only is it difficult to get a child to comply when statements

Remember to use specific positive commands.

rather than direct commands ("Hold the glass with both hands." "Put your bike away.") are given, but the critical aspect of such an approach is likely to breed resentment.

Yet another type of unclear order is the "Let's" command: "Let's wash the toy dishes," "Let's get ready for bed." This can be confusing for young children especially if their parents have no intention of becoming involved. For instance, a mother who has been playing with her two sons in the kitchen now wants them to put away the toys. She says, "Let's put the toys away." If she isn't willing to help them, they probably won't do as requested and she will probably become cross with them for not complying with her unclear command.

Be specific about the behavior you want from your child when you give a command. If Kim asks you to play with her, instead of saying "Just a minute," you might say, "Wait five minutes, then I'll play with you." Don't tell Robbie "Be careful," when he is spilling juice; say, "Use both hands to pour the juice into your glass." Instead of "Let's put the toys away," say, "It's time to put the toys away."

Give "Do" Commands

Question commands can be particularly confusing for children. At issue here is the subtle distinction between a request and command. A request implies that the child has the option of choosing whether or not to do what is requested. If you expect your child to comply but phrase your command as a question, you are providing a confusing message. Another problem with question commands is that you may find yourself backed into a corner. If you say, "Would you like to have a bath now?" and your child says no, you are stuck. You asked a question, received an answer you didn't want, and now must decide how to convince your child to take a bath.

Deliver your commands as assertive statements rather than as questions. Give "do" commands, with the verb at the beginning of the sentence: "Put away the toys," "Go to bed," "Walk slowly," "Speak softly." Here the action verb is the first word in the command and therefore, your child cannot miss it.

Polite Commands

If parents are angry when they give a command, they often seem to encourage noncompliance by including criticism or a negative comment. Billy's dad might say, "Billy, why don't you sit still for once in your life!" Or he might tell Billy to sit still in a sarcastic tone of voice. Sometimes put-downs are included with a command as a way of venting frustration because your child has not done something that you've asked him to do many times before. However, the feeling that is expressed behind the command is just as important as the actual words that are used. The child who senses your frustration may choose not to comply as a way of retaliating for your criticism.

Avoid criticizing your children when you give a command. Negative commands cause them to feel incompetent, defensive and less inclined to comply. Children's feeling about themselves as worthwhile people should be considered at least as important as obedience. Commands should be stated positively, politely and with respect.

Use Start Commands

A stop command is also a type of negative statement because it tells a child what not to do. "Stop shouting," "Don't do that," "Quit it," "Shut up," "Cut it out," "Enough of that" are all stop commands. Not only are these critical of the child, but they focus on the misbehavior instead of telling the child how to behave correctly.

Sports psychologists have found that if the coach tells the pitcher "Don't throw a fast ball," a fast ball is just what the pitcher is likeliest to throw—not out of orneriness but simply because that is what the coach's words have made him visualize. It's worth making every effort, therefore, to give positive commands that detail the behavior you want from your child. Instead of saying, "Stop yelling," or "Stop splashing," say, "Please speak quietly," or "Keep the water inside the tub." Whenever your child does something you don't like, think of what alternative behavior you want and then phrase your command to focus on that positive behavior.

Allow Time to Comply

No-opportunity commands do not allow children a chance to comply with requests. For instance, Nina's dad says, "Put away your clothes," and then he starts putting them away himself before she complies. Or Rino's mom says, "Get down from that swing," and removes him from the swing before waiting to see if he will comply. While immediate compliance is sometimes necessary, especially around safety issues, for the most part children deserve an opportunity to succeed at complying.

After giving a command, pause. If it helps you wait patiently, you might want to count silently to five. If your child has still not complied, then you can consider this noncompliance. However, when you give children time to comply, you will often find that they do. Waiting after you give a command also forces you to pay attention to whether your child has minded or not. Then, you can reward compliance or follow through with consequences for noncompliance.

Give Warnings and Reminders

Some parents give commands abruptly, without any warning. Picture this scene: Jenny is totally absorbed in building a castle with her blocks. Suddenly her father walks into the room and tells her to go to bed. What happens next? Probably much unhappiness, protesting and resistance from Jenny.

Whenever feasible it is helpful to give a reminder or warning prior to a command. This can be an effective way of preparing children to make transitions. If Jenny's dad had noticed that she was engrossed in playing with her blocks and said, "In two more minutes, it will be time to put your blocks away," Jenny would probably not have made a fuss. There are many ways to give warnings. For young children who don't understand the concept of time, a timer can be helpful. Then you can say, "When the timer goes off, it will be time to put these blocks away." For older children, you can refer to a clock.

Children's requests and preferences should be considered, as well. For instance, if your eight-year-old is busy reading a book, you might ask, "How many more pages do you have to finish the chapter?" If your child replies, "One more page," you could say, "Okay, when you finish that page, I want you to set the table." If you are responsive to your children's wishes and give them some lead time, you are more likely to obtain compliance than if you expect immediate obedience.

"When—Then" Commands

Occasionally parents give commands that sound like threats: "You keep watching TV and you're asking for trouble!" or "You're going to be sorry you did that." While the intention may be to warn or signal children that they are getting in trouble, these kinds of threats and their vaguely implied consequences tend to cause children to be defiant and negative rather than compliant.

Use "when—then" commands that tell your children in advance the exact consequences of their actions: "When you've set the table, then you can watch your television program," or "When you finish washing the dishes, then you can go play with your friends." First you get the appropriate behavior that you want and then you provide some positive consequence. This type of command gives your children the choice to comply or not to comply, and knowledge of the consequences of each choice. However, it is important in giving a "when—then" command to ignore all protests and arguments, and to follow through with the consequences. Obviously, this kind of command should only be used if you can allow your children to decide whether or not to comply. If you need compliance to your command, then give a direct positive command.

Give Options

Many times parents' commands prohibit their children from doing something they want to do, such as playing with friends or watching more television. In such instances parents may tell their children what they cannot do but forget to tell them what they can do instead. When children feel rigidly restricted and prohibited from fun activities, they may react with protests and noncompliance.

Commands that prohibit your child from doing something should include suggestions for what to do instead. You might say, "You may not watch TV now, but you can play with this puzzle with me," or "You can't play with Daddy's tools, but you can build a fort in the basement." Such an approach can help reduce power struggles because, instead of fighting about what your child cannot do, you're focusing on some other positive activity.

Give Short Commands

Smothered commands are shrouded in explanations, questions or a flurry of words. For instance, Stan says to his son, "Put away your crayons," followed by many questions about why all the crayons are out and what he is drawing. The result is that the original command is forgotten. A related problem is that parents sometimes give too many explanations with a command. They probably believe that giving a long explanation will increase the likelihood that their children will cooperate, but this approach usually has the opposite effect. Most children will argue with the rationale and try to distract their parents from the original command.

Keep your commands clear, short and to the point. It also helps to have eye contact with your child. If you give some rationale for the command, it should be brief and either precede the command or follow your child's compliance. Suppose you ask your daughter to tidy up the living room. As she does so you might add, "Thanks, you're doing a great job. I really needed this room cleaned up because we're having guests for dinner." *Remember to ignore arguments and protests about your commands as giving attention to them may actually reinforce noncompliance.*

Supportive Commands

Another problem may arise when two parents give commands that counteract one another. Sometimes counter-commands are given when one parent is unaware that the other has given a command. As you can imagine, this is bound to cause noncompliance and escalate conflict in the family.

It is important for the adults in the family to listen to the commands that each one gives and be supportive of one another's commands. Be sure to let your children complete a request made by one person before giving them another one.

Follow Through with Praise or Consequences

Sometimes parents do not notice whether or not their children comply with their commands. If there is no follow-through and children are neither reinforced for their compliance nor held accountable for their noncompliance, then parents must expect that their commands will be ignored.

Praising compliance encourages your children to be more cooperative and to value your requests. If your children don't do as they're told, then you must give a warning statement. This should be an "if—then" statement: "If you don't put your boots away Kevin, then you'll have to go to Time Out." You should wait five seconds to see whether or not the child does as requested. If the child complies, he should be praised and if he still doesn't comply, he should be taken to Time Out.

To Sum Up...

Giving effective commands does not require you to be authoritarian and rigid or to expect 100 percent compliance from your children. Rather, the emphasis is on thinking carefully before giving a command to be sure that it's necessary and that you're prepared to follow through with the consequences. It's important to strike a balance between a child's choices and adult rules. Sometimes you can involve your children in the decision regarding a rule. This works best with youngsters four and older. Consider two preschool children who are fighting because they both want to play with the bubbles and there is only one bubble blower. Their father might respond by giving a command: "First, Doug, you will use it. Then, Susie, it will be your turn." An alternative approach would be for the father to involve both children in deciding how to handle the problem. He might say, "There is only one bubble blower and two of you. What should we do? Do you have any ideas?" If Doug and Susie come up with some solutions, then Dad can reinforce their problem solving ability. In this way, he has avoided being authoritarian and encouraged the children to learn how to figure out a solution to a problem.

Giving effective commands is harder than you might first expect. In some situations, parental commands should be given as absolutes. In situations involving seat belts, hitting, not taking bicycles out onto the street, limitations on television, for instance, you need to have control over your children and must state your commands in a positive, polite and firm manner. There are other situations where you can give up control and avoiding unnecessary commands or unrealistic expectations. Why not allow children to have control over decisions such as what clothes to wear, whether or not to eat all the food on their plates, what stories to read before bed? Under yet other circumstances you and your children can problem solve and learn to share control. While this will be a slow process, and becomes effective only when they are teenagers, introducing negotiation and discussion with children as young as four or five can provide excellent early training.

*Follow through on commands
or children will learn to ignore you.*

Remember:
- Don't give unnecessary commands.
- Give one command at a time.
- Be realistic in your expectations and use age-appropriate commands.
- Use commands that clearly detail behaviors required.
- Use "do" commands.
- Make commands positive and polite.
- Don't use "stop" commands.
- Give children ample opportunity to comply.
- Give warnings and helpful reminders.
- Don't threaten children; use "when-then" commands.
- Give children options whenever possible.
- Make commands short and to the point.
- Support your partner's commands.
- Praise compliance or provide consequences for noncompliance.
- Strike a balance between parent and child control.
- Encourage problem solving with children.

CHAPTER FIVE

Ignore

Inappropriate behaviors such as whining, teasing, arguing, swearing and tantrums are not dangerous to children or other people, and can often be eliminated if they are systematically ignored. Some parents may feel that ignoring is not discipline. In fact, it is one of the most effective techniques that can be used with children. The rationale for ignoring is straightforward. Children's behavior is maintained by the attention it receives. Even negative parental attention such as nagging, yelling and scolding is rewarding to children. Parents who ignore their children when they behave inappropriately give no payoff for continuing misbehavior. If the ignoring is consistently maintained, children will eventually stop what they are doing. And as they receive more approval and attention for appropriate behaviors, they will learn that it is more beneficial to behave appropriately than inappropriately.

While ignoring is highly effective, it is also probably the hardest technique for parents to carry out. The following chapter will help prepare you to deal with the main problems parents encounter when trying to ignore their children's misbehavior.

Avoid Discussion and Eye Contact

Sometimes parents think they're ignoring their children's misbehavior when they are actually giving it considerable attention. They may have stopped talking to a child but continued glaring, grimacing, or in other ways letting her know that the misbehavior is affecting them. Some parents ignore by avoiding eye contact with their child but continue to make critical or angry comments. In both instances, the misbehaving child is successful in receiving attention and, perhaps, a powerful negative emotional response as well.

Effective ignoring occurs when you are able to neutralize your reaction to what your child is doing. Your facial expression should be neutral, you should avoid eye contact, and stop all discussions. Ignoring also involves moving away from the child, especially if you have been in close contact. Just as the most powerful form of positive attention includes a smile, eye contact, verbal praise and physical touching, the most powerful form of ignoring is a neutral expression, involving no eye contact, no communication and a turning away of the body.

Use Consistent Ignoring—Be Prepared for Misbehavior to Get Worse at First

Sometimes well-intentioned parents start to ignore misbehavior such as tantrums or arguments without being prepared for their child's response. Most children will initially react with an increase in negative behaviors to see if they can get their parents to back down. For instance, five-year-old Megan wants to go outside and argues with her mother about this for several minutes. Finally her mother tells her she may not go outside and proceeds to ignore any protests. Megan escalates her demands to see if she can get what she wants. This goes on for ten more minutes until her mother, exasperated and worn down by the arguments, says, "All right, go outside!" By giving in for the short-term benefit of making life more peaceful, the mother has created a long-term problem: Megan has learned that if she argues long and hard enough, she will get what she wants. Thus, she has been reinforced for inappropriate behaviors.

Remember, when you first start ignoring a misbehavior it will usually get worse. You must be prepared to wait out this period if the behavior is to improve. If you give in, your children will learn that behaving inappropriately is an effective way to get what they want.

Be prepared for testing when you ignore.

The example of Megan and her mother is not unlike an experience you may have had with a vending machine. You put your change in for a soft drink, but don't get one, nor can you get your money back. You press the return button several times and when this doesn't work you try the drink button again. Depending on how thirsty or cross you are, you may persist in pressing the buttons and even try banging on the machine. Finally, if no soft drink appears, you give up and move on to something else because there has been no payoff for your banging. However, if by some stroke of luck a soft drink pops out during your banging, then you know that the next time you can't get a soft drink, the trick is to bang hard and long enough. Children can learn to be persistent bangers. This is one of the reasons that ignoring is so difficult for parents to carry out. All children will test their parents' ignoring skills by escalating their misbehaviors. If you decide to use the technique you must be prepared to wait out this period by remaining firm in your resolution to ignore.

Ignore and Distract
Choosing to ignore misbehavior doesn't mean that there is nothing positive you can do to improve the situation. In fact, failure to provide distractions or suggestions for alternative, more appropriate behavior can lock parents and children into a power struggle and cause the children to prolong the misbehaviors. Consider this scenario: Tony asks his father to buy him a toy while they're out shopping. His father refuses and Tony starts yelling and screaming. His father effectively ignores this by walking away, and in a couple of minutes the screaming subsides. At this point, Tony's father might try to distract him with a new activity or something else to think about. Instead, he just waits for Tony to come and join him. Tony, feeling ignored, begins to scream again in an attempt to gain his father's attention.

Sometimes you can use distraction to reduce your children's reaction to being ignored. Distractions are particularly useful with two-and three-year-olds, but they also work with older children. Once Tony stopped screaming, his father could have told him that when he saved up enough money from his allowance, he could buy the toy he wanted. If your daughter starts whining when told she can't have a sugared cereal she wants, ignore her until she stops whining and then ask her to help look for a different food item. The idea is to ignore her misbehavior in response to being told she can't have something, and then distract her as soon as she starts behaving more appropriately. Of course, if she misbehaves again in response to the distraction, you will need to resume ignoring.

Another way to combine distraction with ignoring is to distract *yourself* from your children's inappropriate behaviors. You can do this by talking to yourself or another person, or involving yourself in another activity. If you are ignoring a child who is having a tantrum, you may want to go over to the kitchen sink and peel potatoes, or you might comment on something that is occurring outside the kitchen window. If the child thinks you have been distracted, he or she may quickly stop misbehaving.

Move Away from Your Child but Stay in the Room

It may seem reasonable to ignore your child's misbehaviors by walking out of the room. This can be an effective technique if the child is clinging and physically demanding attention. However, the difficulty with leaving the room is that you won't be able to pay attention to and reinforce appropriate behavior.

When ignoring, it is best to physically move away by standing up and walking to another part of the room. This way you can monitor your child's behavior and reinforce him as soon as he stops misbehaving. If he follows you, holding to your legs or arms, it may then be necessary to leave the room. However, you should return as soon as possible to respond to appropriate behaviors as soon as they occur.

Ignoring Teaches Self-control

Some parents do not use ignoring because they feel it is disrespectful and harmful to their children's self-esteem. They are concerned that this approach will damage their relationship with their children. Other parents do not ignore because they feel it does not punish their children enough. They say, "How can you ignore things like swearing or yelling? These behaviors need discipline."

Research indicates that ignoring is an effective discipline approach because it maintains a positive parent-child relationship based on respect rather than fear. If you can ignore screaming or swearing instead of yelling or criticizing, you show your child that you can maintain self-control in the face of conflict and anger. And because you don't get upset by these behaviors, she'll see that they have little effect or payoff and learn that there is no value in continuing to use them.

Teach Others to Ignore

Sometimes ignoring backfires because even though the parent ignores the child's misbehavior, others give it attention by teasing the child or attempting to console the child. If this is happening, your ignoring will not work because the child is still managing to get attention for the misbehavior. If others are giving your child's misbehaviors attention, they need to be taught the wisdom of ignoring. For example, you can say, "We can best help Ramone right now if we ignore him until he has got himself under control."

Limit the Number of Behaviors to Ignore
Whereas some parents have the problem of ignoring too rarely, others ignore too much. Such people effectively ignore their children's initial misbehavior but then continue to withhold attention, support and approval for several hours or even days at a time. A related problem occurs when parents deal with too many misbehaviors at once—whining, yelling, screaming, arguing and messy eating, for example. Ignoring so many things will cause children to feel neglected and leave parents feeling overwhelmed. Not only will they find it difficult to be consistent in their ignoring, but they will find it hard to remember to give attention for the opposite, positive behaviors.

It is important to identify specific behaviors to focus on when ignoring. Choose only one or two to systematically ignore at any given time. By limiting yourself this way, you can more realistically expect to be consistent in ignoring the misbehavior every time it occurs. As well, you will be able to observe and monitor the effects this discipline technique has on the particular behavior.

Certain Behaviors Should not be Ignored
Some parents ignore *all* their children's misbehaviors, regardless of their severity or the setting in which they occur. This is not an appropriate approach for behaviors that are destructive to children themselves, other people or property. It is also inappropriate in situations—a tantrum on the bus, for instance—where children receive attention from someone else, or for behaviors such as lying, stealing, noncompliance or forgetting chores.

In most circumstances, annoying behaviors such as whining, pouting, screaming and tantrums can be dealt with effectively by ignoring. On the other hand, dangerous or abusive behaviors, including hitting, verbal abuse, running away, setting fires and damaging property must not be ignored. Bullying a sibling or stealing, which provide children with immediate benefits while inconveniencing or harming others, should not be ignored either. In these situations a stronger consequence, such as a Time Out, a work chore or loss of a privilege, needs to be used in order to change the behavior. Therefore, it's important to select the behaviors you are going to ignore with care and to remember that ignoring an inappropriate behavior will only be effective with those for which parental attention is the primary reinforcement.

Examples Of Behaviors That Can Be Effectively Ignored In Preschool Children

- Whining, pouting
- Temper tantrums
- Swearing
- Facial grimaces
- Smart-talk
- Minor squabbles between children
- Brief crying period in the middle of the night
- Picky or messy eating
- Protests when prohibited from doing or having something
- Nose picking and nail biting
- Thumbsucking
- Garbled baby talk

Pay Attention to Positive Behaviors

Some parents become so engrossed in their own activities that they fail to pay attention when their children speak nicely, share toys, solve a difficult problem, or play quietly. If these positive behaviors are ignored, they will disappear. Parents often develop a reflex response, reacting to their children only when they get into trouble. This negative cycle of paying attention when they misbehave and ignoring them when they are behaving appropriately actually increases the frequency of misbehavior.

If you use ignoring, it is crucial that you give attention and praise to positive behaviors, particularly those that are the opposite of the one you are ignoring. If you've decided to ignore whining , for instance, you should make a conscious effort to praise your children whenever they speak appropriately. "I really like it when you use your polite voice," you might say. It's important to focus on the positive behavior you want to see replace the problem one. If you're concerned that your daughter is grabbing and hitting, you need to praise her for sharing and playing nicely.

Another effective technique involves combining ignoring and praise in a group of two or three children. When one child is misbehaving, give your attention to the one demonstrating appropriate behaviors. Imagine a dinner scene with Peter throwing peas on the floor, while David is eating nicely and cleaning up his plate. Your natural first response is to focus on the child who is misbehaving: "Peter, don't do that." However, this would reinforce Peter's inappropriate behavior. If instead you ignore Peter and praise David, Peter will probably begin to behave because he sees that appropriate behavior gains attention and misbehavior doesn't.

Give Back Your Attention as Soon as Possible
Once in a while parents may be so distressed and angered by inappropriate behaviors that they cannot focus on good behaviors. It's important to remember that as soon as your child stops misbehaving, you should quickly return your attention (within five seconds) and praise some appropriate behavior. Only by combining the withdrawal of attention for inappropriate behaviors with consistent attention for appropriate ones will you reverse the cycle of negative attention for negative behavior. So, just as soon as the misbehavior stops, begin to smile, talk to your youngster and look for something to praise.

Use Subtle Ignores
Parents can be too dramatic in the way they ignore their children. If a youngster begins to pout or swear, they make an exaggerated gesture of pulling away and disregarding the misbehavior. This can be almost as reinforcing as giving attention for the misbehavior because it shows the child she has been able to produce a strong emotional response in her parents.

Although it is advisable to withdraw physical contact, eye contact, and verbal contact when ignoring, it is also important that you neutralize your emotional reactions and be subtle. If your child is whining, you should matter-of-factly look away and perhaps comment to yourself or another person about something else that's going on. This is effective because it reveals no hint that you are affected in any way by your children's misbehavior.

Stay in Charge
Sandra is running late for work and her four-year-old son is dawdling and won't put on his shoes. She is so frustrated that she finally says, "Jimmy, if you don't hurry up and get dressed, I'll leave without you!" When he keeps on dawdling, she walks out of the house and gets into her car. Of course, she waits there, though she may hide for a bit or drive around a corner.

Parents who take ignoring to an extreme and threaten to leave their children believe that the fear caused by their leaving will mobilize the children into being more compliant. While such threats may get Jimmy out the door, they have several long-term disadvantages. In order to continue to be effective, all threats need to be backed up with the threatened consequence. Once your child realizes you are only pretending to leave, he will respond with similar threats: "Go ahead and leave me. See if I care!" You are then left in a powerless position because your child has called your bluff. If you don't leave, you're not following through. Yet leaving isn't really an option since a young child is not safe alone at home. The emotional hazard is also great as threats to abandon children make them feel insecure and create further problems of poor self-esteem. Furthermore, you are teaching your child a powerful strategy to use in relationships when faced with conflict. He may begin threatening to run away or may leave home to test the power of this tactic for getting what he wants.

Never threaten to leave or abandon your children, no matter how great the temptation. Think about other strategies that are effective in helping them to be more compliant. Perhaps if you can ignore the behavior that makes you feel so cross that you are ready to leave them, they will begin to behave more appropriately. If you can't use ignoring, you may need to try another discipline technique such as Time Out, work chores or loss of privileges. While these strategies will take more of your time in the short run, they will teach your children that your relationship is secure, regardless of occasional conflict. These strategies are far preferable because they are based on respect rather than on the fear of abandonment.

To Sum Up...

If you decide to use ignoring, you must be determined to ignore your child at all costs until the misbehavior stops. Consistency is the essence of ignoring. When your daughter throws a tantrum you may be tempted to give in. However, each time you do so you actually make the misbehavior worse because you teach her that she can outlast you. The next time, the tantrum will be louder and last longer. Therefore, you must continue ignoring until the behavior changes.

Remember that ignoring is not likely to affect how your child behaves unless a positive relationship has been built up between the two of you. The first task in any plan to change behavior is to increase your attention and praise for positive behaviors. Although ignoring will decrease annoying misbehaviors, it will not increase positive ones. To do this, it must be combined with social approval for good behavior as well as teaching about appropriate behaviors when your child is behaving well.

Also remember these specifics:
- Avoid eye contact and discussion while ignoring.
- Physically move away from your child but stay in the room if possible.
- Be subtle in the way you ignore.
- Be prepared for testing.
- Be consistent.
- Return your attention as soon as misbehavior stops.
- Combine distractions and redirections with ignoring.
- Choose specific child behaviors to ignore and make sure they are ones you can ignore.
- Limit the number of behaviors to systematically ignore.
- Give attention to your child's positive behaviors.

CHAPTER SIX

Time Out to Calm Down

While a child's social and emotional development is built on ongoing and regular deposits of parental love, support, positive attention, understanding and communication, it is also necessary for parents to provide clear limits and appropriate consequences for misbehavior. Many parents have tried some form of physical punishment, lecturing and disapproval. However, research has shown that these are ineffective methods of discipline. In fact, nagging, criticizing, arguing, shouting or reasoning with children while they misbehave constitutes a form of parental attention that can actually reinforce the particular misbehavior and may result in children learning to shout, criticize and argue in response to their parents.

Hitting, smacking or spanking children, on the other hand, is quick and most likely will stop the inappropriate behavior in the short term. Yet, the problem with hitting children is that it has long-term disadvantages. The first is that parents model an aggressive response to misbehavior and so their children learn to use an aggressive response when they are frustrated. Even worse is that parents may lose control when they are spanking. This is frightening for their children and can also be frightening for the parent whose feelings of loss of control may create feelings of guilt once they calm down. They may then respond by overcompensating with reassurance or gifts (sometimes causing a child to withstand spanks in order to get the rewards), or by avoiding the use of discipline in the future. We have already talked about the need for consistency so that our behavior is predictable for our children. If smacking only occurs when the parent has become really cross, not when the problem behavior first started, this makes it hard for the child to learn how to avoid it. A second difficulty with spanking or hitting is that it tends to "wipe the slate clean" for children, leaving them with no ongoing sense of remorse or guilt for misbehavior without teaching them what we want them to do instead. The result is children may obey in the parents' presence but are more likely to behave inappropriately in other settings or with other adults. They also learn to hide or lie about problems in order to avoid being hit. In fact, the more hurtful the discipline, whether it be degrading criticisms or physical punishment, the more devious and resisting children become and they may even come to dislike the parent, making it even harder for the parent to get the child to do what they want them to do.

The task for parents is to provide an ethical approach to discipline that teaches children which behaviors are inappropriate, while giving them the positive expectation that they will be able to do better next time and that they are deeply loved. Methods such as ignoring, using logical and natural consequences, loss of privileges, and problem solving are effective discipline approaches for many problems, and these are discussed in other chapters. In this chapter we will discuss another discipline method, called Time Out, which is reserved specifically for high intensity problems, such as aggression and destructive behavior. It is also useful for highly noncompliant, oppositional or defiant children (defined as a child who refuses to do what you want him or her to do more than 75% of the time), since compliance is the cornerstone of a parent's ability to socialize a child.

The term Time Out is short for "Time Out from positive reinforcement" and is actually an extended form of parental ignoring in which children are removed for a brief period from all sources of positive reinforcement, especially adult attention and are given an opportunity to calm down. Used correctly, Time Out offers several advantages over other time-honored disciplinary practices such as lecturing and spanking. It models a nonviolent response to conflict, stops the conflict and frustration, provides a cooling off period for both children and parents, and maintains a respectful, trusting relationship in which children feel they can be honest with their parents about their problems and mistakes. Time Out provides an opportunity for children to reflect on what they have done and to consider other solutions, and fosters their development of an internal sense of responsibility, or conscience. Also teaching children how to take brief time away to calm down or self-regulate is an anger management approach that children can use throughout their lives.

Steps to Setting Up Time Out

Many parents have tried some form of Time Out with their children and may have experienced that it didn't seem to work. In fact, there has been considerable research showing the most effective ways to set up a successful Time Out. Two important points should be noted to making

Time Out work. First it is short (generally 5 minutes is sufficient) and second, the parent must control the start and the end of the Time Out process. Here are some of the other steps that need to be considered in planning for Time Out...

Time Out location

You need to carefully consider where you will have Time Out for your children. Preferably it is a chair placed in an empty corner of a room or hall away from all family activities and the television. It is important that this not be called the "naughty chair" but rather can be called the "Time Out" or "calm down place" or, "thinking chair." At first, it may also be necessary to have another room that can be used as a backup room in case your child will not stay on the chair. Preferably this back up room should be in a dull, boring, and safe place for your child to be in alone. Guestrooms are often good choices, if available. Bathrooms are not usually a good choice because of the dangers presented by water, medicine, and cleaners. Some families who have little space will need to use the child's room for Time Out. This works for some children but may not for others. The problem with the bedroom is that it usually contains interesting toys and games. For the highly aggressive child, these items will need to be removed for a while until the child's behavior has been brought under control. In general, if needed, this back up room will only be used at the beginning when your child may be testing to see if you are going to follow through on using Time Out. In fact, this is true of the Time Out process itself when applied to a particular problem. If you are still using Time Out regularly after six weeks for the same problem it is worth looking again at the problem to see if your child is capable of avoiding the Time Out – that is have you taught your child the alternative behavior? Or, is Time Out enabling your child to avoid something unpleasant?

Describe the challenging behaviors that will result in Time Out

You should decide which specific misbehaviors will result in Time Out. Those that can't be ignored, such as extreme noncompliance or oppositional behavior and hitting and destructive behaviors, are good ones to choose. Remember though, all young preverbal children frequently engage in mild pushing or aggressive behaviors and sometimes biting. These mild aggressive behaviors can usually be handled with a redirection, a prompt by the parent for the child to use his words, or a direct command to stop. Likewise, typical children disobey their parents one out of every three requests and a warning from the parent is usually sufficient to handle this problem. Time Out should be saved for serious and intentional aggression or persistent noncompliance. Remember, the parenting pyramid where you are first building your relationship with your child through play, praise and support and using proactive strategies to prevent problems when possible before initiating Time Out.

Time Out length
A general rule of thumb is three minutes for three-year-olds, four minutes for four-year-olds and five minutes for children five and older. Time Outs longer than five minutes are not more effective. However, children should not be let out of Time Out until there has been two minutes of quiet, signaling that they have calmed down. This means that when you first use Time Out it may last longer (30 to 40 minutes) if your children continue to scream. Once they learn that screaming does not get them out and quiet calm behavior does, the Time Outs will usually be short (five minutes or so). The main idea is to make it as brief as possible and then to immediately give your children opportunity to try again and be successful. Do not use Time Out for children younger than 3 years of age. (Ignore and redirect strategies will be sufficient for toddlers.)

Keys to Initiating Time Out
Scenario For Child Who Is Aggressive:
Derrick is a highly aggressive 5-year-old child and his parents have explained to him that if he breaks the household rule of hitting he will go to Time Out in the corner of the living room. No warning is given before Time Out in the case of aggressive behavior. In this case if you observed Derrick hitting his sister it would not be appropriate to say, "If you hit Sally again, you will go to Time Out," as this would give Derrick a second chance to hit his sister. Hitting should result in an automatic Time Out because "no hitting" is one of your non-negotiable household rules. For example:

> PARENT: Derrick, you cannot hit your sister. You need to go to Time Out now to calm down.

Scenario For Child (Age 4 And Older) Who Is Chronically Noncompliant:
You have clearly and politely asked your child to do something and he defiantly refuses and ignores your request. You have waited 5 seconds to see if he will follow through despite his attitude, but it is apparent he is not going to comply. Next, you give a clear, polite warning, "If you don't

put the toys away now, you will have to go to Time Out." You again wait 5 seconds and see that he is still refusing. Next you tell him in a firm, respectful, calm voice to go to Time Out.

Here's an example of initiating Time Out for noncompliance with a 7-year-old boy who was disobeying his parents' requests about 95% of the time:

> PARENT: Derrick, hang up your coat please. (wait 5 seconds)
> CHILD: No, I'm watching TV.
> PARENT: If you don't hang up your coat, you will have to go to Time Out.
> CHILD: I'll do it later.
> PARENT: (wait 5 seconds) Derrick, I asked you to hang up your coat and you disobeyed. Go to Time Out now.

Set a timer
Once your child is in Time Out, you should set a timer for three to five minutes and ignore him while he is in Time Out. Using sand or egg timers for keeping track of time in Time Out is important. Most young children don't understand the concept of time, so they may panic when asked to sit for any period of time. Focusing on the timer can be calming for children and it provides a visual symbol of how much time is left to sit on the chair. You will probably want to put the sand or egg timer where your child can see, but not touch it. You might try a "chill bottle" —that is a plastic bottle filled with colored water and sparkling items. You shake the bottle and the children know they must sit in the Calm Down or Time Out chair until the sparkling items have settled to the bottom of the bottle. It is important not to talk to your child while he or she is in Time Out.

End of Time Out: calm for two minutes
When the timer goes off, if your child is calm and quiet, you can say, "Derrick, your Time Out is over, you may come out now." If your child is still crying or yelling, you should wait until he or she has calmed down for at least 2 minutes. Remember some children take longer than others to calm down and individual differences should be respected.

Follow Through: repeat the command for noncompliance
If you used Time Out because your child was oppositional, then once Time Out is over you need to *repeat the original command*.

PARENT: Derrick, hang up your coat please.
CHILD: Okay.
PARENT: I'm pleased you hung up your coat.

If Derrick refused to hang up his coat, then the entire sequence would have to be repeated. If Time Out is used for hitting or some destructive behavior, then once Time Out is over you should look for your child's first positive behavior that can be reinforced.

PARENT: Derrick, that's nice sharing with your sister.

Responding to Children Who Refuse to Go to Time Out
If your child is six years of age and younger and refuses to go to Time Out, give your child a warning. *"You can go to Time Out like a big girl, or I will have to help you go."* This choice is usually enough to motivate most children to go by themselves. However, if your child still refuses to go on her own, then gently and calmly take your youngster by the arm and walk to Time Out.

If your child is old enough to have a sense of time (around 7 years of age) and refuses to go to Time Out in the first place, add on one extra minute for arguing and not going to Time Out. You can continue that up to ten minutes. At that point, give a warning to go to Time Out or lose a privilege—no television for the evening, or bike is locked up for 24 hours.

PARENT: Derrick, hang up your coat please.
CHILD: No, I'm watching TV.
PARENT: If you don't hang up your coat, you will go to Time Out.
CHILD: I don't care. You can't make me!
PARENT: That's one extra minute in Time Out.
CHILD: Who cares? I like it there anyway.
PARENT: That's seven minutes now.
CHILD: So you can count, huh? (.......add time up to 10 minutes)
PARENT: That's ten minutes now, if you don't go to Time Out now, you will have no computer tonight.
CHILD: But that's not fair!
PARENT: No computer tonight.

Once you have followed through with removal of a privilege, your child will quickly learn that it is better to go to Time Out in the first place. The advantage to this approach is it gets you out of the power struggle and your child has been given a choice: either he chooses to go to Time Out (for 10 minutes) or chooses to miss using the computer. Take notice—if you take a privilege away, it is important that you take it away briefly the same day and then return it the same day or the next day. Longer punishments are not more effective. Briefer consequences allow children to have fresh starts and new learning trials and chances to be successful. Finally, it is ideal if your child has experienced the consequence of refusing to go to Time Out before you initiate another Time Out. For example, if Derrick's hitting of his sister is the problem, then his parent would need to supervise in order to reduce the opportunities for hitting until he has experienced the first consequence. This way the next time he gets the choice of Time Out or a consequence he knows that you will follow through and be more likely to choose the Time Out option.

Refusing to Stay in Time Out
Again your child is given a set of choices. If your child comes away from the Time Out chair location, *calmly return her* with one warning: "If you get off the chair again, you will have to go to the Time Out room." If your child does not stay in the chair location a second time, then gently take her to the Time Out room leaving the door open. If she comes out of the room, give another warning, "If you can't stay in the room with the door open, I will need to close it." If she comes out of the room a second time, then you will need to close the door. There are different opportunities in this scenario for your child to make a better choice. While your child may test the scenario to the limit the first few times, she is unlikely to try that again once she learns that you are prepared to follow through with consequences.

Be prepared to ignore the child who tries to "huff and puff and blow the door down."

If your child is over seven years old and comes out of Time Out, you can try a different approach involving a privilege removal. Give one warning: "If you don't go back into Time Out now, you'll lose your bike use for the evening." (Or "There'll be no bedtime story tonight" or "No soccer game after dinner.") If your child still refuses, then you must enforce the loss of the privilege and the Time Out sequence is dropped.

Initially Misbehavior Will Get Worse
Remember, when you first use Time Out the inappropriate behavior will get worse before it gets better. Be prepared for testing. Sometimes children resort to extreme behaviors in an effort to get your attention. Remember that messes and damage to property can be cleaned up or fixed.

Be Positive
When Time Out is over, do not scold or lecture. Look for new learning opportunities in which your child can be successful.

Teach Your Child How to Take a Time Out
Children are less likely to resist Time Out if you have explained to them the meaning of Time Out and practiced going there before it is needed. For example, you might say, *"You will have to go to Time Out if you make a mistake and hit someone. When you are in Time Out you will have time to calm down and think about what you have done. When it is over, you will have a chance to try again."* This explanation will have little meaning for most young children until they actually experience Time Out, but, nevertheless, it models a respectful approach. It is also a good idea to rehearse with your child how he will behave when he goes to Time Out and what he will do and think to himself when he is on the chair. You can coach your children to say to themselves, "Stop. Calm down. I can calm down. I can do it. I can handle this. I'll take a big breath. I'll try again." Practicing this self-talk will help your child to gain self-control and learn to calm down more quickly. But remember, this coaching can only occur when you are introducing Time Out to your child not during an actual time out because once you start a real Time Out you must ignore the protests.

There are many pitfalls to be avoided in the use of Time Out. On the following pages, you will find an outline of problems you may encounter and ways to overcome them.

Pitfalls to Implementing Time Out
Edit Criticisms and Nagging
It can be extremely difficult to keep your cool in the face of blatant non-compliance or aggressive behavior. Sometimes parents criticize their children or say insulting and hurtful things when using Time Out. A few examples include "You can't do anything right. Go to Time Out," "I'm fed up! You never obey me! Go to Time Out," "You've been terrible today. How many times do I have to tell you to stop?" This is a destructive

process and is more likely to result in children refusing to go to Time Out or responding with insults. Parents may then respond with more anger, resulting in an escalation of bickering.

It is understandable that parents feel hurt and angry when their children misbehave, disobey or challenge their authority. However, in order to avoid an escalation of negative exchanges, parents must decide to stop their own criticisms and be polite and stay calm at the very time their children are being impolite, obnoxious and unreasonable. This means doing some mental work called "editing" in which you delete negative comments and reactions, and state exactly what you want your child to do and why in an assertive but courteous fashion. For instance, "You need to go to Time Out for not doing what I asked you to do," or "Remember hitting is not allowed. Go to Time Out."

This also means *not lecturing* your child when Time Out is completed. Sometimes parents feel they have to remind their children why they had to go to Time Out—"You were put in Time Out because you hit. Remember not to hit. It makes me really angry." This is rubbing the child's nose in the mistake. It's better to say, "Now let's try again. I know you can do it." Once Time Out is over, you should view this as a clean slate or a new learning trial—a chance to try again and be successful.

Identify Problems Early
Sometimes parents try to ignore annoying behaviors such as constant whining, bickering with a sibling, or loud squealing. Then suddenly they feel they can't stand another minute of it and explode with anger. "You get into Time Out now, you're driving me crazy! I said now before you get into big trouble!" There are several problems here. First, these parents wait until they are boiling with anger and about to lose control. Second they give the child no warning, and third they don't make it clear why the child is being put into Time Out. This approach does not teach children anything except an explosive response to frustration.

You may not even be aware of the mounting anger that a particular inappropriate behavior triggers in you, until you explode. If this is the case, try to think about and monitor your reactions to particular misbehaviors. Then, if you find that interrupting or whining triggers a strong emotional response, you may decide that it isn't possible to ignore this behavior for very long. This is when you should present your children with the Three Strikes and You're Out Rule. Tell them that interrupting (or whining) three times will result in a Time Out. The first time a child interrupts, you might say, "That was your first interruption." Then "That was the second interruption," and finally "That was your third

Three strikes and you're out!

interruption. Go to Time Out." This warns your child that the behavior is inappropriate and alerts you to your mounting annoyance level. With this approach, you are clear about exactly what type of behavior will result in Time Out and you model an effective, calm and rational approach to a problem behavior. The key to success is staying calm.

Expecting Remorse

Some parents believe that in order for Time Out to be an effective form of discipline it must result in a child expressing pain or remorse or crying over the misbehavior. If this doesn't happen, they mistakenly think it isn't working and stop using it. They may consider spanking and hitting more effective because it is more likely to result in tears and expressions of remorse. However, as we have seen, physical punishment, even when it eliminates undesirable behavior in the short run, tends to cause more problems because it teaches a violent approach to conflict. Spanking also doesn't help children to learn how to problem solve or cool down so that they can cope with a problem. Tears may satisfy a parent's need for "just desserts," but they don't necessarily reflect effective discipline. In our experience a genuine apology is much more likely to be offered if not demanded.

Time Out doesn't need to result in tantrums, crying or expressions of guilt in order to be effective. In the beginning, young children may react violently when Time Out is used, but if it is used consistently and frequently, most will eventually take it without much anger. We have even found that some children put themselves in Time Out when they feel they are losing control. Thus, Time Out helps children learn self-control.

Don't be surprised if your children tell you Time Out doesn't bother them, and don't be fooled. They're only bluffing. Remember, the purpose of Time Out is not to get revenge or make children experience pain, but rather to stop the conflict and withdraw the reinforcing effects of negative attention for a misbehavior. It gives children a cooling off period and a chance to self-regulate and reflect upon what they have done.

Five-Minute Time Out with Two Minutes of Quiet

It's easy for parents to believe that Time Out is more effective if they make it longer—especially if their children have done something really bad like lying or stealing. Some parents add time on whenever their children yell or misbehave in the Time Out room. This is especially problematic if parents are also yelling through the door, "That is one more minute for that scream," since this attention will actually increase the misbehavior. Overly long Time Outs tend to breed resentment in children, and the isolation imposed keeps them from new opportunities to learn from experience, to try again and be successful.

Some parents have just the opposite problem. They use Time Out for a minute and then let their children out when they bang on the door, cry or promise to behave. Unfortunately, letting children out when they are still misbehaving reinforces that particular inappropriate behavior. The message communicated is, "If you kick (or cry or promise) hard enough, I'll let you out."

The most effective Time Out need only be three-five minutes (depending on age) provided there has been two minutes of quiet at the end. So if your child is yelling for the first 3 minutes of Time Out and quiet for the last 2 minutes, you can let him out of Time Out. (You do not need to add on time for the yelling, just be sure that your child has been calm for 2 minutes before coming out of Time Out). Adding time on for misbehaving doesn't make it more effective or eliminate the problems and in fact, it may do just the opposite. Remember, with children, there's no need for the punishment to fit the crime. Time Out is not meant to be like a jail sentence for adults. Its purpose is to provide a cooling off period, an opportunity to self-regulate and a clear, unrewarding consequence for misbehavior. The objective is to get your children out of it as quickly as possible so as to give them another chance to be successful.

Overuse of Time Out

Time Out is often used for many different misbehaviors, from whining, yelling and screaming to throwing, hitting and lying. Some parents report using it 20 to 30 times a day! This overuse is inappropriate and removes misbehaving children from opportunities to learn or demonstrate good behavior. It doesn't teach them any new and more appropriate ways to behave. While it keeps them out of your hair in the short run, in the long run it can cause bitterness and make children feel that they can't do anything right.

If you are a Time Out junkie, select the misbehavior you are most concerned about (e.g., aggression), and for the first three-four weeks, use Time Out only for that misbehavior. After Time Out has effectively reduced the frequency of this misbehavior, then you could add Time Out for another misbehavior (e.g. verbal abuse). For more minor disruptive behaviors such as whining and tantrums, try ignoring or a logical consequence instead of Time Out. More importantly, you must ensure that you are spending more time *supporting, teaching and encouraging appropriate behaviors* than you are focusing on negative ones. Time Out will only work if there are frequent positive consequences and parental attention and praise for appropriate behaviors. Remember Time Out is only effective if it is used infrequently. If you are using it alongside a positive plan to encourage children's appropriate behavior you should not have to use it for too long.

Don't Wait to Explode
Some people have a natural tendency to avoid confrontations and conflict, wanting everything always to be smooth and happy. These people don't change when they become parents, and they probably avoid using Time Out whenever possible. Often they store up annoyances and deal with problems only when they reach an explosion point. Avoiding conflicts with children doesn't help them to learn that there are negative consequences for misbehaving.

You need to be honest with yourself about which behaviors are annoying, inappropriate, or likely to result in your children alienating friends or getting into trouble at school. This means dealing with annoyances clearly and assertively as soon as they occur. For instance, you might say to one of your children, "I am not happy when you disobey me. If you don't clean up the living room, you will go to Time Out."

Freedom within Limits
Some parents avoid using Time Out because they want discipline and relationships with their children to be democratic and equal. They believe that parents should never impose their authority or exercise the power they have over their children, and that reasoning with youngsters about their problems is preferable to putting them in Time Out. They may feel that Time Out is disrespectful to children and even a form of rejection.

First of all, it is important not to equate Time Out with a general style of childrearing. Some parents are autocratic and expect complete obedience from their children. Such people may use Time Out to crush children's independence, creativity, problem solving and questioning of values. Other parents are democratic; they solicit children's input and explain why certain behaviors are appropriate or inappropriate. These parents use Time Out in a respectful way to teach children how to self-regulate and that there are consequences for misbehaving. It also teaches children that it is necessary to calm down before handling a conflict situation. Democracy does not mean unlimited freedom with no rules, but rather freedom within limits. These limits have to be set and imposed, and within most families they usually include not hurting people or destroying things and cooperating in a respectful way with each other.

Secondly, Time Out should not be perceived as a substitute for reasoning with children and teaching them. It is only one tool to be used briefly when a child's anger or frustration level is high. Later when things calm down and the child is behaving appropriately, parents can model, teach and talk about other more appropriate problem solving behaviors.

"If—Then" Warnings and Follow-Through

Occasionally parents threaten Time Out with no intention of following through. They might say, "Do you want a Time Out?" or "You're asking for a Time Out!" or "Are you ready for a Time Out?" These threats have the effect of nagging and, because they are rarely carried out, they dilute the parents' authority. Children come to believe that Time Out won't be used, especially if the threats are carried out only one time in ten, and the result will likely be an escalation of resistance to Time Out when it is actually imposed.

It is more effective to use an "if—then" statement than an empty threat of Time Out. "If you don't close the refrigerator door, then you will have to go to Time Out." Then, follow through once you have given your child an opportunity to comply. Only mention Time Out if you have the time and energy to carry it out. Otherwise it's better to ignore the misbehavior.

Following through also means that you must be prepared to repeat the Time Out if your child doesn't comply after the first one is over. If Donna's mom put her daughter in Time Out for refusing to wash the dishes, then as soon as the Time Out is over, she must repeat the command. If Donna refuses again, the warning and Time Out must be repeated until she washes the dishes. If you miss this important part of the follow-through, your children may learn to use Time Out in order to avoid doing something they don't want to do. Letting the child choose when to come back is one of the things that must be avoided as there is lots of evidence that this makes Time Out ineffective. You must control both the start and the end of the process.

Avoid Interaction During Time Out

Some parents inadvertently give attention to their children while they are in Time Out. For instance, Timmy yells in the Time Out room and

Timmy's dad responds to each yell with "You must be quiet before you can come out." Other parents respond to their children each time they ask, "How many more minutes?" Still others go in and out of the Time Out room, either to check on their children or to return them when they come out. All these actions defeat the purpose of Time Out and are very reinforcing for children.

There should be no communication with children when they are in Time Out. If you are likely to feel compelled to enter a Time Out room for fear that your daughter will break something, any items she could break should be removed from the room or a new location found. If you use a Time Out chair and your child manages to attract the attention of the dog, siblings or other adults, it may be necessary to move the chair to a less interesting location away from the rest of the family.

Avoid Physical Restraint

Sometimes when children repeatedly come out of Time Out, parents physically restrain them in Time Out. Others drag their children back into Time Out or spank them in order to get them to go. They justify such spankings and physical restraint by saying that it was used as a last resort after all else failed or that since it works it must be all right. The problem with this the-end-justifies-the-means approach is that it defeats the purposes of Time Out and focuses only on the short-term goals of getting children to comply and maintaining control. Unfortunately, the long-term disadvantages far outweigh the short-term benefits, increasing children's aggression and providing a model for a violent approach to conflict situations. Such situations are much better handled by combining Time Out with a loss of privileges. For example, at any point where you find you are starting to physically try to enforce Time Out, either to get your child into Time Out, or to keep him in Time Out, you need to shift gears and give your child either the choice of going voluntarily or taking a different consequence. This technique models a nonviolent approach that maintains good relationships with children.

Refusals to Come Out of Time Out

Another form of standoff commonly instigated by children involves children refusing to come out of Time Out once it's over. If your child was sent to Time Out for noncompliance, then it's important that you restate the original command (e.g., "Derrick you need to come out of Time Out and take out the garbage.") If your child refuses to come out of Time Out to take out the garbage, you should add two minutes to the Time Out. This can be continued for up to ten minutes and then a privilege can be withdrawn. It is important that you follow through by asking your child to comply with your original request, otherwise children may learn that they can get out of doing something by staying in Time Out.

However, if your child is in Time Out for hitting, you can say, "Your time is up. You can come out now." In this instance, it is fine if your child refuses to come out because there is nothing that you need him or her to do. You can simply respond, "Come out whenever you are ready," and ignore any refusal. This results in you not giving any power or attention to the child's noncompliance.

No Time Out Room Available
Some families don't have a suitable backup room available for the child who refuses to stay on the chair or go to the backup room. This does not mean you cannot enforce Time Out, but rather that you need an alternative plan. If this is the case you can use the strategy recommended for withdrawing a privilege when an older child refuses to go to Time Out. For example, you can say, "if you come off the Time Out chair again, you will lose 30 minutes of television," or, "you will not go to baseball practice tonight." Then if the child comes off the chair a second time, you end the Time Out sequence and follow through with the consequence. Think about possible privileges that you can remove immediately after the child's refusal to stay on the Time Out chair. Some examples include, loss of computer, TV, bike or phone privileges or of an activity planned for that evening. Once your child has experienced this consequence, he will learn that it is preferable to complete the time on the Time Out chair than lose the privilege.

Other Power Struggles
Another type of standoff happens when a parent has trouble forgiving a child after Time Out, and might continue to ignore him or her for an hour or even a whole day. As mentioned earlier, this does not teach children how to deal with conflict in an appropriate fashion; rather it teaches them to withdraw from conflict. Refusing to speak to your children for long periods after misbehavior only escalates tension and anger. In this situation, you should think about what is bothering you, what behavior you expect and then state this clearly. For instance, "I'm angry that you broke my vase. You will have to clean up the mess now and pay for it out of your allowance. I'll help you pick up the pieces."

Other Principles of Time Out

Hold Children Responsible

When some children are put in a Time Out room, they react violently by throwing things around, breaking things or even hammering holes in the door. Parents may react by opening the door and spanking the child. Others may avoid using Time Out again for fear of getting the same response.

It's not uncommon for children to react strongly to Time Out, especially in the beginning. If your child damages things in a room during a Time Out, you can respond in several ways. First, the original command (if this is a Time Out for noncompliance) must be repeated. For example, if your son was in Time Out for not putting his bike away, then he will first have to put it away. Afterwards, he should be asked to clean up the Time Out room. If he has broken something, then he should be held responsible for paying for it out of his allowance or have some privilege removed for that day.

If you are using your child's bedroom for Time Out and messes in Time Out are a frequent problem, then you will need to find another room or use a consequence. A dull room, as bare as possible, will be less interesting or reinforcing because it will provide a minimum of opportunities for making messes or breaking things.

Expect Persistence

A child yelling, screaming, swearing and banging on the door during Time Out can be an exhausting experience for parents. It's difficult to listen to children misbehaving without feeling anxious, depressed or angry. "Will she ever stop this?" or "What did I do wrong?" or "It can't be good for him

Time Out hangover.

to get so upset." Such feelings make it hard to continue Time Out for the full time needed or to use it again. In a sense parents may suffer a "hangover" from trying to use Time Out and avoid its use in the future. This may feel better in the short term, but has taught the child that tantrums are a successful strategy to get parents to back down on the rules.

Expect that Time Out will be difficult at times because all children will test the limits. If you use Time Out for hitting, your children will hit again several times in order to determine if it is a predictable and consistent response. If they don't experience a similar response, they will continue to use hitting as a method of handling conflict. In order to remain consistent and cope with the stress of enforcing a Time Out (while your child screams loudly) try distracting yourself by calling a supportive friend, turning up the volume of the TV, listening to some calming music on headphones, or doing some deep-breathing exercises (see Self-Control chapter).

Time Out in Public

When children misbehave in public places such as restaurants, movie theaters and grocery stores, parents are often reluctant to use their normal form of discipline. Some worry about how other people will react if they use Time Out with their children in public. Others are afraid their children will escalate their misbehavior into a full-blown tantrum, so they avoid discipline. Still others do not see how Time Out can be used anywhere but at home and resort to threats and spankings. As a result, many children have learned that grocery stores and restaurants are places they can get their own way because their parents will give in to avoid a scene.

Try to avoid using Time Out in public places until you've established consistent Time Outs at home for certain misbehaviors. In fact, it is a good idea to avoid public places with children until you have achieved some success with Time Out at home. Once you feel confident that this approach is working then the next important step will be to impose Time Out when aggressive behavior occurs in public places as well. This may mean leaving the grocery store to do a modified five-minute Time Out in the car or next to a tree in a park. If there is no place for a Time Out, you can say, "If you don't stop yelling (or whining or whatever), then you'll have a Time Out when we get home." You *must* follow through with this as soon as you get home. Once you have followed through once or twice at home, its effectiveness will be increased for future use. Your children will learn that the rules apply regardless of where they are, and they'll stop testing and learn to behave more appropriately.

Be prepared to do Time Out in public.

Pace Yourself

Often parents feel they have no time to carry out a Time Out. They might be late for work, on their way to an important appointment, or talking on the telephone when their children misbehave. When confronted with doing a Time Out and being late for work, they decide to overlook or give in to the misbehavior. This makes the use of Time Out inconsistent and usually results in an escalation of inappropriate behaviors during these hectic periods.

If your children misbehave as you are rushing to get ready for work, you need to plan a new strategy. At first this will mean getting up earlier so there is plenty of time for you to reinforce positive behaviors and carry out Time Out for inappropriate ones.

Support Each Other

Occasionally, while a parent is doing a Time Out, the other parent or a grandparent or friend will disrupt the process by talking to the child or by arguing about using Time Out. This makes it difficult to enforce Time Out and will result in the child seeing an opportunity to divide and conquer.

Research has shown that conflict with children can spread or deflect to create conflict between spouses, between parents and grandparents, and between parents and teachers. Consequently, if a parent is doing a

Time Out, there should be an agreement that other family members will be supportive even if there is a disagreement. Later when the adults are calm they should discuss, problem solve and agree on the following:

- which behaviors will result in Time Out
- how to determine who will take the lead in carrying out the Time Out
- ways for each to show support while supervising a Time Out
- how one parent can signal to the other that he or she is losing control and may need help to finish the Time Out
- acceptable ways to give feedback about the use of discipline.

If family members support one another as a team there will be fewer opportunities for children to wedge between them and fewer negative exchanges between parents and children around the use of Time Out. This is also great modeling for children in how people can work together.

There Is No Instant Solution

Some parents claim that Time Out doesn't work for them. The reason may be any of those we have discussed, or it may simply be that they have tried it a few times and then given up. It's a mistake, however, to expect four or five Time Out trials to eliminate a problem behavior.

Time Out is not magic. Children need repeated learning trials. They need *many* opportunities to make mistakes and misbehave and then to learn from the consequences of their misbehaviors. Just as it takes hundreds of trials for a baby to learn to walk, learning appropriate social behaviors also takes multiple practices. So remember, even when Time Out is used effectively, behavior changes slowly. Be patient. Remember that it will take your children at least 18 years to learn all the mature adult behaviors you'd like to see.

Remember to build up your bank account.

Build Up Your Account with Love and Support

Sometimes parents are clear with their children about the consequences for misbehaving but do not provide attention and encouragement for appropriate behaviors. In other words, much emphasis is placed on what children should not do, and there is considerably less emphasis on what to do instead.

Time Out is only one aspect of discipline. By itself it is not enough. You must capitalize on the many opportunities to teach your children appropriate behaviors. Praising, encouraging, and building self-esteem whenever your children do something positive is the core of parenting. Moreover, your ability to model effective communication, conflict resolution, problem solving, positive self-talk, playfulness and empathy for another's feelings is integral to the development of your children's social and moral development. In a sense, what you do is build up your family bank account with deposits of love, support and understanding. Then every now and again you temporarily make a withdrawal and use Time Out. Therefore, it is important to constantly keep your account growing.

Time Out for Parents

Parents can sometimes overreact to their children's misbehaviors because they are exhausted, angry or depressed about some other events in their life. A father who gets angry at his daughter may really be angry at his wife for ignoring his efforts with the children. Or a mother who has had an exhausting day at work and been criticized by her boss, may become cross with her children for making noise and not letting her relax. Depending on the mood and the energy level of the parent, a child's behavior can seem cute one day and obnoxious the next.

Even the kindest and most well-intentioned parents get frustrated and angry with their children. No one is perfect. But the important task is to recognize the filters and mood you bring to your perceptions of your children, and to learn to cope with the anger or frustration. If you're depressed because of work problems, it may be a good idea to take a Time Out yourself away from the children in order to relax and gain perspective. If you're angry with your spouse, you may need Time Out to problem solve. In helping your children to be less aggressive and more able to problem solve and handle conflict constructively, it is vital that you use Time Out when you feel anger building, to model conflict resolution and ways to support and care for each other. Remember children learn more from positive models than they do from critics. (See Chapter on Controlling Upsetting Thoughts.)

Remember to use Time Out for yourself.

Moving Beyond Discipline

Children who are impulsive, oppositional, inattentive, hyperactive and aggressive will need constant parental monitoring and socialization involving redirection, warnings, reminders, and consistent follow through with consequences. However, one of the hardest things to do when a child is disruptive is to move beyond the Time Out to repair and rebuild your relationship with your child. This means not holding onto grudges and resentment after consequences have been implemented and continued praising, encouragement for positive behaviors as well as teaching in problem solving, emotional regulation skills, and self-management. Be patient with your children as well as with yourself.

To Sum Up...

• Be polite.
• Be prepared for testing.
• Monitor and control personal anger in order to avoid exploding suddenly; give warnings.
• Give 5-minute Time Outs with 2-minute calm at the end.
• Carefully limit type of behaviors for which Time Out is used.
• Use Time Out consistently for chosen misbehaviors.
• Don't threaten Time Outs unless you're prepared to follow through.
• Ignore child while in Time Out.
• Use nonviolent approaches such as loss of privileges as a backup to Time Out.
• Follow through with completing Time Out.
• Hold children responsible for cleaning messes in Time Out.
• Use Time Out regardless of setting.
• Support a partner's use of Time Out.
• Don't rely exclusively on Time Out—combine with other discipline techniques, such as ignoring, logical consequences and problem solving.
• Expect repeated learning trials.
• Plan backup loss of privileges for older children who refuse to go to Time Out or stay in Time Out.
• Build up bank account with praise, love and support.
• Use personal Time Out to relax and refuel energy.

CHAPTER SEVEN

Natural and Logical Consequences

One of the most important and difficult tasks of parenting is to prepare children to be more independent. This training begins at an
early age. An important way to foster decision making, a sense of responsibility and the ability to learn from mistakes is through the use natural and
logical consequences. A natural consequence is whatever would result
from a child's action if there were no adult intervention. For instance, if
Ryan slept in and missed the school bus, the natural consequence would
be that he would have to walk to school. If Caitlin did not want to wear
her coat, then she would get cold. A logical consequence, on the other
hand, is designed by parents as a negative consequence inherently related
to the misbehavior. A logical consequence for a youngster who broke a
neighbor's window would be to do chores in order to make up the cost
of the replacement. A logical consequence for bed-wetting would be to
require the child to strip the sheets and put them in the wash. In other
words, when parents use this technique, they refrain from protecting
their children from the negative outcomes of their behavior.

Examples of Natural Consequences
- If child breaks her toy when angry, she will have no usable toy.
- If clothes are not put in hamper, the clothes will be dirty.
- If child jumps in mud puddles, he will have to wear wet shoes.
- If child is late for dinner, the food will be cold and family members
  will have left the table.
- If child doesn't eat at meals, there will be no food until the next meal
  and she'll be hungry.

Examples of Logical Consequences
- If child can't keep crayons on the paper, they will be taken away.
- If child refuses to eat dinner, there will be no snacks or dessert.

- If child doesn't keep her gum in her mouth, it will be taken away.
- If water is splashed out of the bathtub, the bath will end.
- If child can't use a quiet voice in the library, then he will have to leave.
- If child can't stay in backyard, then she'll have to play inside.
- If glasses are left in the living room, children cannot drink there the next day.
- If child hasn't had his afternoon snack by 4:30 pm, there will be no snack before dinner.
- If child watches more television than allowed, then the same amount of television is taken away the next day.
- If the child doesn't put her bike away in the garage, then use of the bike is restricted that evening.

Natural and logical consequences are most effective for recurring problems where parents decide ahead of time how they are going to follow through. This approach can help children to learn to make decisions, be responsible for their own behavior, and learn from their mistakes. In the following pages, we will discuss some of the problems that can occur when setting up logical and natural consequences and effective ways to overcome them.

Be Sure Your Expectations are Age Appropriate
Most natural and logical consequences work best for children five years of age and older. They can be used with younger children, but parents must first evaluate carefully whether the children understand the relationship between the consequences and the behavior. For instance, if Alexandra is not ready to be toilet trained but she is made to clean her underpants or change her bed, she may feel unduly criticized or humiliated. Moreover the logical consequence is an undue punishment. However, to deny dessert or snacks to a child who has refused to eat dinner is an appropriate consequence since the child learns that not eating dinner causes hunger. Of course, natural consequences should not be used if children may be physically hurt by them. For example, a preschooler should not be allowed to experience the natural consequences of sticking a finger into an electrical outlet, or touching the stove or running in the road.

When thinking through the natural consequences that may result from your children's inappropriate behaviors, it's important to be sure that your expectations are appropriate for their age. Because of the cognitive skills involved, natural consequences will work better for school-age children than for preschoolers. Logical consequences that young children do understand are "if—then" statements. For instance, "If you don't keep your gum in your mouth, I will have to take it away." Or for a child who points scissors at someone, "If you can't use the scissors carefully, then I will remove them." In these examples, the logical consequence of not using something properly is having it removed.

Be Sure You Can Live with the Choices

When attempting to carry out natural and logical consequences, some parents find it difficult to allow their children to experience the outcomes of their actions. They are so sympathetic towards their children that they feel guilty for not coming to their aid and may intervene before the consequence occurs. For instance, Carla tells her daughter Angie that the natural consequence of dawdling in the morning and not being ready for day care on time will be to go in pajamas. When the time comes to enforce this, however, she can't bring herself to let Angie go in her pajamas and dresses her instead. Such over-protectiveness can handicap children by making them incapable of handling problems or mistakes.

Be sure you can live with the consequences.

When using consequences it's important to think about the pros and cons of applying this technique to particular misbehaviors. Be certain that you can live with the consequences and that you are not giving idle threats. In the example above, Carla should have first considered whether or not she would be willing to follow through and take Angie to day care in her pajamas if she continued to dawdle. Failing to follow through with an agreed-upon consequence will dilute your authority and deprive your children of opportunities to learn from their mistakes.

Consequences Should Be Fairly Immediate

The natural and logical consequences approach doesn't work when the consequences of misbehaviors are too distant. The natural consequences of not brushing teeth would be to have cavities. However, since this might not occur for five to ten years it would not be effective. Similarly, overeating may have long-term consequences that are too distant to affect children's behavior in the short-term. Permitting youngsters to neglect homework and watch television every night until the end-of-the-year report card

Avoid consequences that are too distant.

shows they have failed is another consequence that is too delayed to have any influence on their daily study habits. Such long-term punishers may instead lead children to feel hopeless about their abilities.

For preschool and school-age children it's important that the consequences closely follow the inappropriate behavior. If Daniel damages another child's toy, then it should be replaced as quickly as possible and he should have to help pay for it through chores or from his allowance. If Lisa does not put her clothes in the laundry hamper, she should have to wear dirty clothes. In this way, Lisa and Daniel will learn from their inappropriate behavior and will probably behave more appropriately the next time.

Give Your Child Choices Ahead of Time

Sometimes parents use this approach in a punitive way, not letting their children know the possible consequences in advance. Linda's father comes into her room one morning and says, "You aren't dressed and it's time to leave, so you're coming right now in your pajamas." She is given no warning and does not have the choice of deciding to be ready by 8 o'clock or to change in the car on the way to school. Not surprisingly, Linda will probably feel resentful and will probably not see herself as responsible for the consequences of her behavior.

Discuss the various consequences with your children ahead of time so that they can think about them and know that they are responsible for the decision. Linda's dad could say, "Since you're having a hard time getting ready in the morning, you can have an alarm clock or go to bed half an hour earlier." Or he might say, "Either you get dressed by 8 o'clock, or you'll have no breakfast and will have to get changed in the car." Another example of giving a child choices would be to say, "If your toys aren't picked up by seven, there will be no snack or story." It is up to the child to decide how to respond. These approaches can help children to see, through positive consequences, that it is better to respond positively rather than negatively.

Consequences Should Be Natural or Logical and Nonpunitive
Occasionally parents come up with consequences that are not logically or naturally related to an activity. Consider a mother who washes her son's mouth out with soap because he said something bad. While she might argue that it is logical to clean out the mouth of a youngster who has been swearing, this is more likely to make her son feel dirty, degraded and angry. Other parents create consequences that are too punitive. "Since you wet your bed last night, you can't have anything to drink after noon today," or "Because you didn't eat your dinner, you will have to eat it for breakfast," or "Since you hit me, I'm going to bite you." Children will feel resentful and perhaps even retaliate against such consequences. They will be more likely to focus on the cruelty of their parents than on changing their own behavior.

A calm, matter-of-fact, friendly attitude is essential for deciding upon and carrying out consequences. The natural consequence of not wearing a coat when it's cold outside is to become chilled. The logical consequence of not doing homework might be to miss a favorite television program. The natural consequence of not putting clothes in the hamper is that the clothes don't get washed. These consequences are not degrading nor do they cause physical pain. Instead, they help children to learn to make choices and to be more responsible.

Involve Your Child Whenever Possible
Some parents set up a natural and logical consequence program without involving their children in the decisions. This may well cause the children to feel cross and resentful. Instead, you should consider this an opportunity for you and your children to work together to promote positive behaviors, allowing them to feel respected and valued. For instance, if your children are having problems fighting over the television, you might say, "You seem to be having trouble agreeing about what to watch on TV. I feel bad about yelling at you and I want to make the

evenings better for all of us. You can decide either to take turns choosing programs or not watching it. Which would you prefer?" Involving your children in the decision making about consequences often reduces their testing when there is a problem and encourages cooperation.

Be Straightforward and Friendly

Parents may sometimes undermine their consequence program by becoming angry with their children and criticizing them for being irresponsible. This defeats the program's purpose of letting children discover for themselves, through experience, the negative consequences of their behavior. Moreover, the anger and disapproval may reinforce the misbehaviors.

It's important to be straightforward and assertive about consequences, to be prepared to follow through with them, and to ignore your children's protests or pleading. If they refuse to accept consequences, you should use Time Out or the loss of a privilege, whichever best fits the situation. Remember, your children will try to test the limits, so expect testing. But it is important not to lecture or criticize them or offer sympathy after the consequence occurs. Instead, once it is completed, they should be given a new opportunity to be successful.

Consequences Should Be Appropriate

Sometimes parents come up with a consequence that lasts too long and unduly punishes their children. Say seven-year-old Ben rides his bicycle in the road after being told to stay on the driveway. The logical consequence would be for the parents to lock it up. Locking it up for a month, however, would be excessive and bound to make Ben feel cross and resentful. Moreover, it wouldn't allow him any new opportunities to be more successful in handling his bicycle responsibly. Although some people believe that the stronger and longer the punishment, the more effective it will be, the opposite is true.

A more appropriate consequence in Ben's case would have been to lock up his bike for 24 hours and then allow him the chance to be successful in the way he rides it. If four-year-old Kathy is using crayons and starts coloring on the kitchen table, a logical consequence to present her with might be, "If you can't keep the crayons on the paper, then I will have to take them away." If she continues to color on the table, then the crayons would have to be removed. However, they should be returned within half an hour to give her another opportunity to use them appropriately. The principle is to make the consequences immediate, short, to the point, and then to quickly offer your child a chance to try again and be successful.

Remember that the consequences approach, like any other parenting technique, take time, planning, patience and repetition. Most of all if requires a calm, respectful attitude.

To Sum Up...

- Make consequences age-appropriate.
- Be sure you can live with consequences you set up.
- Make consequences immediate.
- Give child choice of consequence ahead of time.
- Make consequence natural and nonpunitive.
- Involve child whenever possible.
- Be friendly and positive.
- Use consequences that are short and to the point.
- Quickly offer new learning opportunities to be successful.

Avoid consequences that are too severe.

CHAPTER EIGHT

Teaching Children to Problem Solve

Young children usually react to their problems in ineffective ways. Some cry, others hit and still others tattle to their parents. These responses do little to help children find satisfying solutions to their problems. In fact, they create new ones. But research shows that they use these inappropriate strategies either because they have not been taught more appropriate ways to problem solve or because their inappropriate strategies have been reinforced inadvertently by parents or other children's responses. Parents can help by teaching their children how to think of solutions to their problems and how to decide which solutions are most effective.

It also has been shown that children's temperament influences their ability to learn more effective problem solving skills. In particular, children who are hyperactive, impulsive, inattentive and aggressive are more likely to have cognitive difficulties with social problem solving. Such high-risk children perceive social situations in hostile terms, generate fewer prosocial ways of solving interpersonal conflict, and anticipate fewer consequences for aggression. They act aggressively and impulsively without stopping to think of non-aggressive solutions or of the other person's perspective. On the other hand, there is evidence that children who employ appropriate problem solving strategies play more constructively, are better liked by their peers, and are more co-operative at home and school. Consequently, parents have a key role in teaching children who are aggressive and impulsive to think of more prosocial solutions to their problems and to evaluate which solutions are better choices and more likely to lead to positive consequences than others.

While teaching effective problem solving will be particularly helpful for high risk children, efforts should be made to improve social skills and cognitive problem solving for *all* children. Indeed, it is the job of parents to prepare today's children to be responsible citizens who are capable of thoughtful decision-making and coping with interpersonal conflict. Children's successful development into adulthood is dependent on their ability to use critical judgment, effective decision-making skills and perspective-taking regardless of their innate ability and cultural or family background.

Parent as Model
Undoubtedly, you are already teaching your children more appropriate problem solving tactics without realizing it, especially if they have opportunities to observe you using problem solving skills (see Chapter Problem Solving between Adults). It is a rich learning experience for them to watch you discussing problems with other adults, negotiating and resolving conflict, and evaluating the outcome of your solutions. While you may not want your children to observe all your problem solving meetings, many daily decisions you make provide good opportunities for them to learn. For instance, children learn from noticing how their parents say no to a friend's request. They watch with interest as Dad receives Mom's suggestion to wear something different. Is Mom sarcastic, angry or matter-of-fact in her request? Does Dad pout, get angry, cooperate or ask for more information? Watching parents decide which movie to see on Saturday night can teach much about compromise and negotiation. Your children learn much of their behavior by observing how you react to life's daily hassles. You can help further by thinking your positive problem solving strategies out loud. For example, you might say, "How can I solve this? I need to stop and think first. I need to stay calm. What plan can I come up with to make this successful?"

For children, the process of problem solving can be divided into six steps and presented as the following questions:

- What is my problem? What am I supposed to do? (Define the problem and feelings involved)
- What are some solutions? What are some more solutions? (Brainstorm solutions)
- What are the consequences? What happens next?
- What is the best solution or choice? (Evaluate consequences in terms of safety, fairness and good feelings)
- Am I using my plan? (Implementation)
- How did I do? (Evaluating the outcome and reinforcing efforts)

For children between the ages of three and eight, the second step—generating possible solutions—is a key skill to learn. While implementation and evaluation are more easily done by older children, youngsters first need to consider possible solutions and to understand that some solutions are better than others. The ability to think ahead to possible outcomes for each solution is a big developmental step and will be particularly difficult for young children or children who are hyperactive and impulsive.

STEP ONE: Discuss Hypothetical Problems
A fun way to begin problem solving discussions with your children is to ask them to pretend being 'detectives' who are trying to solve a problem. Then through the use of stories or puppets you can create problem scenarios and ask them to come up with as many solutions as possible. More of these problems can be found in two colorful children's books, *Wally's Detective Books for Solving Problems at Home and at School* (Webster-Stratton, 1998). Here are some hypothetical problem situations you could try to solve together with your child using the six steps outlined in this chapter:

- Suppose a child much younger than you started hitting you. What would you do?
- Suppose a boy had been playing for a long, long time with a toy, and you wanted to play with it. What would you do?
- Suppose there was only one piece of pizza left and you and your sister both wanted it. What would you do?
- Suppose you broke your dad's favorite lamp. What would you do?
- Suppose you are constantly teased by another child at school. What would you do?
- Suppose you want to meet a new neighbor. What would you do?
- Suppose your mother sent you to your room for calling your brother a name when he called you a name first. What would you do?
- Suppose you lost a brand-new pair of shoes that your father bought you for soccer. What would you do?
- Suppose you really want to watch a special program on TV, but your mother won't let you. What would you do?
- Suppose you ask some kids to play with them and they won't let you. What would you do?
- Suppose another child teases you for your new hair cut. What would you do?
- Suppose you ask another child to play ball with you and he or she refuses. What would you do?
- Suppose your brother wrecks a model you've been working on for two weeks. What would you do?

The first step in helping children understand if they have a problem is for them to be aware of their feelings. If they are feeling uncomfortable (sad, or angry or worried) this will be an important clue that there is a problem to solve. Therefore when talking about these problems, help your child identify the feelings of the characters involved in the situations. Some children have limited vocabulary for expressing feelings. For such children to become effective problem solvers it will be necessary to help them expand their feeling vocabulary. Once they are able to recognize and label their feelings then you can help them learn how to accurately define the problem. For example, "So you feel angry because your classmate won't share the football with you."

Another aspect of this problem definition phase also involves trying to help your child think about the feelings of the others in the situation. For example, "How do think the boy who has the football feels?"

Some children have difficulty reading the feeling clues of others in a situation or may misinterpret others' feelings, leading to inappropriate decisions.

STEP TWO: Brainstorm Solutions
After defining the problem, the next step is for you to help your child come up with as many different solutions, options or choices as your child can in order to solve the problem. If your child cannot think of any solutions to begin with, suggest a few ideas. Try to make these problem solving discussions fun by using cartoons, stories or puppets. You might even suggest that you write a story together about solving the problem. Avoid criticizing or ridiculing any of your children's ideas, no matter how silly they are. Instead, encourage imaginative thinking and try to model creative solutions yourself. Be sure to praise them for their attempts to solve the problem. In particular, it is helpful to praise them for their different solutions (e.g., 'Great job, that is a different idea') because it will encourage a broader variety of solutions rather than variations of the same idea.

Here are some solutions that might be proposed to the first three hypothetical situations:

- Yell at him or her. Look sad or cry. Walk away. Laugh at him or her. Hit back. Tell her not to hit. Get a parent.
- Take it. Hit him. Wait a while. Ask him. Say please. Do something else fun.
- Trade something. Talk about your feelings. Beg. Offer to share. Say please. Take it. Cut it in half.

Join your child in problem solving.

STEP THREE: Think Through Consequences

After generating possible solutions, the next step is to look at what would happen next if each solution were carried out. Once the consequences have been discussed, help your children to assess which solution or choice may be the best one. If for instance, your daughter said that tricking or hitting a friend to get a toy is a solution, help her to consider the possible outcomes, such as losing a friend, getting into trouble, or getting the toy. Then consider the possible consequences of a different solution, such as asking the friend for the toy: she might be turned down by the friend, ignored, or she might get the toy. Often, children are surprised or upset when things don't go according to their plan. Part of this can be avoided if they stop and predict several outcomes that might result from their behavior. Be sure that this does not become a burdensome or compulsive activity. They don't have to discuss the consequences of every single solution.

STEP FOUR: What Is The Best Solution or Choice?

After reviewing possible outcomes of a few solutions, the next step is to help your child decide what one or two might be the best choice to try. By phrasing it as a choice it gives your child the responsibility for the problem.

Choosing the best solution involves children asking themselves three questions: Is the solution safe? Is it fair? Does it lead to good feelings? If the solution meets these criteria then the children are encouraged to try it out. You might ask them to act it out with you.

STEP FIVE: Implementation of Problem-solving Skills
The fifth step when engaged in hypothetical problem-solving games is for your child to think of a situation where they might use the agreed upon solution. Then later in the day if you observe a similar real-life problem occurring, you can help your child use the solution to try solving the problem. For example, after you have been having these problem solving discussions, your son comes running to you complaining that his sister took away his favorite book, or your daughter comes to you in tears because her baby brother bit her. You can respond by following the problem solving steps outlined above. While it may be tempting to tell them what to do, it is more effective to help them think about solutions. Problem solving in the midst of a conflict is much harder than problem solving in a hypothetical or neutral situation. Children may be so angry and upset that they cannot think clearly. You may be able to calm them through discussion, so they can come up with some solutions. Sometimes children may be so emotional that they need to go for a brief Time Out until they cool off. Occasionally a problem is so distressing that it is best discussed later when both you and your child have had time to calm down and gain some perspective.

STEP SIX: Evaluating Outcome
How often have you heard yourself say, "Max makes the same mistakes over and over again. He doesn't seem to learn from experience or remember what happened the other times." The reason for this is that some children lack the skill of using the past to inform the future. They do not know how to recall past experience or to see how those experiences apply to what is happening now. This is why the sixth step is important because it will help your child learn how to evaluate how successful s/he was in solving a problem (whether hypothetical or real life) and whether they might use it again in the future. Thus it encourages them to rethink the past event and anticipate whether this would be a good choice in the future. You can help your child evaluate the solution and its consequences by asking the same three questions they asked themselves when they were choosing a good solution:

• Was it safe? Was anyone hurt?
• Was it fair?
• How did you feel about it and how did the others feel?

If the answer is negative to any of these questions then encourage your child to think about different solutions. You might say, "Okay so that was not the best choice and we wouldn't want to do that again because it led to bad feelings, what other choice could we make if this happens again?" Finally, the most important aspect of this step is to reinforce your child for his efforts at problem solving. Praise him and get him to pat himself on the back for his own good thinking—regardless of the quality of the solution that was proposed.

The following pages focus on some of the problems parents may encounter when they try to teach problem solving to their children. It also includes some effective ways to be successful.

Discover Your Child's View of the Problem First
Sometimes parents are too quick to come to a conclusion about what exactly is their child's problem. For instance, Tanya's mother may decide that her daughter is having trouble sharing without understanding that from Tanya's point of view, the problem is that her friend grabbed *her* crayons away in the first place. Or perhaps Tanya shared her crayons with her friend but then the friend refused to give them back. If her mom makes a quick decision about the problem, she may focus her energies in the wrong direction. By misinterpreting the situation, she may lecture Tanya about sharing. This can lead to the child's resistance for several reasons. No one likes to be blamed for things they didn't do and Tanya will likely become upset about unfair treatment. And if she is preoccupied with thinking about the injustice and how to retrieve the crayons, she won't hear a word of her mother's good ideas.

Your first task is to try to understand the problem from your child's point of view. You will usually need to ask questions like, "What happened?" "What's the matter?" or "Can you tell me about it?" This kind of question not only helps your child to clarify the problem in his or her own mind, but also insures that you won't jump to the wrong conclusion about what's going on. Once you are sure you understand, you might say in a situation like Tanya's, "Now I understand what the problem is. You shared your crayons, but your friend played with them too long and wouldn't give them back. And that made you mad." In order for children to learn anything from a problem, it is important that the solution be relevant to *their* perception of the situation. Believing that you understand your child's point of view is likely to increase his or her motivation to deal with the problem cooperatively.

Encourage Your Child to Come Up with Multiple Solutions
Many parents believe that telling their children how to solve a problem helps them learn to problem solve. For example, two children may have

trouble sharing a bicycle and the parent responds by saying, "You should either play together or take turns. Grabbing is not nice." Or "You must share. Johnny will get mad and won't be your friend if you don't share. You can't go around grabbing things. Would you like that if he did it to you?" The problem with this approach is that the parents tell their children what to do before they have found out what the problem is from their viewpoint. Moreover, it does not help them to think about their problem and how to solve it. Rather than being encouraged to learn how to think, they are told *what* to think and the solution is imposed upon them.

It is more effective to guide your children into thinking about what may have caused the problem in the first place than to tell them the solution. Invite them to come up with possible solutions. If you want to help them develop a habit of solving their own problems, they need to be encouraged to think for themselves. They should be urged to express their feelings about the situation, talk about their ideas for solving the problem and anticipate what might happen if they try a particular solution. The only time you need to offer solutions is if your children need a few ideas to get them started.

Guided Problem Solving

The opposite problem occurs when parents think they are helping their children to resolve conflict by telling them to work it out for themselves. This approach might work if the children already have good problem solving skills, but for most young children it won't. In the case of Max and Tyler fighting over a book, it will probably result in continued arguing and Tyler, the more aggressive child, getting the book. Therefore, Tyler is reinforced for his inappropriate behavior because he got what he wanted and Max is reinforced for giving in because the fighting ceased when he backed down.

Your role is to teach your children to work it out on their own by guiding them through the problem-solving steps. You can encourage them to talk aloud as they think and you can praise their ideas and attempts at solutions. In this way, you reinforce the development of a style of thinking that will help them to deal with all kinds of problems. Encourage them to come up with many possible solutions. Then help them to shift their focus to the consequences of each solution. The final step is to help them to evaluate which are the best ones.

Be Positive and Fun

Sometimes parents try to be helpful by telling their children when their solutions are silly, inappropriate, or not likely to be successful. This can make them feel ridiculed and they'll probably stop generating solutions. Another type of problem occurs when parents become obsessive about this process and they force their youngsters to come up with so many solutions and consequences that the discussion becomes confusing.

Avoid ridiculing, criticizing, or making negative evaluations of your children's ideas. Instead, urge them to think of as many solutions as possible, and to let their imaginations run free. If they have a short attention span or become bored, not all the solutions have to be looked at in detail regarding the possible consequences. Instead, focus on two or three of the most promising ones.

Encourage children to problem solve with each other.

Ask about Feelings

When some parents problem solve they avoid discussing feelings. They focus exclusively on the thinking style, the solution and the consequences. Yet, they forget to ask their children how they feel about the problem or how the other person in the situation may have felt. It is also important for parents to be aware of their own feelings. Hearing your daughter report that she has been sent home from Julia's house for hitting may provoke feelings of anger, frustration or helplessness. You would need to gain control of these emotions before trying to help your child with her feelings about the situation.

Encourage your children to think about their feelings in response to a problem or to a possible outcome of a solution. Urge them to consider the other person's point of view in the situation. You might ask your daughter, "How are you feeling about being sent home?" "How do you think Julia felt when you did that? How did you feel when she did that?" Raise the question about how she might discover what someone else feels or thinks. "How can you find out if she likes your idea? How can you tell if she is sad or happy?" This will help your children to be more empathetic and, because they try to understand other people's feelings and viewpoints, result in more willingness to problem solve, compromise and cooperate. Discussing your feelings also helps them to realize that you empathize with them.

Encourage Many Solutions

As your children come up with solutions, be careful not to criticize them because they are not good enough. Allow them to think of as many as possible without comments from you as to their quality or potential effectiveness. Then you can offer a few of your own creative ideas—as suggestions however, not as orders. Research has shown that one difference between a well-adjusted and a poorly-adjusted child is that the well-adjusted one is more likely to think of a greater number of solutions to problems. The goal, then, is to increase your children's likelihood of generating numerous ideas.

Use Open-Ended Questioning and Paraphrasing

Using open-ended questions will maximize a child's thinking about the problem. While you may be tempted to ask "why" questions ("Why did you do that?") or multiple choice questions ("Did you hit him because you were angry or because he was making fun of you...?") or closed-ended questions ("Did you hit him?"), avoid these approaches because they either result in a yes or no answer or close off discussion because of feeling defensive or blamed. Instead ask "what" or "how" questions such as, "What happened?" or "How are you feeling?" or "What other feelings do you have?" or "What do you think the other person feels?" These open-ended questions will be more likely to engage the child in the problem solving process.

Paraphrasing or reflecting back on what your child is saying also helps them feel listened to and valued for their ideas. The advantage of paraphrasing is you can rephrase some of your child's statements to more appropriate language. For example, when your child was asked how he felt, he responded, "He's a real dummy." This can be paraphrased as, " You sound really angry with him." This will help your child eventually to develop better problem solving vocabulary.

Think about Positive and Negative Consequences

When parents discuss the possible consequences of solutions, they occasionally focus on negative ones. For instance, a father and son may be talking about outcomes of a proposed solution that hitting his friend may allow him to get the ball he wants. One obvious consequence is that the other child will cry, be unhappy, and get the hitter in trouble with his parents. Most parents would predict this consequence. However, many would overlook the fact that hitting might work to get the desired ball. It is important to be honest with children and explore both the positive and negative consequences. If hitting works in the short run, the child then needs to think about what effect such behavior might have on his friend's desire to play with him in the long run. By evaluating all of the possible outcomes, children can make a better judgment about how effective each solution is.

Model Your Thinking Out Loud
Some parents schedule their own problem solving sessions when their children are in bed because they are not comfortable allowing them to watch. Such people may feel that they must present a united front to their children. While this is true with regard to discipline, it is not always true in other areas. Children can learn to handle differences of opinion if they can observe adults resolving problems effectively. While they should be protected from watching heated arguments about major issues, exposure to well-managed discussions of disagreement provides a positive learning experience.

While you may not want your children to be present for all of your problem solving sessions, it is helpful for them to observe daily problem solving that goes on in the family. They can learn by watching you and your spouse decide who is going to find a baby sitter for the weekend, who will do the shopping, or how to decide where to take a vacation. For single parents there are countless opportunities for children to observe you discussing a problem or conflict, generating solutions and then working to evaluate what the best solution might be. You can model problem solving out loud as you sort out plans for a party, or make car-pool arrangements or determine how to make your budget work out. It is also helpful for them to see you evaluate a solution that may not have worked out well and to hear you decide on a different strategy for the future. Research suggests that the opportunity for children to observe adults discussing and resolving conflict is critical, not only for developing their problem solving skills, but also for reducing their stress and anxiety about unresolved issues.

Focus on Thinking and Self-Management
Often parents believe that the objective of problem solving is to come up with the best solution to a particular situation. While this would be nice if it happened, the real purpose for going through the process with your children is to teach them a thinking strategy and a method of self-management rather than generating the "correct" solution.

When you are problem solving with your children, focus on how they are thinking rather than on specific conclusions. Your goals are to help them become comfortable thinking about conflict, develop a knowledge base for generating good solutions or choices, and understand strategies for thinking ahead to possible consequences of different solutions. These cognitive social problem solving skills will eventually lead to self-management when faced with real-life conflict. Try to use the problem solving methods whenever you can throughout the day to help your children find solutions to their problems.

Consider the following examples of poor versus effective problem solving with children:

Poor Problem Solving:
Two children are fighting over a doll and each is grabbing it.

PARENT: I've told you a million times not to grab each other's toys.
1ST CHILD: But it's mine.
2ND CHILD: She took it. I had it first.
PARENT: Can't you two learn to play together? You must learn
            to share!

Fighting resumes.

Effective Problem Solving:
Tina is crying and holding her arm.

MOTHER: Who hit you?
TINA: Sarah.
MOTHER: What happened? (Mother elicits Tina's view of problem.)
TINA: She just hit me.
MOTHER: Do you know why she hit you? (Mother encourages Tina
            to think of causes.)
TINA: Well, I hit her first.
MOTHER: I guess you were mad. Why?
TINA: She wouldn't let me look at her book.
MOTHER: That must have been frustrating. How do you think she felt
            when you hit her? (Mother helps Tina think of the feelings
            of others.)
TINA: Mad.
MOTHER: I guess that's why she hit you back. Do you know why she
            wouldn't let you look at the book? (Mother helps Tina to
            see the point of view of the other child.)
TINA: No.
MOTHER: How can you find out?
TINA: I could ask her.

MOTHER: That's a good idea. (Mother encourages Tina to seek facts and discover the problem.)

Later

TINA: She said I never let her see my books.

MOTHER: Oh, now you know why she said no. Can you think of something you could do so she'd let you look at the book? (Mother encourages Tina to think of solutions.)

TINA: I could tell her I won't be her friend if she doesn't give it to me.

MOTHER: Yes, that's one idea. What would happen if you did that? (Tina is guided to think of consequences of solution.)

TINA: She might not play with me again or be my friend.

MOTHER: Yes, that's a possible result, do you want her to be your friend?

TINA: Yes.

MOTHER: Can you think of something else so she would still be your friend? (Mother encourages further solutions.)

TINA: I could trade her one of my books.

MOTHER: That's a good idea. What might happen if you did that?

In this example, Tina's mother helps her to think of why she was hit and recognize the problem. When she learns that Tina hit first, she does not lecture or offer advice, but helps her daughter to think about Sarah's feelings. Through problem solving she encourages Tina to consider the problem and alternative ways to solve it.

Poor Problem Solving:

MARTY: Dad, come play with me.

FATHER: I can't, I'm busy.

MARTY: Please, Dad, please play with me.

FATHER: I have to get dinner. I'll play with you later.

MARTY: Please? I want you to play with me now.

FATHER: Just go play by yourself while I get dinner. You have to learn how to play by yourself. You can't have everything the minute you want it.

Five minutes later

MARTY: Dad, are you finished with dinner?

FATHER: I'll tell you when I'm finished, don't bother me or I won't play with you at all.

Effective Problem Solving:

MARTY: Dad, will you play with me?

FATHER: I'm making dinner right now. When I finish this salad, then I can play with you.

MARTY: Please Dad, please play with me now.

FATHER: I can't play now even though I'd like to. We're having your grandparents over for dinner and I want to have this made by the time they get here.

MARTY: Oh Dad!

FATHER: Can you think of something different to do while I finish this salad? (Father helps Marty think of alternative activity.)

MARTY: No.

FATHER: You're just teasing me. What would you like to do?

MARTY: I could help you make the salad.

FATHER: Yes, that's one thing you could do.

MARTY: Or, I could watch TV.

FATHER: Yeah, now you've thought of two things. And if you still want me to play with you when I'm finished, let me know.

Emotional confrontation can be avoided when both Marty and his dad recognize the problem and each other's point of view. Marty accepts that he can't have what he wants immediately and is willing to wait for it because he is guided to think how his father is feeling and knows his father understands how he is feeling.

Praise and More Praise

Throughout the day look for times when your children are making good choices and effectively problem solving and pause to praise your children using these strategies. For example, say, "Wow you two worked out that problem like real detectives! You are getting very good at solving problems and staying calm."

To Sum Up...

Teaching these social problem solving steps is no harder than teaching any other set of skills such as how to ride a bike or learn to read. First you teach the step-by-step procedures to follow and then you provide modeling, repeated practice and reinforcement with different situations. Gradually with time and practice and persistence these 'scripts' will become automatic and with ongoing experiences they will be broadened and integrated. Just as when learning to read there is no expectation that these skills will all be mastered in one year or on one course, but instead will require continued instruction and support. Moreover, just as some children have difficulty with learning to read or write so do some children have more difficulty with reading social cues, understanding another's point of view, understanding how to express their feelings and learning appropriate strategies to solve their problems. With persistent encouragement on the part of the parent, children will come to perceive themselves as competent decision-makers and will be armed with the necessary skills for meeting the challenges of adolescents and adulthood.

Remember
- Use games, books and puppets to present hypothetical problem situations for children to practice the problem solving steps.
- Help children clearly define the problem and to recognize the feelings involved.
- For preschool children, focus on generating many solutions.
- For primary age children, focus on helping them think through to the various consequences of different solutions.
- Be positive, creative and humorous.
- Model effective problem solving yourself.
- Help children anticipate what to do next when a solution doesn't work.
- Remember it is the process of learning how to think about conflict that is critical, rather than getting correct answers.

CHAPTER NINE

Helping Children Learn to Regulate Their Emotions

Billy's Little League was leading a close game against the league leaders, and the team was ecstatic. In the final inning, the game turned and the other team pulled ahead by three runs. The pressure was on! The pitcher for Billy's team panicked and threw the ball to first base rather than home, permitting another runner to score.

Finally, the other team struck out and Billy went up to bat, trembling. When he struck out, he was so mad that he threw his helmet onto the field. His father griped, "What drama! Can't he learn to control himself?"

A second boy, Eric, struck out and stoically left the field. Jack and Ian, on the other hand, burst into tears over the loss. One parent yelled, "Ten-year-old boys are too old to cry! Don't be babies." Another parent advised, "Don't cry—get mad!"

As the dejected team left the field one boy said, "I'm going to break their pitcher's leg."

As this scenario shows, there are dramatic differences in children's and parents' responses to emotionally charged situations. Understanding the forces behind emotional reactions is the first step in helping children deal with life's frustrations and disappointments.

First, it is important to define the terms: Emotions are responses to stimuli or situations that affect a person strongly. Watch how different teammates demonstrated the three levels of emotional response.

- The first—and most basic—level involves neurophysiological and biochemical reactions, including all the bodily processes regulated by the autonomic nervous system: heart rate, blood flow, respiration, hormone secretions and neural responses. For example, a person who is angry feels her heart race and her face get red. Billy's trembling was a neurophysiological expression.

- The second level of emotional response is the motor and behavioral, where a person expresses emotion through actions, such as facial expressions, crying, sullen gazes or withdrawal. Jack and Ian expressed their emotions behaviorally when they burst into tears, as did Billy when he hurled his helmet in anger. Leaving the field showed Eric's use of withdrawal, another behavioral expression of emotion.
- Still another boy expressed his feelings through his words, revealing his cognitive or subjective response to the event. It's the third level, using language (spoken, written, or thought) to label feelings as in, " I feel frustrated."

What is Emotional Regulation?

Emotional regulation refers to a person's ability to provide adequate control over his or her emotional responses (neurophysiological and biochemical, behavioral and cognitive) to arousing situations. The term *emotional dysregulation* refers to someone whose emotional responses are often out of control, like the child whose anger and aggression keep him from making and keeping friendships, or the child whose withdrawal from emotional challenges leads to avoiding any new activity.

Just as walking, talking, and toilet training are developmental steps, emotional regulation is a developmental achievement that is not present at birth—i.e., it must be learned. At first, regulation must be provided by the environment. The young infant who has a wet diaper expresses her distress in the only way she can—through crying. She needs outside help to reduce her internal tension. The parent helps by trying to understand the meaning of the baby's cries and taking the necessary action to calm her. And as we all know, some babies are easily calmed and others are more difficult. This suggests that infants are born with individual differences in their ability to self-regulate.

In toddlerhood and the preschool years the child's emotional regulatory system starts to mature, and the burden of emotional regulation begins to shift from parent to child. As children develop language skills they become increasingly able to label their emotions, thoughts, and intentions, which helps them regulate their emotional responses. In part, this means letting their parents know what they need in order to calm themselves. However, children at this age still need adult help to regulate intense emotions.

By school age, children take greater responsibility for their own emotional functioning, but parents continue to have a major role. At this age, emotional regulation becomes more *reflective*, guided by the child's sense of self and the environment.

The extreme emotional responses of anger, distress, and excitement have been dampened to some extent by this age. Instead of hitting someone or exploding in a tantrum when they're angry, many school-age children will argue, or perhaps even be able to verbalize that they are mad. Instead of expressing impatience by whining, children begin to be able to wait. Instead of expressing excitement by running around in circles, children can talk about how excited they are.

Moreover, as children develop their own capacities for emotional regulation, they start to separate their internal reactions from external expressions. Thus we see the school-aged child who can be internally distressed by an event but outwardly show no sign of emotion.

During adolescence, hormones enter the picture and create an upheaval in the child's emotional systems, challenging the emotional regulation learned over the years. Parents may feel as if their adolescent has regressed to the emotional regulatory stage of a preschooler!

How Quickly Do Children Learn Emotional Regulation?
Just as there is a wide variation in when children start to walk or talk or learn to use the toilet, some children's self-regulatory systems develop more slowly than others'. We know little as yet about what contributes to these differences in timing. However, research suggests that at least three processes underlie children's growing ability to regulate their emotions:

- *Neurological maturation.* The growth and development of the child's nervous system provides the "hardware" required for controlling emotional reactions.
- *Temperament and developmental status.* Some children are more vulnerable to emotional dysregulation due to learning difficulties, language delays, attentional deficits or difficult temperament.
- *Parental socialization and environmental support.* Differences in how families talk about feelings (their own and others') are related to later differences in the ways children express their feelings and regulate their

emotions. Children who experience chronic stress, or lack predictability and stability in their environment, have more problems with emotional regulation.

We cannot change a child's neurological system or her temperament and developmental status, but we can help children learn to regulate their emotions through the third factor, socialization and support.

Here Are Some Ways You Can Help:
Provide stability and consistency
Consistent limits, clear household rules and predictable routines help children know what to expect. When the home feels stable and secure, children develop the emotional resources to deal with the less predictable world outside.

Accept your child's emotions and emotional responses
Children's emotional outbursts are not intentional, nor are they deliberate attempts to make parenting difficult. It is normal for children at times to sulk, to respond by yelling, cursing, or breaking something, or to withdraw and want to be left alone. "Tuning in" and understanding your child's emotional states helps your child tolerate and cope with increasing amounts of emotional tension. Even a simple statement such as "I see that you are mad that you can't have a cookie now," will help a child identify the emotional turmoil occurring in his or her body.

Talk about your own feelings
Use the language of feelings with your children, and they will begin to identify emotions accurately and put them into words. For example, in the example at the start of this article, the father might have said something like this to his son:

> "I felt really frustrated to see your team lose after doing so well throughout the whole game. I feel sad that you lost. But the important thing is you played a really good game. You guys were doing your best and you were good team members—you all really worked together. I was proud of you. Next time maybe you'll win!"

Parents who frequently use the language of emotions to express their own emotional states and to interpret others' (nonverbal) emotional expressions are providing their children with a powerful mechanism for emotional regulation. This frequent talk about feelings helps children learn to identify emotions accurately and models ways to cope with those emotions through verbalizing the feelings. Children who hear "feeling talk" from adults will be less likely to resort to inappropriate behavioral expressions of negative emotions. Research suggests that children who learn to use emotional language have more control over their nonverbal emotional expressions, which in turn enhances the regulation of emotions themselves.

Using the language of feelings also shows how parents cope with particular emotions. In contrast, parents who intellectualize or defend against emotional experiences may be encouraging children to bottle up their feelings.

Encourage Children to Talk Freely About Feelings

We are trying to teach control over behavior, not feelings. Be sure children understand that while it is not always OK to act on their feelings, it is always OK to talk about them, and that all feelings are normal and natural.

Avoid saying, "Don't be sad," or "You shouldn't be angry about that." Instead, label your child's feelings accurately and encourage him or her to talk about the emotion. As your child tells you about her experience, listen carefully without judging or giving advice. Sometimes it helps to share a similar past experience of your own.

Children also need to understand that, just as one person likes broccoli and another doesn't, people may have different feelings about the same event and may even have more than one feeling at the same time. The crucial lesson is that all feelings are OK—some are comfortable and nice inside while others hurt, but they are all real and important.

I'M GETTING FRUSTRATED WITH THIS GAME. PERHAPS YOU CAN GIVE ME SOME TIPS.

Model Emotional Regulation

How do you handle your own emotions? Do you fly off the handle, or withdraw in sullen protest? Your children are likely to imitate (or model) your example. Talk about your emotions and your strategies for coping.

For example, if you are getting frustrated trying to repair your lawnmower, instead of exploding in a torrent of swear words, you might say, "I better stop, calm down, and relax a little before I continue. I'm so frustrated that I seem to be making things worse. Maybe if I get away from it for a while I'll figure out what it is I need to do." As always, it is important to model the kind of behavior you expect your child to exhibit. If you want your child to manage his emotions, it is important that he see you doing the same and that he see how you do it.

Also stay calm during your child's emotional outbursts. Try to offer calm and soothing words of advice, perhaps even cuddle the child or stroke his arm or back. If your child is very upset, however, your attention and comfort may make the outburst worse. At times like this, after offering brief reassurance, it is often best to walk away and let your child's upset behavior run its course. As your child starts to calm down, you can say "I know you were disappointed, but you are really trying to calm yourself down now. As soon as you want some help to solve the problem, I'm ready to help you." With such coaching, the child may calm herself enough to be able to state how she is feeling.

Teach Positive Self-Talk

Often underlying thoughts intensify, or even cause, negative emotions such as anger, frustration, fear or discouragement. These thoughts are known as "self-talk," although children may express them aloud. For example, a child who is feeling discouraged may say to you or to himself, "I'm just a failure," " I can't do anything right," or " I hate you."

In the example outlined at the start of this chapter, Billy and Eric react differently because they are telling themselves different things about the incident. If we asked Billy why he got angry, he might have said, "The pitcher didn't know how to throw a good ball." If we asked Eric why he didn't get angry, he might have said, "I'm no good at baseball—I can't hit the ball anyway." While Billy responds by blaming the other guy and Eric responds with negative self-talk, in both cases they were caught up in negative behavioral responses and negative emotions that might have been averted if they had said something different to themselves such as, "I did my best, I struck out but next time I'll do better" or "I can do it, it just takes practice, everyone strikes out sometimes."

Research indicates that children who have negative self-talk get angry more easily than children with positive self-talk. Teach your children to quietly tell themselves thoughts that calm them down, help them gain control over, or put the situation in perspective. For example, a child who's being teased can stay calm by thinking to himself, "I can handle it. I will just ignore him. It is not worth getting upset about. I can stay calm, I am strong."

Examples of positive self-talk include:

- "Take three breaths."
- "Think happy."
- "I'm not going to let it get to me."
- "Everyone gets teased at times."
- "Everyone has parents who get mad at them sometimes."
- "I can handle this."
- "I can calm down."
- "I have other friends who like me."
- "He didn't do it on purpose, it was an accident."
- "Everyone makes mistakes. No one is that perfect. I'll do better next time."
- "With more practice, I'll get it."
- "I'll calm down and use my brave talk."
- "My friends still like me even if I make mistakes in baseball."
- "I'll feel happier in a little while."

Identify Tough Situations and Use Them as Springboards to Teach Problem Solving

Often children resort to emotional outbursts because they haven't learned strategies for getting what they want. They can be taught to think through various ways of responding to a situation and the consequences of those responses. These are the fundamentals of problem solving.

The basic idea is to teach your child to generate several possible solutions to a problem. When he has an idea, be encouraging and ask for another. When you are convinced that he has come up with as many solutions as he can, you can offer other possibilities. Next, ask him to think about the consequences of each solution. For example, you can help him to understand that if he hits his sister in order to get the bike, he might get himself in worse trouble. Finally, reinforce his thinking and problem solving efforts with your praise.

Practicing how to handle hypothetical situations that normally make them angry helps children learn to control their anger in the future. Role play around situations that typically provoke emotional outbursts (e.g., being teased or left out, losing at a game) and break the problem solving process into six steps:

- Define: What is the problem and how am I feeling in this situation?
- Brainstorm solutions: What could I do about it (no matter how far-fetched)?
- Evaluate possible solutions: What would happen if I did this?
- What is the best solution? (according to what is fair, safe and leads to good feelings)
- Implement: Am I doing what I decided to do?
- Evaluate results: How did it turn out?

Another strategy to teach problem solving is to review a problem that has recently occurred, label the emotions involved, and go over how your child might have handled the situation in a different way. Do not blame or criticize; focus instead on helping your child identify what he felt in the situation and to think of effective ways to manage his feelings and face the problem in the future.

Teach the "Turtle Technique"

Positive self-talk and problem solving strategies help children learn emotional regulation on the cognitive, or thinking, level. But sometimes they need help dealing with the neurophysiological/biochemical aspects of emotional arousal. For example, some children, or all children in some situations, become so agitated that they have no control over their self-talk and cannot do the necessary problem solving; their physiological arousal produces cognitive disorganization. Learning positive self-talk

THIS IS GETTING WORSE.
I NEED TO WALK AWAY AND
CALM DOWN. IT WON'T SEEM
SO BAD LATER. BUT IF WE
FIGHT WE'LL GET INTO
TROUBLE AND SOMEONE
MIGHT GET HURT.

will relieve some of this over-arousal, but the child may need additional suggestions for calming down first. The "turtle technique" is an effective way to calm down and a good first step before problem solving.

First ask your child to imagine she has a shell, like a turtle, that she can retreat into. Next teach how to go into the shell, take three deep breaths, and say to herself, "Stop, take a deep breath, calm down." As she takes these slow deep breaths, ask her to focus on her breathing and to push the air into her arms and legs so she can relax her muscles. Sometimes it helps to picture a particularly relaxing scene. As your child continues this slow breathing she is coached to say to herself, "I can calm down. I can do it. I can control it. I can stay out of fights." She can stay in her shell until she feels calm enough to come out and try again.

Model this "turtle technique" for your children. Say you're all in the car, waiting for someone to move out of their parking spot. Suddenly, someone else darts in and takes the spot. You say, "I am so mad at him! I was waiting first! Oh well, better go into my shell for a while and calm down. Guess I better use my turtle power and take some deep breaths. Well, I feel better. Let's start looking for parking again." For young children, it can be very effective to practice and reinforce the turtle technique using a small turtle hand puppet. This provides the child with a visual image of the turtle going into its shell. If you don't have a hand puppet, you might instead check turtle picture books out of the library.

Help Children Recognize Stages in the Build Up of Tension

The first "early warning" stage of anger or negative emotion is familiar to every parent. The child grumbles, looks grouchy, sulks around the house. In the second stage, the child becomes increasingly tense, restless, and moody; no matter what you suggest, nothing seems to satisfy or interest him. An explosive outburst may occur at the slightest provocation. The child usually resists parental efforts at control of this outburst stage and they may increase his opposition to anything the parent says. In the third stage, after the tantrum subsides, depression replaces aggression; it is the "leave me alone" stage. The child is sad or placid and does not want to interact with his parents. In the fourth and final stage the child is ready to resume normal activities and may act as if nothing had happened.

During the first stage, it is possible that parental intervention can help a child to re-regulate. Intervene with suggestions of "turtle technique" or calming self-talk before the child has become too agitated. Often children do not realize they are becoming angry or frustrated and therefore don't voice these feelings until they emerge in a full-blown tantrum. In this early warning stage, encourage children to talk about feelings and to express their frustrations in socially acceptable ways. If your child has difficulty expressing herself, you might try to put into words what you suspect the child is thinking and feeling. Parental understanding and concern can go a long way toward reducing build up of negative feelings at this stage.

It is also possible to intervene in the fourth stage, after the incident is over. At this point, the parent can lead the child through problem solving and discussing what happened and how the child might handle it differently next time. Include how you and the child each felt about the episode, the causes and early warning signals, and alternative ways to solve the problem in the future.

During the second and third stages, children are usually too dysregulated to respond to parental intervention. Indeed, at this stage intervention may make the tantrum worse, or may just provide attention that reinforces the child's tantrum. During these stages, it is best for the parent to ignore, while monitoring to make sure that the child is safe. If the child's behavior is so disruptive or aggressive that it can't be ignored, then it may be effective to use Time Out.

Use Time Out for Inappropriate Emotional Angry Outbursts

As we have learned in an earlier chapter, Time Out is an effective method for discouraging children's inappropriate behavior. When a child who has hit another child or has been destructive is sent to a Time

I NEED TO RELAX. I'LL TRY TENSING AND RELAXING MY MUSCLES AND THINKING OF MY HAPPY PLACE.

Out spot, he is deprived of adult attention for the aggressive behaviors. Children hunger for attention—even negative attention is preferable to none at all, and will reinforce the behavior. Thus yelling at the child for his misbehavior or giving in to the child's emotional outbursts actually increases the likelihood they will continue in the future. However, if there is no payoff for the misbehavior and if the parent withdraws her attention, the aggressive behaviors will subside—especially if you are teaching alternative responses which you reward with your approval.

First, at a time when your child is calm, explain that aggressive behaviors such as hitting others, being verbally abusive, and breaking objects will result in Time Out. For example, parents might introduce a program as follows:

> *"Lee, I'm so proud of you for getting ready so quickly in the morning. You jump right out of bed and get dressed when I call you. Now, I want to help you be more successful controlling your anger. It is normal to get angry, but we can't allow you to hurt others. So from now on, we are going to help you learn to control your anger by putting you in Time Out every time you hit someone. You will have to go to Time Out in the chair in the corner of the room for five minutes. And you will have to be quiet for at least 2 minutes before you can get off the chair. You can help yourself get calm in Time Out by using your "turtle technique." In addition, we also are going to keep track on this chart of all the times you do stay calm in frustrating situations and talk about your feelings in an acceptable way. Then you can turn in these points on your chart for something you want."*

When sending a child to Time Out for hurting someone be sure you are matter-of-fact when enforcing the rule (show no sympathy or anger).

Teach Appropriate Expression of Negative Feelings

As mentioned earlier, children need to know that all feelings are okay—anger, anxiety, sadness and other negative feelings are unavoidable and normal—but that there are different ways of expressing those feelings, and that they have a choice in how they react. Children should be taught to put their negative feelings into words in ways that are assertive but not hostile. You can help them learn the difference between sticking up for their rights and attempting to hurt someone else, and praise them when they express difficult emotions in appropriate ways. "It's okay to tell Jonathan that you really don't like it when he takes your ball. It's not okay to yell at him and tell him that he is stupid."

Avoid Letting it All Hang Out

It used to be faddish when treating angry children to encourage them to scream and hit pillows or punch bags. The theory was that humans were like a closed tea kettle and needed to release the steam or bottled up anger from their system. However, there is no evidence that encouraging aggression in any way reduces problems with anger control. In fact, children who are encouraged to act out their aggression, even by hitting a pillow or doll, actually become more aggressive! Thus it is never a good idea to allow children to behave aggressively, not even to toys and other objects. Instead, encourage appropriate verbal expression of anger. This is far more likely to help a child cool off.

Angry children often are preoccupied by their anger and do not recognize times when they are experiencing other feelings. In fact, they may confuse sadness, disappointment and frustration with anger if they don't have any other feeling vocabulary. You can help your children learn words for their different feelings by labeling their feelings of frustration or sadness. In addition for children who are frequently angry, it is helpful to make them aware of times when they are having positive feelings such as being happy, excited, proud, curious or calm. During playtimes with your children, describe their positive feelings by saying such things as, "You look so proud of your model airplane" or, "You really stayed calm and patient even when it was difficult to figure out how to put that hard puzzle together" or, "You were curious about how to put that together and worked hard to figure it out." Whenever you do label a negative feeling, pair it with a positive coping statement. For example "I see that you're really frustrated that it's not your turn. But I bet that you're going to be able to wait a few more minutes." Or, "I can tell from looking at your face that you are very angry. But I'm proud of you because you are trying to keep your body calm and your hands to yourself." Becoming literate in emotional language will give children greater capacity to regulate their emotions and communicate with others.

Praise Children's Efforts to Regulate Their Emotions

Be sure to praise your children for handling their frustration without losing control of their anger. "I am really pleased that you worked so hard even though you were losing." Research has shown that aggressive, impulsive and hyperactive children receive more critical feedback, negative commands and less praise than other children—even when they are behaving appropriately. In essence, they train their parents not to praise or reinforce them for their positive behaviors because their emotional responses are so exhausting to deal with. In addition, since they have trouble noticing their own feelings, they may not be aware of times when they are regulating their emotions. But labeling these times, and providing children with praise for their emotion regulation efforts, you are providing much needed positive attention as well as making them aware of their internal regulation processes.

It is particularly important to try to praise behaviors involving self-control and persistence, appropriate expression of feelings (be they positive or negative) and control of emotional outbursts, especially with children who dysregulate easily or are impulsive and inattentive. Reinforce any calm, purposeful activities following a disappointment or frustrating event. For instance, you might say, "That was great. You calmed yourself down," or, "That was really strong. You were patient and kept trying even though you were getting frustrated with that difficult math assignment."

You can also teach your children to reinforce themselves. Teach them to praise themselves through positive self-talk such as, "I did a good job," or, "I stayed really calm, I was patient with myself and it worked in the end."

Alter Child's Self-image and Paint a Positive Future
Through your praise, you will help your child change her self-image. Have your child begin to perceive herself as someone who is becoming successful at handling emotions. You can predict your child's success by saying such things as, "You are becoming a person who can really control your anger well. You are very strong inside."

To Sum Up...
- Provide as much stability and consistency as possible.
- Accept your child's emotions and emotional responses.
- Talk about your own feelings (positive and negative).
- Encourage children to talk about feelings—avoid directives about feelings.
- Model emotional regulation.
- Teach children positive self-talk strategies.
- Identify typical situations that result in emotional explosions and use them as springboards to teach problem solving.
- Teach the "turtle technique" for managing anger.
- Help children be aware of build up of tension.
- Use Time Out for destructive behavior.
- Encourage appropriate expression of feelings.
- Praise your child's efforts to regulate emotions.

CHAPTER TEN

Teaching Children Friendship Skills and Ways to Cope with Peer Problems

My son, Robbie, is a 7-year-old, and he is never invited over to other classmates' homes after school. He doesn't get any invitations to birthday parties either. One day Robbie came home from school in tears saying, "No one likes me. Why don't kids like me around?" I decided to send him to summer camp so he could learn some social skills and make some new friends in a different setting. Two days after camp started, the camp director met me at pickup time and told me that Robbie was disruptive and noncooperative with the other children. He was not fitting in—the other children were isolating him. The director wondered if he was ready for camp. What can I do to help him be liked by other children and to be more cooperative? Should I take him out of camp?

It is so sad for me. My son doesn't have any friends at school. He's alone most of the time. The kids tease him constantly. It is heartbreaking to see your son be that one kid in class you remember when you were in school that everyone went, "Yuck, we don't want to be with him, he's weird." My goal for him is to be happy, find some friends and have some peace.

Stories such as these are not uncommon among parents. As an adult, you know the lifelong value of friendship, and you want your child to develop close, abiding friendships. Yet you also know you cannot make other children (or adults) like your child.

Watching your child be left out and rejected over and over by peers can be emotionally devastating. You see the impact of this isolation on your child's self-esteem and the loneliness it creates. Even though you know you can work with your child at home to solve problems and teach social skills and emotional control, you feel helpless in terms of what happens with peers at school or in other social settings. You may even find you are avoiding enrolling your child in summer camps or outside school activities for fear you will receive negative calls from the supervisors about his or her behaviors. As a result your child is spending more and more time alone, which you realize is counterproductive.

Why Are Children's Friendships Important?
Few parents really need to be convinced that friendships are important for children. Through the successful formation of friendships, children learn social skills such as cooperation, sharing and conflict management. Friendships also foster a child's sense of group belonging and begin to facilitate children's empathy skills—that is, their ability to understand another's perspective. The formation of friendships—or their absence—has an enduring impact on the child's social adjustment in later life. Research has shown that peer problems such as peer isolation or rejection are predictive of a variety of behavior problems and later maladjustment including depression, school drop out, and other psychiatric problems in adolescence and adulthood.

Why Do Some Children Have More Difficulty Making Friends?
For many young children, making friends is not easy. It has been found that children who have a more difficult temperament—including hyperactivity, impulsivity, and inattention—have particular difficulty forming and maintaining friendships. Their inadequate impulse control leads to aggressive responses, poor problem solving, lack of empathy and a failure to consider the potential consequences of their actions. These children also have significantly delayed play skills that include difficulties waiting their turn, accepting their peers' suggestions, offering an idea rather than demanding something, or collaborating in play with peers. It has also been found that children with poor conversation skills are more likely to be peer-rejected. They have difficulty knowing what to say to get a conversation going and how to respond positively to the overtures of others. As a result, they have difficulty joining in groups. Children with social difficulties often misjudge what is expected of them in social situations: they may be impulsive or disruptive when entering a group, have trouble sharing and waiting their turn, or make inappropriate or critical remarks. Consequently their interactions are often annoying to other children, especially if the other children are trying to play a game together or concentrate on their individual work. Other children may

be threatened by how easily impulsive children become emotionally upset or aggressive. These peers may respond by isolating, rejecting or by making fun of them. Young impulsive children who are having these kinds of peer difficulties also report internal distress, such as loneliness and low self-esteem. These self-perceptions contribute further to their peer difficulties by causing them to be overly sensitive to peer comments, to lack confidence in approaching other children, and eventually to withdraw from interactions and group activities. Their isolation results in fewer and fewer opportunities for social interactions and fewer chances to learn more appropriate social skills. The end result can be a bad reputation among classmates and other peers, and social isolation.

What Can Parents Do?

Trying to teach a child social skills can be a major challenge for parents— because parents normally aren't there to prompt their child to inhibit impulsive urges or to stop and think about how to behave with peers. But the first step is to teach and practice these skills with your child at home. Once your child has learned the appropriate behaviors, then your task becomes one of encouraging your child to use these skills when friends come home to play and working with teachers to foster their use with peers at school and other large group settings.

Teach Children How to Initiate an Interaction and Enter a Group

One of the first social skills to teach young children is how to enter a conversation or begin an interaction with another child or group of children. Some children will be shy and afraid to start a conversation, or to ask to join in when a group of children are already engaged in an activity. Other children have trouble not out of shyness but because they are overly enthusiastic. They barge into a group of children engaged in play without asking or waiting for an opening. As a consequence they are frequently rejected by the group. Both types of children need to learn how to approach a group, how to wait for an opening in the conversation, and how to ask to join in. They need to practice these skills with parents. You can teach these skills by role-playing scenarios where the parent first models the appropriate behaviors and then the child rehearses them.

Role Play Example:

Parent approaches the child: (pauses and watches child play for a while)

PARENT: Gee, that's an interesting game. (waits for child's response)
PARENT: Would you mind if I played with you?

CHILD: Okay.
PARENT: Thanks, which pieces can I work with?

Alternative Variation:
Parent approaches the child: (pauses and watches child play for a while)

    PARENT: Gee, that's an interesting game. (waits for child's response)
    PARENT: Would you mind if I played with you?
    CHILD: No, I'm working on this by myself.
    PARENT: Okay, maybe another time. When you're done, if you want
           to work on my model with me, that would be fun.

Change Roles: Parent role-plays child and child practices skills.

Play Daily with Your Child to Model and Encourage Social Skills
While parents need to encourage and praise all children for friendly play
skills, they will need to give particular attention to coaching children
who are developmentally delayed (such as children with Autism or
Asperger's syndrome), or who are isolated, insecure and socially withdrawn, as well as those children who are impulsive, inattentive, and
hyperactive. These children are delayed in their play skills and many
have not learned the principles of co-operation and balance in give-and-
take relationships. They lack the skills necessary for good co-operative
and reciprocal interaction.

    You can do this teaching by setting up daily play periods (lasting 10-
15 minutes) utilizing unstructured and cooperative toys such as blocks,
Lincoln Logs, drawing materials, and so forth. During these play periods
model taking turns, sharing, waiting and giving compliments. Whenever
you see your child or children doing any of these behaviors, praise them

and use the social and emotion coaching strategies we discussed in Chapter One. It is important that these play periods be "child-directed"—that is, don't give commands, intrude on your child's play, be impatient, take over, or criticize, but rather follow your child's lead by listening, commenting descriptively, staying calm and praising his ideas. Remember, children learn from you as you are a model for cooperative play.

Help Your Child Learn How to Talk with Friends
Poor conversation skills have been linked repeatedly to poor social competence and peer rejection. On the other hand, training in conversational skills has been found to enhance unpopular children's social functioning. During play interactions, puppet role plays and games with your children you can practice and coach your child to learn skills such as introducing oneself, listening and waiting to talk, asking another child's feelings, taking turns in conversation, suggesting an idea, showing interest, praising someone, saying thank you, apologizing and inviting someone to play. Begin by working on only one or two of these conversation skills by first practicing them and then prompting and praising them whenever you observe your child doing any of them at home. For example, "That was very friendly to say thank you, I appreciate that," or, "You waited for me to take a turn, that was generous of you, " or, "You really listened to your friend's idea and followed his suggestion, that is very friendly."

Set Up Play Dates at Home—and Provide Careful Monitoring
Encourage your child to invite classmates over after school or on weekends. Choose classmates to invite over who are positive role models for peer relationships. You can ask your child's teacher which classmates

s/he thinks would have similar interests to your child and would work well with your child's temperament. At first while you are teaching your child social skills, avoid inviting home another child who is impulsive and hyperactive but rather someone who complements your child's temperament. Help coach your child when setting up these invitations by practicing what to say on the telephone and by talking with the friend's parents so they know about the invitation.

When friends are invited over, *do not leave this play time unstructured.* Plan cooperative activities such as building a tree fort, conducting an experiment, building a model, working on a craft, baking cookies, playing basketball, and so forth. Plan with your child what the other child would enjoy, and set up the visit so that it has a clear purpose and structure. Monitor these play activities closely and watch for signs that interactions may be getting out of control. Increased silliness, horse play, roughhousing, escalating frustration or hostility are signs that the children need to take a break with a snack, or change to a more structured or calmer activity. Show interest in your child's friend by asking what s/he likes to do after school, what sports s/he is involved in, whether s/he has a favorite food, and so forth. Avoid letting the children spend their time together watching TV or playing on the computer as there will be very little social interaction and less chance to get to know each other. Make these first visits relatively short and pleasant.

Coach and Praise Social Skills During Peer Play at Home
Start by choosing one or two social behaviors you would like to increase (e.g., sharing, taking turns). First be sure you have taught your child

what these skills look like during your one-on-one play times with your child. You might even list them on a chart. This chart will serve to remind you and your child of the specific behaviors you are working on. Then when your child's friend comes over to play, watch for these behaviors to occur. When you see them, praise them for their friendly behaviors. You might want to make a game and give the children points, stickers or tokens every time you see them share, take turns or help each other. Children aged 7 and older will be less embarrassed if you call them away from the play group to praise and reward them out of earshot of others.

When praising, be sure to clearly describe the social behaviors that you are encouraging. Don't just praise your own child for the target behaviors; praise both children for their cooperative behavior and talk about how they are becoming good friends. For example, "You two are cooperating and working very well together! You are being very friendly with each other and helping each other make this a cool structure. Wow you are team players!" Several times during the week review your child's chart and the social skills you are working on. Remind your child to use the skill when s/he goes off to play at someone else's house. Once your child has learned the first social skills then you can move on to some different behaviors to give your attention to.

Here are some typical social behaviors that children may need help learning: sharing, waiting, taking turns, asking (versus demanding), giving a compliment, cooperating, offering a suggestion, accepting a peer's idea, expressing a positive feeling, helping a friend, being patient with another and problem solving.

Teaching Problem Solving/Conflict Resolution

Starting a friendship is one thing; keeping a friend is another. The key skill your child needs to keep a friend is knowing how to resolve conflict. In the absence of this skill, the most aggressive child usually gets his or her way. When this happens, everyone loses—the aggressive child may learn to abuse friendships and will experience rejection by peers for the aggression, while passive children may learn to be victims. And yet it is important for parents to help children settle conflict without taking over. You can take the role of "coach" on the sidelines and when disagreement occurs involve the children in the process of defining the problem, brainstorming solutions and picking a solution to try. Follow the problem-solving steps outlined earlier in Chapter Eight.

For instance, let's say that 6-year-old Anna and 7-year-old Cary both want to play something different. Anna shouts, "I want to play house!" and Cary shouts, "No, I want to make beads, we played house last time," and Anna retorts, "No, we didn't, we did what you wanted." In this case, you might say, "Okay, we have a problem here. You both want to play something different. Do you have any ideas how to solve this problem?" Next they come up with solutions such as taking turns, combining the activities, or doing something different. Once they decide which solution to try, they both may have had to compromise, but they have begun to learn how to handle conflict. Be sure to praise their teamwork and good problem solving.

One game you can play with your children is called the "pass the hat" game. In a hat place small, rolled-up pieces of paper with questions written on them. The children sit with you in a circle and pass the hat while the music is on. When the music stops, the person who has the hat in his or her lap gets to choose a piece of paper and try to answer the question. If s/he can't answer the question, s/he can ask someone for help. See below for some suggestions for the hat. Add in some jokes too to make the game fun.

- A friend comes to you and wants to know what to do when he is teased. What would you say?
- You see your friend being left out of a game and even bullied and pushed away by some kids on the playground. What should you do?
- What is a solution?
- How do you know when you have a problem?
- What is a consequence?
- What questions can you ask yourself to decide whether your solution will have a "good" consequence?

- Your friend just lost his new shoes. What can you say?
- Your dad seems angry and says he's having a bad day. What can you say?
- You notice someone crying on the playground. What can you say or do?

Teach Your Child to Use Positive Self-Talk

When children experience a peer's rejection or a disappointment, often they have underlying negative thoughts, which reinforce and intensify the emotion. These thoughts are sometimes referred to as "self-talk," although children will often express them aloud. For example, a child who tells you, "I am the worst kid, no one likes me, I can't do anything right" is engaging in negative self-talk which s/he is sharing with you. Children can be taught to identify negative self-talk and to substitute positive self-talk in order to help cope with their frustrations and to control angry outbursts. For example, when a child's request to play is refused by another child, s/he can say to herself or himself, "I can handle this. I will find another child to play with" or "I can stay calm and try again" or "Count to 10. Talk don't hit" or "Stop and think first." In this way children learn to regulate their cognitive or thought responses, which in turn will affect their behavioral responses. Positive self-talk provides children with a means of emotional regulation with their peers.

Helping Your Child Control Anger

Aggression and inadequate impulse control are perhaps the most potent obstacles to effective problem solving and successful relations in childhood. There is also evidence to suggest that aggressive and inattentive children are more likely to misinterpret another peer's or person's situation as hostile or threatening. When a child becomes agitated (with a racing heart and rapid breathing) due to anger, fear, anxiety or aggression, they cannot use problem solving or other social skills. Therefore, children need to learn emotional control strategies to use in situations that provoke their anger. The "turtle technique" asks the child to imagine

s/he has a shell, like a turtle, that s/he can retreat into. When the child goes into his or her shell, s/he takes three breaths, and says, "Stop. Take a deep breath. Calm down." The child visualizes a happy and relaxing scene during this slow breathing and then says to herself, "I can calm down. I can do it. I can try again." Once you have taught your child this technique you can use the word "turtle" as a cue whenever you see your child beginning to get emotionally dysregulated. Teachers might also use this cue in the classroom and respond by putting a turtle stamp on the child's hand or giving out an "I can control my anger" sticker. (See Chapter Nine for more information on emotional control.)

Encourage Positive Peer Contacts in the Community

Enroll your child in organized community activities such as Scouts, sports, and summer camps. If your child is impulsive and inattentive we suggest you choose programs which offer structured activities with adequate adult supervision. Small groups will work best. Try to avoid peer group activities which involve a great deal of coordinated activity or complex rules, and stay clear of activities that involve passive sitting time such as Little League. The worst place to put a distractible child is in a field position because he will quickly become disengaged from the game—it would be better to have him close to the action because it will maintain his attention. Avoid too much competition, which can trigger emotional arousal, frustration, and increasingly disorganized behavior. Of course, an exception to this rule would be if the child has a clear talent in a particular sport. In such cases, you would want to encourage that activity as it will increase his or her self-esteem.

Collaborating with Teachers

Parents have relatively few opportunities to see their children in settings where they are with large groups of children—and these are the very settings where children need to practice these skills! Behavior in the classroom may be very different from behavior at home. While your child might do well when a single friend comes to visit at home, s/he may still have substantial peer problems in larger group settings. It is important to meet with your child's teacher to discuss your child's behavior management at home and at school. Collaborate with the teacher to identify a few positive social skills you both want to start encouraging. Set up a chart for these behaviors, and offer to make copies of the charts for the teacher so s/he has one for each day. The teacher can put check marks on this "friendly report card" for each time that the child puts up a quiet hand, cooperates with peers, participates appropriately (versus impulsive

talking out), etc. At the end of the day this "report card" can be sent home with the child, and the parents can add checks earned at school to their home reward chart. For example, earning 5 checks at school might equal an extra story time or a special activity at home.

It also is ideal if you can work with the teacher to set up an incentive program at school. For example, each day the child earns an agreed-upon number of checks s/he gets to choose a special activity such as extra computer time or starting the lunch line or leading a class discussion. It is also helpful if the teacher assigns your child some special responsibilities so other children can see him or her in a positive light.

For highly distractible children, you might need to work with the teacher to advocate for a school counselor, aide or teacher to be assigned as a "coach." This coach can meet with the child three times a day for a brief 5-minute check-in. During this check-in the coach reviews the child's behavior chart and praises any successes in interactions with peers. S/he also makes sure the child has his or her books ready and his or her assignments written out in his or her notebook for the rest of the morning. At lunch s/he would review expectations for lunch period or recess and again, before going home, s/he would review the day's behavior as well as see that the child had his or her behavior chart, books, and homework ready to take home.

Cooperative learning activities, where children work in small groups, also help prevent peer rejection. It is important that the more hyperactive and impulsive children be put in different groups with socially skilled children. Children who are isolated or who tend to be victimized should be placed with positive, friendly students. Carefully planned cooperative group activities, where the focus is on the performance of the entire group, create mutual positive dependence among group members and by extension a feeling of cohesiveness in the whole group. When each member of the group is given responsibility for every other member's learning of the prescribed task, children begin to feel responsible for each other.

Empathy Training

A key aspect to your child's social success is his ability to begin to consider the concerns, goals, and feelings of others. If your child cannot take the point of view of another person, then s/he may misperceive social cues and not know how to respond. While the development of empathy takes years, and all children are self-centered and "egocentric" at this age, it is still possible to promote children's awareness of others' feelings and perspectives.

Finally, of course, a warm trusting parent-child relationship with you greatly improves your child's chances of developing healthy friendships. Reinforce your child's self-image as a valuable person who can be a friend. Self-acceptance and confidence affect how much a child craves the approval of peers. Strive to be a model and a coach.

To Sum Up...

- During one-on-one play times with your child model and practice how to enter groups, how to play cooperatively, and how to talk with friends.
- Continue during your daily play times to label and praise friendly behaviors.
- Invite your child's playmates home and use this as an opportunity to do social and emotional coaching.
- Set up co-operative games during visits to help children to practice friendship skills.
- Encourage your child to use positive self-talk and self-regulation strategies to stay calm during conflictual interactions.
- Praise and establish reward programs for children with social difficulties to enhance targeted social skills.
- Collaborate with teachers to develop coordinated behavior plans and incentive systems that promote children's targeted social skills at school as well as at home.

PART TWO

Communicating and Problem Solving

CHAPTER ELEVEN

Controlling Upsetting Thoughts

All parents feel angry, depressed, frustrated and guilty when dealing with their children's misbehaviors. Upsetting feelings are not only to be expected but are essential and beneficial. They signal the need for change and problem solving, and provide motivation. Danger arises, however, when these feelings so overwhelm parents that they are immobilized by depression or lose control of their anger. The idea, then, is not to avoid these feelings or eliminate conflict, but to learn to cope with emotional responses to conflict in a manner that provides more self-control.

Researchers have demonstrated a clear relationship between what we *think* about a situation, how we *feel* about it and how we *behave*. Let's look at the model of how thoughts determine emotions.

To see how this works, let's consider the various ways a parent might react to this situation. Eddie has left food, toys and papers strewn all over the living room. Annoyed with the mess, his father might say to himself, "He's impossible, inconsiderate, irresponsible, and lazy." As he thinks these negative thoughts, his anger mounts and he begins criticizing and yelling at him. On the other hand, he might view the situation as hopeless or think that he is to blame. He might say to himself, "He'll never outgrow it" or "It's all my fault for being a lousy parent" or " There is nothing I can do." In this case, he is more likely to feel depressed, and tentative, and to avoid making a request or disciplining the child. If, however, he kept his thoughts focused on his ability to cope and be calm, he might say to himself, "I'm going to have to remind Eddie to tidy up this room." This would facilitate more rational and effective responses to his misbehaviors.

The same event triggered three different emotional and thinking responses in this example. The truth is that we become angry not because of the event itself but because of the view we take of it. You may have already noticed that some days a messy room is not bothersome to you and other days it is very irritating. Your view of the situation

Responses to Situations

The first two diagrams—Depression Cycle and Anger Cycle—illustrate the vicious circle that results if negative thoughts are allowed free reign. The third diagram—Positive Response—shows how positive thoughts produce a more effective response that leads to improved behavior.

Depression Cycle

Messy living room.

IT'S MY FAULT

Negative thoughts about self: "I'm a terrible parent."

Increased criticism and spanking.

Increased child misbehavior.

Increased emotions of depression and helplessness.

Withdrawal from discipline.

Anger Cycle

Messy living room.

HE'S IMPOSSIBLE AND LAZY

Negative thoughts: "He's impossible and lazy.

Emotions of anger.

Physiological changes: Blood pressure rises, etc.

Increased criticism and yelling.

Increased child misbehavior.

Positive Response

Messy living room.

I CAN COPE...

Substitution of positive for negative thoughts: "I can cope—my job is to help him."

Decreased stress.

Increased coping response.

Decreased child misbehavior.

may be influenced by other events in your life such as how things have gone at work that day or whether or not you had a fight with your partner. The purpose of this chapter is to help you identify some of the common negative self-statements you make that increase your distress and learn how to substitute coping responses during periods of conflict.

STEP ONE: Be Aware Of Your Negative And Positive Thoughts

Your thoughts are always with you, and they're under your control and no one else's. But since they're always with you, you take them for granted and pay little attention to them. Unless you learn to pay attention to your thoughts, you will not be able to change them. Imagine the following scene:

> You have two children aged four and six. It is supper time and you have had a stressful day at work and have been home from work five minutes. Both kids are yelling and arguing in the living room. You are trying to get dinner ready and you tell them to be quiet and stop fighting. The fighting continues and you feel yourself getting more and more tense. Suddenly you hear the sound of a lamp falling on the floor. What are your thoughts? They are probably negative.

STEP TWO: Decrease Your Negative Thoughts

After becoming aware of your negative thought patterns, the second step is to decrease them. There are four ways to do this.

Use Thought Interruption

As soon as you realize that you're having a negative thought, stop the thought. You might say to yourself, "I am going to stop thinking about my problems at work now. I need to give the children some attention." Some parents wear a rubber band on their wrist and snap it every time they have a negative thought to remind them to stop it. "Stop worrying. Worrying won't help anything."

Reschedule Worrying or Anger Time

Constantly going over in your mind your worries such as all the ways your children are causing you trouble and have made you angry is very draining. Decide how long you need to spend on these thoughts and then schedule this time into the day. For instance, tell yourself that at 9:30 p.m. you will let yourself be as angry as you want. During the rest of the day don't allow these thoughts to interfere with your mood, work or play. The idea is not to stop having unpleasant thoughts altogether but to decide when is the best time to think about them. One half an hour each day should be enough.

Objectify the Situation

The third approach towards stopping negative self-talk is to ask yourself during moments of conflict whether what you are thinking or doing is helping you reach your goal.

- What is my goal? (for my children to improve their behavior)
- What am I doing now? (getting angry, getting depressed)
- Is what I'm doing helping me reach my long term-goal? (no, we're arguing and I'm about to spank them)
- If it isn't, what do I need to do differently? (think more positively, get away for a while, do some calm down exercises and so on)

This has been called the "turtle technique" because you withdraw into a shell momentarily to assess your behavior. One father described this to us in a parent group. He was trying to leave for work and his son wasn't ready and persistently dawdling. He put him in his bedroom and the boy started screaming. The father's anger increased until he opened the door and grabbed his son saying, "You want negative attention, you're going to get it!" Suddenly he thought about what he was doing and realized that this was getting him nowhere. He left the room, went outside and a few minutes later his son joined him fully dressed. The father discussed how he was able to become more objective, to stand back and assess what was happening and realize that losing control or getting revenge would only aggravate the situation. The ideal is to use this technique before you lose control, but at least this father was able to stop his response mid-stream. Next time he will catch himself earlier in the sequence.

Normalize the Situation

Another way to objectify a situation is to normalize it by remembering that all parents have difficult and conflictual days and all children have behavior problems. Moreover, all parents and children have feelings of guilt, depression, anger and anxiety. Once you have normalized your thoughts, then it is important to stop the negative ones. You might say to yourself, "I'm feeling uptight, but that's natural," or "Lots of parents feel discouraged at times. This feeling will pass."

Remember to Normalize the Situation.

STEP THREE: Increasing Your Positive Thoughts
Reducing the number of negative thoughts you have won't automatically increase positive ones. Here are six ways to help you increase positive thoughts.

Dispute Negative Self-Talk
Combat self-talk that contains "should" and "ought" and "must" statements or generalizations that include words such as "awful" or "terrible." Instead of thinking, "I should be a better parent," say to yourself, "Why do I feel I have to be the perfect parent?" Don't moan to yourself, "My children are terrible!" say, "My kids aren't so bad." The thoughts normalize and the misbehaviors are objectified. If you can recall a situation when you overreacted, it's useful to go over it, identify the negative self-talk and think of ways to dispute it.

Substitute Calming or Coping Thoughts for Negative Ones
Another approach is to replace upsetting thoughts and negative self-statements with alternative calming ones. If you find yourself thinking about your child in hostile terms ("She is misbehaving because she hates me. She likes to get me upset."), then thought-stop and try to substitute thoughts that emphasize your ability to cope ("I'm going to have to help her learn to control herself. It's up to me.").

Time Projection
The idea here is to think more positively by mentally traveling forward to the time when the stressful period will have ended. For instance, if you are trying to toilet train your young son, tell yourself, "When he goes to college he won't be wearing diapers." You acknowledge that the behavior problem and the feelings of depression or anger will go away eventually. If your child is misbehaving because he or she was denied something, it will probably take several minutes for the tantrum to stop. If you and your children are reacting to a divorce or separation, it will be much longer before things get better. However, it is still important to acknowledge that the loss and pain you now feel will lessen as time goes by. Time projection recognizes stressful feelings, allows you to see a more satisfying future and reminds you that psychological pain is not fatal.

You can also remind your children of the temporary nature of a problem. You could say to your son who is not toilet trained, "Next year at this time you will be potty trained. You won't have to wear diapers any more." Or, "It is hard to learn to read now, but it will get better every week."

Think and Verbalize Self-Praise Thoughts
A fourth way to think more positively is to give yourself a pat on the back for your accomplishments. Many people don't give themselves credit for what they do, particularly for the difficult job of parenting, and then they belittle themselves when things don't work out right. Remember to look at what you have accomplished each and every day.

Think ahead to a positive time: "He won't be in diapers when he's in college."

Humor

Humor helps to reduce anger and depression. Don't take yourself too seriously. You might say to yourself jokingly as dinner burns and you threaten to send your kids to the moon because they're fighting again, "Oh yes, I'm perfect. I never lose my cool." Laughing at yourself will probably help you to calm down and think about the situation more rationally. You might even keep a joke book to bring out at times when you are feeling particularly tense.

Model Coping Self-Talk and Self-Praise

As you learn to use coping and self-praise thoughts when confronted with a problem, try to say them out loud. You are a powerful model for your children. During the day there are countless opportunities for you to model aloud for your children how you thought about and coped with a difficult situation. By observing these responses your children will eventually learn to use them as well.

Of course, there will be times when you will find it difficult to use self-control techniques. Don't worry—relapses and problems are to be expected. You will become more proficient with practice. Think in terms of small gains and don't belittle gradual progress. And don't forget to praise your efforts. Ask yourself, did you need to get angry in the first place? And don't forget to give yourself credit for trying.

Refute Negative Labels and Focus on Specific Positive Behaviors

Labeling categorizes children's personalities in a negative manner. A label implies that they always behave in a particular way and are incapable of changing. Diane, who does not put out the garbage, might be labeled by her father as "totally irresponsible, inconsiderate, lazy and spoiled." People who have learned to view the world in this extreme manner may also do this in regard to spouses, other family members, co-workers or friends. This global negative thinking will increase the level of frustration and anger when such people are in an upsetting situation.

Avoid focusing on a single problem behavior and believing that it reflects your child's or spouse's entire personality. One way to keep from labeling is to refute negative thinking by asking yourself, "Is this always true?" or "Is this totally accurate?" Most likely the behavior is only true for the moment. Next, think about the specific behavior that is annoying you and come up with a coping self-statement. For instance, Diane's dad might say to himself, "I seem to be labeling her. She's not really lazy. She's just having trouble remembering to take out the garbage. I'll talk to her about ways to remember." Another way to refute labels for your children is to normalize their behavior. Remind yourself that all children throw tantrums, disobey, forget to do chores, and behave aggressively from time to time.

Avoid Speculations about Intentions

Some people assume they know the reason why their child or spouse behaved in a certain way. Often they attribute motives to misbehaviors and act upon these beliefs as if they are true. Unfortunately, these assumptions can become self-fulfilling prophecies. For example, two children are bickering in the den while their mother is trying to watch the news. She mind-reads, "They are being loud on purpose. They want to make me mad!" Or when a father who comes home from grocery shopping and finds his wife talking on the phone while the kids mess up the living room. He mind-reads, "Nobody cares about me. If she cared about me, she would make the kids behave properly." This kind of negative mind-reading is bound to increase resentment and anger towards his wife and children.

It is important to focus on the behavior you want to change and to avoid speculations about motives. Instead of the mother thinking, "They are doing it on purpose to make me mad," she might say to herself, "I don't know what has upset them today. Perhaps I should ask them." She asks them about their problem instead of making assumptions. In the second example the father might tell himself, "I need to talk to her about helping the kids keep the living room tidier." He avoids mind-reading and focuses on the behavior he wants to change. He has chosen to see himself as a facilitator of change rather than a victim of his family.

Think Positively

Individuals who mind-read often engage in fortune-telling, or predicting a dismal future. They assume that because an event occurred in the past, it will determine future events. For instance, five-year-old Connie has been stealing small things around the house. Her father thinks, "She will become a delinquent and drop out of school." Other examples of fortune-telling are, "He'll never stop," "Oh no, it's starting again. It will be just the same as last time." This kind of gloomy prophesying causes parents to feel depressed, act passively or withdraw from helping their children behave more appropriately. Moreover, making negative predictions about the future sets up a self-fulfilling prophecy. If parents are convinced that their children will never behave any better, then they probably won't.

Remember to stop negative thoughts and substitute coping thoughts.

A more positive way of thinking about Connie stealing would be, "I can help her learn not to steal." This focuses on coping effectively with the problem and results in the child receiving more hopeful messages about her capabilities. If prophecy is to be helpful, one must mentally travel forward to a time when the stressful period will have ended and predict a positive outcome. For example, the mother of six-year-old twins who fight constantly might say to herself, "It is hard to have two six-year-olds. They bicker all the time. But in a few years they will probably get along well and be good friends." Making a positive prediction will remind you that there will be a more relaxed future and encourage your children to behave more appropriately.

Thought-Stop and Substitute Coping Thoughts

Some parents catastrophize and imagine the worst possible outcome or exaggerate the importance of a negative event. If a father was trying to read and his children were whining, he would be catastrophizing if he said to himself, "I can't stand it. They're driving me crazy!" This kind of thinking heightens emotional arousal, anger and explosive outbursts by convincing parents that they are out of control.

You will recognize yourself exaggerating a problem situation if you are thinking in terms which use words such as "always," "never," "everybody," and "nobody." Say to yourself, "Stop! I'm not going to think that way."

Instead, substitute more coping thoughts: "I can control my anger," "Things could be worse," "I can stay calm and deal with this." You focus on your ability to stay in control no matter how unpleasant you find the situation. In the above example, the father might make a coping statement such as, "This is frustrating, but I can stand it. It's not the end of the world. All children whine sometimes."

Normalize and Dispute Negative Self-Talk

Self-talk that includes "should" and "must" implies that one has a right to something and that it is intolerable if it does not occur. The first part of this may well be true, however, the second part causes the difficulty. Circumstances do not always allow for the ideal, and to react as if the resulting situation is unfair is to invite emotional upset. Parents might feel that they have the right to silence, read the newspaper or watch a program on the television. This kind of attitude, especially when it excludes the rights or needs of others, can be the basis for a lot of anger. By expressing preferences in the form of absolutes, they feel victimized when desires are not met. The resulting sense of injustice and the desire to punish or set things right sustains anger and fuels further conflict. For instance, Sally is having trouble with her son, Jessie, in the grocery store. He is hyperactive and won't listen to a word she says.

Challenge irrational thoughts.

She thinks, "He should not treat me like this. He must treat me more fairly." As these thoughts travel through her mind, she feels more and more irritated.

You need to rewrite self-statements that use absolutes to include more flexible standards for yourself and others. Accept yourself and others as imperfect and fallible and give people choices in ways to respond. In a sense, this means learning to expect unpredictability and mistakes as a part of life. In the above example, Sally could say to herself, "He's a little squirrelly today. He must be having an off day. All children do from time to time." Another tactic would be to mentally dispute all self-talk which includes "musts," "oughts," and "shoulds." "Who says children should treat parents fairly?" "Why should I expect him to be perfect when no children are." "Who says I ought to be perfect?" Many parents find that challenging the "shoulds" they set for themselves can lead to a refreshing release from unattainable standards for their own behavior. Interestingly, these unrealistic standards reflect the "shoulds" they heard from their own parents.

Think about Long-Term Goals

Sometimes parents say to themselves, "This isn't fair! Why do I have to have a child like this? I don't deserve this. My child deserves to be punished." They feel victimized by their children and their anger serves the purpose of justifying their revenge. They may think they are in control of the situation even though their anger is out of control.

It is hard to let go of anger, especially when you feel you are the victim of unfair treatment. Being angry can make you feel righteous, energized and powerful. Giving it up can be difficult because it is sometimes confused with passive defeat and loss of power. In such situations, it is useful to think in terms of long-term goals rather than the short-term satisfaction of obtaining revenge. You might say to yourself, "In the long-term, it is better for my child to see me cope by taking charge of my anger rather than to let it control me." Another constructive self-statement would be, "The long-term cost of letting my anger explode would be far greater than the momentary satisfaction of showing my child I won't be pushed around." If you are feeling really angry, it can be useful to do relaxation breathing exercises or to have a Time Out to help you gain control.

Objectify and Normalize

Another type of upsetting self-statement occurs when parents blame themselves for problems with their children. When confronting a problem, they say to themselves, "I'm a total failure as a parent. I can't do anything

Controlling anger can be difficult at times.

right." Or they may focus on their situation and say, "If only I hadn't gone back to work, maybe they would behave better," or "It's because I'm a single parent that I'm having these problems." In these instances, parents generalize and interpret problems with their children as a reflection of their parenting skills or life style. Not only does this oversimplify a complex problem, it leads them to feel hostile and passive, and may eventually cause them to withdraw.

Depersonalize your self-critical thinking by remembering that all children have behavior problems and they are not necessarily a reflection of your parenting ability. It's also important to remember to objectify your children's behaviors and ask yourself:

- How can I help my child learn more positive behaviors?
- What is my goal for my child?
- Is what I'm doing helping him or her learn more positive behaviors?
- If it isn't, what do I need to do differently?

For instance, you might think, "Getting angry won't help him. He is just testing the limits of his environment. I can help him learn not to ride his bike on the road." Or "All kids do this with their parents. She's not a monster. I need to stay calm with her." One way to normalize self-criticism about your life circumstances is to remember that every family experiences a major stressful event such as divorce, death, chronic illness, unemployment, or a move. The goal is not to avoid or deny these stresses but to help your children learn how to cope with them in a productive and flexible way.

If you are self-critical you need to learn not only how to stop negative thoughts but also to increase positive and self-praising thoughts. Many people are reluctant to praise themselves, perhaps because they feel it is self-centered or vain. However, if it is good to compliment other people, it is also good to do the same for yourself. Some examples of self-praising thoughts are: "I'm a good parent," "I try hard," "I'm proud of myself for taking charge of the situation," "I'm making progress" and "It's getting better each time I do this." Consider all the things you accomplish each day and give yourself credit.

Focus on Being Calm and Using "I" Messages to Receive Support

Occasionally when parents are frustrated with their children, they blame their partner for the problem. An example of this is a mother who thinks, "I do all the work around here. I'm not getting any support from my husband, and the children don't listen to me. It's his fault for not backing me up." Or a father might say to himself, "After working all day, I'm tired. When I get home, all I get are hassles. The kids yell and squabble. If Joan was better at disciplining the kids, they would behave better!" People who make this type of blaming self-statement are likely to find themselves in conflict with their spouse as well as their children.

Another way that parents blame one another for their children's problems is to accuse each other of setting a bad example. For instance, "Laura is aggressive, just like her mother," or "Tom is as messy as his dad." This kind of thinking can become a self-fulfilling prophecy. It is likely to be verbalized in anger or despair, and children are thus taught that they are expected to imitate their parents' undesirable behaviors.

If you have thoughts that blame your spouse for the way your children behave, you need to stop them. Coping thoughts that focus on giving a clear "I message" about what behavior you would like should be substituted. The mother who felt a lack of support could say to herself, "I better calm down before I say something I'll regret. What I need is help. I'll ask my husband to help me. Then maybe I can have a nice relaxing bath." The father could tell himself, "Take it easy. Take a few deep breaths. What I need is a few minutes of peace. Maybe if I ask Joan to play with the kids while I read for a bit, then I could play with them later."

If you blame your spouse's personality for your children's inappropriate behaviors, you should stop this type of thinking. Instead, try to focus on how their positive behaviors are similar to your spouse. For instance, "She has a lot of energy just like her dad. She will probably be an athlete too." Or "He likes reading as much as his mother. Maybe he'll become a librarian."

Focus on Coping

When some parents make self-statements, they focus on giving up. A mother who has worked with her son but finds he continues to get poor grades may say to herself, "I'm tired of this. Why try at all? Nothing will work"; or "I can't deal with this. He's just not capable." The adoption of a defeatist attitude usually results in withdrawal from the problem, avoidance of discipline and a simmering level of annoyance or anxiety. Eventually, parents will either explode with anger or become depressed. Moreover, saying that a child is not capable of changing has the possibility of becoming a self-fulfilling prophecy.

A more useful coping response is to think about what you can do to help your children. You might think, "This is frustrating and I'm tired but I can cope," or "No one can make me give up. Things will get better. It just takes time." The important message to give yourself and your children is that you can all cope with the situation. Even if things are bleak, you can reflect a positive outlook for the future. Even if your intervention doesn't improve the situation dramatically, it will certainly prevent things from getting worse.

Modeling Coping Self-talk

As you learn to use coping, calming thoughts when confronted with a problem, try to say them out loud. While a family is seated at the dinner table, Mom might say to Dad, "Peter, I think I coped well with Alice's problem at school. I told myself not to overreact, that all children have difficulty at school from time to time. I set up an appointment with her teacher to talk about ways we can help her learn to share better. I feel good about that." Here Alice's mother is modeling not only how she stopped herself from overreacting but also how she praised herself for her control.

Parents are powerful models for their children. During the day there are countless opportunities for you to model out loud for your children how you coped effectively with a difficult situation. As your children observe these positive thinking responses, they will eventually learn to use them as well.

Empower yourself.

To Sum Up...

People often say that a particular event made them feel angry or depressed. Although this is not a conscious attempt to avoid responsibility, it tends to put them in a victim role. Such people rarely feel they have any influence over their emotions, and alternate between holding in their feelings or exploding with rage. However, there is really only one person who can make you angry or depressed, and that is you. Remember, you always have a choice as to whether to get emotional or to use a coping strategy.

Remember:

- Refute negative labels that may come to mind.
- Avoid speculating about intentions.
- Paint a positive future.
- Use thought-stopping when tempted to catastrophize and substitute coping thoughts.
- Normalize behavior and use flexible standards.
- Get control of your anger.
- Don't be self-critical; instead objectify and use self-praise.
- Support your partner or others involved in caring for your child and seek support.
- Focus on coping.
- Be positive and use humor.
- Reschedule anger or worry times.
- Model positive, coping self-talk.

CHAPTER TWELVE

Time Out From Stress and Anger

Once you have learned to recognize upsetting thoughts and substitute more positive ones, the next thing you need to do to gain more self-control is to become aware of your physiological responses to stressful events and thoughts. Think about how you react physically during times of conflict. Many people report that in stressful situations they experience such physical tension, rapid heartbeat, headache, hypertension, or muscle tension, that it interferes with their self-control.

Begin by looking at the sources of stress in your life. One of the myths about stress is that it only happens to high-powered leaders or in catastrophic situations. In fact, studies show that everyday hassles may actually produce more stress than a crisis. And as you know, parenting can produce a lot of everyday hassles. Daily tension can result from rushing around doing errands, meeting deadlines, trying to find a baby sitter, or trying to find a way to pay the bills. It can be caused by children misbehaving or being ill, cereal spilled on the floor, or a pile of dirty clothes. It isn't created only by big things like a divorce or being laid off, but also by seemingly little things, such as nothing to do, a lonely night or boredom. The causes of stress are highly individual. What brings one person to the verge of a tantrum may not bother another person at all. Learning to relax and manage your stress level can help you keep control and accomplish your goals without wearing yourself, and those around you, to a frazzle.

In the previous chapter, we discussed one way to manage stressful thoughts by modifying your self-talk to be more positive. Sometimes it is also necessary to learn how to physically relax, or take Time Out to restore calm to your body, before you can gain control of your self-talk. Think about Time Out from stress. In most sports there is provision for Time Out. These breaks give the coach and team a chance to strategize, catch their breath, and then re-enter the game with renewed energy. In our daily lives, however, there are very few scheduled Time Outs. Even coffee breaks are usually filled with stimulation rather than real refreshment. Somewhere along the line, relaxation got dropped. Now it is up to you to reinstate Time Out in order to gain perspective and to re-energize yourself.

On the following pages, you will find six ways to take Time Out for various reasons. Of course, if you are home alone with very small children and you need a Time Out, you will not be able to remove yourself physically from their presence. You will need to modify Time Out to suit your circumstances. Experiment and learn how to release tension and anger, and gain more self-control.

Time Out for a Breather
Breathing deeply and slowly can relieve distress. It helps shed tension, slows the heart rate, relaxes muscles, reduces blood pressure and calms the mind. Many people must learn to relax physically before they can gain control of their self-statements. Here is a relaxation procedure you can learn with a little practice.

- Choose a quiet environment (bathroom, basement, garage).
- Get comfortable sitting down or even lying on the floor. Close your eyes.
- Become aware of your breathing.
- As you breathe in and out, slow down your breathing.
- As you slow down your breathing, with your next deep breath, slowly count as far as you are able from one to 10 in that single breath.
- Now exhale slowly, counting from one to 10 again until you are out of breath.
- Visualize yourself calm and in control. Picture yourself relaxing in a favorite spot.
- Remind yourself you are doing a good job and making progress.
- Repeat this deep, slow inhaling and exhaling as you count until you feel relaxed.
- Relax all muscles as fully as possible. Start with tensing and relaxing your foot muscles and move up to legs, arms and finally your facial muscles.

Practice one or two times a day (10 to 20 minutes).

Learning to relax is like learning any new skill. It simply takes regular practice, patience and time. Don't be concerned if your progress seems slow. Becoming tense or worried about relaxing is of course not very relaxing. One of the most frequent problems during relaxation is the occurrence of distracting thoughts. Don't worry if your mind wanders. Just try to refocus your

Time Out for a breather.

attention on your breathing. Another problem can be external distraction. If possible, try to select a time and place where you won't be disturbed.

After you have practiced relaxation for 10 sessions, then you can begin to use it for a problem situation. For instance, schedule practice sessions before high tension times, such as just before going home from work and picking up the kids, before the kids come home from school, or as you notice your annoyance level starting to increase.

Time Out on the Go

This Time Out technique can be used anywhere, while grocery shopping, doing the dishes or sitting at your desk. Systematically tense and relax certain parts of your body. Close your eyes and visualize your muscles relaxing and releasing tension. As you breathe in, tense your right arm and fist as tightly as you can. Hold for a count of four, then relax fully as you breathe out. Repeat for your left arm and fist, buttocks, right leg and foot, left leg and foot, face and jaw. At the end, tense your entire body, then relax.

Time Out for Visualizing and Imagining

A third way to take a Time Out is to visualize or imagine a calm scene or time in your life. When you visualize something, you can help to set up the conditions for all your thought processes to coordinate smoothly. The results can often be surprisingly productive. Visualization is very personal. There is no single right way to do it. So experiment with it to see what kind of visualizing helps to make you feel relaxed. Imagine a cloudless sky, a sparkling clean house, a quiet library, a time when you felt close to your child or a friend, or...

Time Out to Control Anger

It was once believed that "blowing off steam" by shouting and swearing would drain off violent energy and reduce aggression. People were thought of as tea kettles that could only contain a fixed amount of aggressive energy. Therefore, when this energy increased, it was necessary to release the steam by lifting the lid of the kettle. It is now understood that rather than having a cathartic or beneficial effect, blowing off steam inflames aggression and violence. Studies have shown that couples who yell at each other do not feel less angry afterwards; they feel more angry. The reason for this is that many times angry outbursts are self-reinforcing because they give people a false sense of power. They often feel that their anger forces others to take them seriously or results in others' compliance. Sometimes a tirade is a way of getting revenge. However, all of these are short-term effects. It is of the utmost importance to look at

Time Out for Visualizing.

the long-term effects of anger because they can be both permanent and damaging. Since it is frequently reinforced, it is likely that people who use it will develop a habit of dealing with frustration by lashing out. And parents who model angry outbursts make other family members angrier, defensive and fearful.

All parents find that they occasionally lose control of their anger when things become stressful. Therefore, it is just as important to establish a Time Out procedure for yourself as it is to set up one for your children. The following steps can help you to interrupt the anger cycle.

Be aware of cues that signal increasing anger

Anger increases progressively rather than appearing full-blown. Therefore, it is important to be aware of your body's signals that tell you your anger is increasing. Such signals can include physiological changes such as rapid breathing and increased pulse rate, or thoughts that blame ("That bitch"), catastrophize ("I can't stand it anymore") or mind read ("She's doing it on purpose"). Pacing, shouting or clenching your fists are also signs of escalating anger.

Establish a Time Out signal

Develop a method of signaling your family to let them know that you need to take Time Out to get your anger under control. It should be a neutral sign such as making a "T" with your hands or simply saying "Time Out."

Decide where you will go

Choose a location where you can be alone and make sure the rest of your family knows where you are. Otherwise, they may feel abandoned and try to restrain you.

Decide on the duration of Time Out
A time limit should be decided upon when you call a Time Out. Ideally, it should not exceed 30 minutes. Then you can signal your readiness to resume the discussion or whatever was interrupted. Your family should understand that the interrupted activity will be resumed so that Time Out does not become an avoidance tactic.

Guidelines for Time Out
Guidelines for Time Out should be agreed upon by your entire family so they know what to expect when Time Out is called. Factors to consider might include whether the person will leave the house, go to a friend's or make a phone call. (Drinking or using drugs should not be considered an option since alcohol or drug use do not facilitate self-control and will likely have the opposite effect.)

Self-talk about Stress
Remember that thought stopping and refuting negative thoughts are also ways to manage stress. You can use these coping thoughts to deal with your stress reactions. For example, tell yourself, "This is normal. Stress is what I usually feel when I begin a Time Out." Use these feelings of tension as allies in coping with the situation. They can signal you to say to yourself, "Relax, take a slow breath. Take it easy." Expect your stress to rise at times. Remember, the objective is not to eliminate it totally but to keep it manageable. For instance, you might tell yourself, "I'm getting tense. My muscles are tightening. My body is signaling me to calm down." The idea is to normalize stress and recognize it is a part of family life. Think about it as temporary rather than ongoing, for no matter how tense a situation is, it will eventually pass. When responding to stress focus on what is controllable instead of what is uncontrollable. Turn to thoughts that focus on coping and finding solutions rather than those which blame others. Finally, focus on your strengths and abilities to cope.

Signal early when your anger is escalating.

Personal Time Out
What else might you do? Exercise, eat well, pace yourself, avoid coffee, alcohol or drugs, take a walk, go jogging, read, tell a joke, listen to

Don't let stress take hold.

music, go shopping, watch a movie, get a massage. Personal time for adults and children is one of the most effective ways to reduce stress. If you have an overloaded schedule, think about trimming it so that you have time for spontaneous fun, silly times and doing nothing. Be sure that your children are not overextended with too many lessons or other structured activities.

To Sum Up...

The essence of Time Out is to allow yourself to step back from the stress or anger and regain your focus on what is essential. Instead of being deeply involved in a distressing situation, take Time Out. Once you have gained perspective on the situation, you rob it of the power to overwhelm you. Time Out may last a minute or an hour. You get to choose when and where to take it. Including short but frequent Time Outs in your daily routine will build your sense of well-being and self-control.

Remember:

- Scan your body for tension, and breathe and relax or do the exercises.
- Notice any negative self-statements and replace them with soothing self-encouragement.
- Ask yourself if what is making you feel tense is really that important? Will it make a difference a week from now? A year? When you are 70?
- Visualize some marvelous past event or dream of fun event in the future.
- In the middle of conflict, breathe, cool off, get playful, or get away for a few minutes.
- Take a break (go into the bathroom for a bath, read a magazine).
- Make a list of things that you find pleasureable and plan to do one of these each week.

CHAPTER THIRTEEN

Effective Communication Skills

Some families deal more calmly and effectively with problems than others. These families generally have good communication skills, which help them to work together to resolve current problems and nip future ones in the bud. Unfortunately, few of us are born with effective communication skills. We can learn them however, and then we can model them for our children to learn as well.

To use communication skills to their best advantage, parents must be able to use self-control skills to manage their negative feelings and thoughts. Excessive anger, guilt, anxiety or depression interfere with communication. The following pages discuss blocks to effective communication and some ways to overcome them. We all commit the errors listed to some degree and need to improve in certain areas. The purpose of this chapter is to help you identify areas you personally would like to improve.

Active Listening
Many people do not really know how to listen. They interrupt with questions, arguments, criticism, or advice instead of allowing those who are speaking to say what they want to say. A child or adult who doesn't feel listened to is likely to restate the problem again and again or to withdraw totally. Consider the following adult-child exchange:

KATHY: Marcus won't let me play in his room with him. He doesn't like me.

MOTHER: Well, if you didn't mess up his toys, he'd like you better. (*criticism*)

or

Why don't you go outside and play? (*solution*)

KATHY: No one likes me. They won't play with me.

PARENT: Why don't you stop complaining? (*criticism*)

or

> I like you. (*placating*)

or

> Of course they like you. They just can't come and play right now. (*denial*)

or

> Why don't you ask the new kids who moved in down the street to play with you? (*advice*)

Now consider the following adult-adult exchange:

WIFE: I had a really frustrating day with the kids. I'm at the end of my rope!

HUSBAND: (He has just gotten home from work and walked in the door to see the three-year-old running around and the baby crying.) Hmmm... (Avoids eye contact and picks up a newspaper). (*denial*)

or

> Why don't you get a baby sitter to help you during the day? (solution)

or

> I know the feeling. My day was lousy too. (*discounting*)

Listening attentively is one of the most powerful reinforcers that one person can provide for another. Unfortunately, it is a rare skill and often undervalued. Listening means giving the speaker, whether it's a child or an adult, "the floor," allowing him or her to state feelings or ideas without interruptions. Good listeners are not passive, merely nodding their head with a blank expression or listening while reading the newspaper. Instead, they listen by watching the speaker closely and using appropriate facial expressions. Here are some tips on becoming an effective listener.

- Maintain eye contact. (Turn off the television or put down whatever you're reading.)
- Give the person a chance to finish speaking before responding.
- Listen to both the content *and* the feeling of the speaker. (Every message has both a content component, which is the actual information that is conveyed, and a feeling component, which is the nonverbal message.)
- When the speaker stops, express interest by asking questions about the situation.
- Provide feedback: summarize and then paraphrase in your own words the content of the message and the feelings of the speaker.

- Validate: try to see the problem from the other person's point of view. Let the speaker know that you see his or her point of view as a valid one. Validation can help reduce the gap that may exist between speaker and listener. It's important to admit that there are views that differ from your own and that, given a different position, the perspectives might alter.
- Encourage the speaker to continue.

Note: Of course it's also important for the speaker to give some thought to when to communicate. If the person addressed is absorbed in a television show or almost asleep, effective communication will be difficult.

Here are more effective ways the listener in the previous examples might have responded:

KATHY: Marcus won't let me play in his room with him.

MOTHER: You'd like to play with Billy and he won't let you. That must make you feel bad. (*summarizing and validating content and feelings*)

or

Gee, that must make you feel bad. What can we do to make things better? (*reflecting child's feelings and asking questions*)

or

Can you tell me more about what happened? (*asking questions to better understand the problem*)

WIFE: I had a really frustrating day with the kids. I'm at the end of my rope!

HUSBAND: What happened? (*expressing interest*)

WIFE: Johnny got into trouble at preschool for hitting and has been hitting the baby. The baby has had diarrhea and has been crying all day. The house is a mess and I'm exhausted!

HUSBAND: Wow, that sure would be frustrating to have Johnny acting up and the baby sick at the same time! You sound worn out. How can I help? (*reflection and validation of feeling and content*)

or

That sounds overwhelming. How's the baby now? (*feedback of feelings and expression of interest*)

In both these instances, the speaker's feelings were validated as the listener tried to see the problem from her point of view.

Speaking Up

Some people try to avoid conflict, disagreement or disapproval by not talking about how they're feeling or the things that are bothering them. They may store up grievances and then let them out in an angry explosion. The parents in the next examples have clearly been storing up a lot of resentment.

> MOTHER: I've had it! I do everything in this house. I keep it clean, make all the meals, do the laundry, take Max to school, do the shopping, and work part-time. All you do is read your newspaper!
>
> FATHER: I've had it! I do everything in this family. I work to support you all, pay the bills, fix the cars, wash the windows, help with the dishes, take Max to baseball practice, and all you do is nag!

There are several reasons why people need to level, or speak up, about how they feel. First, if you don't express your feelings or desires, others may mind-read and make decisions for you. Since their assumptions are often incorrect, they may be acting against your wishes. Second, if you sit quietly on your problems you may then explode in a fit of anger or hysteria. Talking about conflicts as they come up reduces the pressure that causes such explosions.

Sometimes a quiet person does not speak up for fear of being punished or criticized for such thoughts or feelings. In such a situation, the listener needs to use the active listening skills described above to provide reinforcement.

Here are some tips to help you speak up about your feelings and problems.

• Use "I" messages instead of "you" messages. "I" messages communicate what the speaker wants or feels. They're a way to confront people without having a destructive effect. "You" messages tend to blame, criticize or pass judgment, and they often generate anger or humiliation. If you think about what your reactions would be if you were on the receiving end of the following remarks, you will see why "I" messages are more effective in eliciting cooperation.

(Carla isn't dressed; she's been dawdling since she got up and her mother will be late for work.)

Don't let grievances smolder until they explode.

MOTHER: You're never dressed on time. You always make me late. Why can't you be ready on time? (*"You" message focuses on what Carla is doing wrong*)

Alternative:

> I feel annoyed when you dawdle in the morning. I want to see if you can beat the clock and be dressed when the timer goes off in 10 minutes. (*"I" message focuses on mother's feelings and desire for change*)

FATHER: Whenever I come home from work this place is totally disorganized. Is that all I get after a hard day's work? Can't you clean up or have the kids fed by the time I get home? (*"You" message focuses on criticizing mother*)

Alternative:

> When I first come home from work I need a few minutes to unwind. (*"I" message focuses on what father wants*)

MOTHER: I've been with the kids all day and you walk in and demand your dinner. Then you go off and read the damn newspaper and don't even help. (*"You" message*)

Alternative:

> When you get home from work I need a few minutes to relax away from the kids before serving dinner. (*"I" message*)

- Be brief, clear and specific. In order to be able to speak up, you must think about exactly what you want rather than focusing on the negative, or what you don't want. Once you have a clear idea of what you want, state it positively and briefly. It's not necessary to recount episode after episode to prove your point about how messy or irresponsible a child or spouse has been. Instead, state the problem briefly and focus on the positive behavior that is desired by using "I" messages.

- Express negative feelings promptly. The longer a problem is ignored, the more likely it is that your feelings of anger will be magnified. Try to deal with a problem as soon as you can discuss it calmly.
- Ask for feedback. Sometimes you may not be sure if whoever is listening to you has understood your point of view. If this happens, you should ask, "Am I making sense?" "Do you see what I mean?" This is much more effective than rambling on and on, and it assures the listener that his or her comprehension of the situation is important.
- Avoid too much leveling. Be selective. Leveling doesn't mean you should be insensitive about where, when or how you express your feelings. Before you start, it's important to ask yourself: "Do I have a legitimate bone to pick or am I in a bad mood?" "Am I overreacting?" "Am I really interested in solving anything?" "Is this the right time for leveling or will I get a better hearing later?"

Feeling-Talk

Many parents talk to their children about ideas, facts, and rules, but they rarely discuss their own personal feelings with their children. For example, how often have you told your child of a situation when you feel anxious, afraid, happy or excited? Ironically, parents often have a similar complaint about their children—that their children don't talk to them about what is bothering them. Moreover, research suggests that when parents do deal with children's feelings they talk to boys and girls in different ways and permit different types of feelings to be expressed. Boys are more likely to be encouraged to talk tough and to be aggressive, while they are likely to be criticized if they express sadness or seem too emotional. Girls, on the other hand, are more likely to be taught that direct expression of aggressive feelings is unfeminine, while expression of sadness, tears and sentiment is more acceptable. Thus in the end, boys learn to express angry feelings and girls learn to discuss feelings of depression. Such talk may actually intensify the feelings themselves—so that boys become angrier and girls sadder. Consider the following scene and a fairly typical parental response:

(Donald is four years old and his sister Anna is 18 months old.)
CHILD: (crying) I hate her! She's always wrecking my stuff. And she bit me!

PARENT: Wow—she bit you.
CHILD: Yes, she bit me here! (points to leg)
PARENT: (looking at leg) That looks sore. What happened?
CHILD: (crying escalates) It hurts. Oh, it hurts.
PARENT: Calm down, calm down. Now, what did you do to make her
         bite you? (crying continues)
PARENT: (getting annoyed) Stop crying. Big boys don't cry. Stop it
         right now! She's just a baby. You should learn to keep your
         belongings away from her.

Feeling-talk, or self-expression, is the skill of informing another person clearly and directly about inner feelings whether they are positive or negative. By putting emotions into words, both parties become clearer about what's going on. For parents this means modeling effective feeling-talk for their sons and daughters: "I enjoyed our time together today. I feel happy," "I understand you feel angry about not going to the movie," "I feel sad that your puppy died." Notice that these are "I" statements and that they are based in the present, not the past. A word of caution: while it is important for you to express yourself, this does not mean that you should "let it all hang out" in a tirade of negative feelings. In fact, you should carefully consider the timing and usefulness of negative feeling-talk. The object should be to learn from one another about negative feelings and areas of conflict so that action can be taken. Venting, blaming and criticizing will interfere with the attainment of this goal.

Parents should not only express their own feelings appropriately but they should try to verbalize their children's feelings and validate them. For instance, a more appropriate way to approach the situation described above is as follows:

CHILD: (crying) I hate her! She's always wrecking my stuff. And she
         bit me!
PARENT: Wow! She bit you. I'm sorry.
CHILD: (pointing to leg) Yes, right here.
PARENT: That looks sore. It must hurt a lot.
CHILD: It does.
PARENT: What happened?
CHILD: I was building a fort out of blocks and Anna knocked it down.
         I pushed her away and she bit me. I hate her!
PARENT: That's too bad. I'm not surprised you were upset.
CHILD: She always wrecks my stuff. But why did she bite me? I'll
         bite her back!

PARENT: Well, you could do that. What do you think would happen? Will that help the problem?

CHILD: I guess not.

PARENT: What do you want to do?

CHILD: Build a fort without her getting in my way. I guess I could do it in my room so she wouldn't bother me.

PARENT: That sounds like a great idea.

Stop Action and Refocus

Occasionally when people are trying to discuss a problem, they end up "unloading," that is dragging in all sorts of gripes that may or may not be related to the original problem. Pretty soon both parties feel overwhelmed.

PARENT: I'm fed up with the house and how badly behaved the kids are. We never get a chance to go out alone together. And you're always too tired for sex.

or

PARENT: You're irresponsible! Your report card was terrible, you're always fighting with your brother and your bedroom's a disaster!

Call a stop action, or truce, and halt all discussion when you realize unloading is occurring. To facilitate calling a truce, your family should decide in advance on how to signal that a discussion is to be stopped. You might simply say, "I need to stop talking about this right now," or "I'm getting upset. Could we talk about this later when I calm down?" (Note the use of "I" messages.) Everyone in the family should agree that even if only one person gives the signal, the discussion will end temporarily. Then you will need to set another time for continuing it. Cooling off periods should be no longer than 24 hours or you may avoid resolving the problem altogether. If you signal each other before you get too upset, you can usually resume the conversation in a few minutes. And the sooner you can discuss the problem the better.

Be Polite and Positive and Edit Your Complaints

It's amazing but true that we are all much more likely to say mean or insulting things to the people we know and love than to strangers. Family members frequently interrupt each other, put one another down and hurt each other's feelings. Put-downs can evoke anger, resentment, defensiveness and guilt or depression, and they undermine effective communication and problem solving. Here are some

When anger escalates signal a truce.

examples of typical put-downs an adult might resort to when dealing
with a child or another adult:

TO A CHILD: You are such a mess! Can't you stay clean for five min-
              utes? You're driving me crazy! What an obnoxious brat!
              Joey, you forgot your coat. If you didn't have your head
              screwed on, you'd forget it too. When are you going to
              be responsible like your sister?

TO AN ADULT: How the hell would you know? So now you're the
              expert, huh?
              I'd better handle it. You get too upset.

Politeness is extremely important in the effective resolution of a
situation, and you can make a conscious decision that *you* will be polite
no matter how anyone else is acting. The fact that someone else is rude
and childish does not make it acceptable for you to behave that way.
You won't always feel polite, however, so you will have to learn to do
a bit of editing before you speak. Here are some tips to help become a
good editor.

• *Say what you can do and what you want to do.* Edit out statements
referring to what you can't do.

HUSBAND: Let's go shopping now.
WIFE: I can't. The baby is asleep. I only have one hour free and I've got a million things to do. *(focus is on what she cannot do, which creates opposition)*
Alternative:
I'll have an hour free at four o'clock after the baby wakes up. (edit focuses on what she can do)

CHILD: Will you play with me? Why can't you play now?
FATHER: I just took you to the park. You always want me to play with you. Can't you learn to play alone? I have a thousand things to do. *(focus is on child being a bother, which discounts child and creates insecurity about relationship)*
Alternative:
After I do the wash I'll play with you. (edit focuses on what father can do)

• *Focus on the positive.* Edit out complaints. Imagine a situation where your child tries to wash the dishes but gets water all over the floor. Or your partner makes dinner but leaves the kitchen in a mess. In these cases you have a choice: you can complain, or edit out the complaint and give an honest statement of appreciation for the effort made. "Gee, it's great to have the dishes all washed. Thanks for taking the time to do them." "I really appreciate your making dinner." (If a messy kitchen is an important issue to you, you can always decide to discuss it at a later time.) Here's another situation:

CHILD OR MOTHER: Here, I bought this cologne for you.
FATHER: (Says to himself, "What am I going to do with this? I wish she'd bought something I like." He edits these thoughts.) Thanks for the gift. It was nice of you to think of me.

Some parents don't make positive statements to each other or their children because they believe that saying something they don't feel would be dishonest. They aren't willing to make any changes until their partner or child changes first. This kind of thinking creates a standoff. Other parents believe it shouldn't be necessary to state their positive feelings because the other person ought to know how they feel. They don't realize how effectively positive statements can influence others to feel better and to behave better. Probably the most common block to making positive statements is a feeling of awkwardness, especially among parents who received little praise themselves as youngsters. If you feel awkward making positive statements remind yourself of what it was like when you first tried to hit a golf ball, play the piano or speak French—the awkwardness passes with practice.

- *Edit self-criticisms.* Say you have a fight with your child or lose your temper and then realize that you were wrong. You might say, "I'm a rotten parent. Why do I always lose control and get angry?" Instead, you should edit these put-downs in favor of more constructive self-statements: "I was wrong for saying that. I'm sorry. What can I do to make things better?" "That was a dumb thing to do," "That wasn't a good idea. Let's think of a better one." The point is to focus on the mistaken ideas or actions and to accept responsibility for error, but not to devalue yourself as a person. Everyone makes mistakes. It is important to model this attitude in an appropriate manner and to provide a positive alternative for future behavior. For instance, you might say, "Next time I'll try to stay calm," or "When this happens again, I'll go outside for a few minutes rather than get so mad."
- *Focus on the present and edit out old business.* Avoid digging up past events and unloading old conflicts. This will only increase the problem and the anger level of everyone involved. Remember that unloading tends to occur most with people who don't communicate about problems as they arise.
- *Think about the other person's needs and point of view.* If you find that you are thinking only of yourself, then edit those thoughts. Instead, think about what your partner or child needs or wants. For example, "I wonder if he's feeling left out because the new baby is taking up so much of my time? Maybe we should get a sitter for the baby and go out." One of the most powerful responses you can make to a complaining child or partner is, "I see your point. What can we do to make things better?"

Focus on Fixing the Problem, Not the Blame:
Sometimes effective communication is hindered by blaming. One person may directly accuse the other of creating the problem, but blaming can also be done much more subtly. Here are some common examples of blaming.

FATHER: She gets her own way and you never discipline her. That's why she's such a behavior problem. You're not tough enough. She's never a problem with me.

MOTHER: I think you spank her too much. That's why she's so aggressive.

MOTHER: You never used to be like this. Now you only think of yourself.

FATHER: All you do is nag. Why do you think I spend so much time at the office?

Blaming sets people against each other rather than uniting them to solve a problem. It is important to focus on fixing the problem. If your children realize that you and your partner are willing to work together they're less likely to try to pit the two of you against each other. For instance, it would have been much more useful for the father (or the mother) in the first example above to say: "The problem seems to be that Gillian is overly aggressive. Each of us uses a different approach to handling her behavior problems. Let's decide how we both want to handle these problems in the future." This approach identifies the differences between the two parents that need to be resolved without implying that one is right and the other wrong.

A Problem Is Always Legitimate

It is common for one family member to bring up an issue only to have the others dismiss it as not being a serious problem. Or they may see some benefits in maintaining the status quo and so not wanting to discuss it. A messy living room, for instance, may bother one person in a family but no one else. Here are some examples of denying or discounting a problem.

MOTHER: This living room is a mess and I always have to pick up old newspapers and toys after everyone.

DAD AND CHILDREN: Oh Mom, it's okay. We like it like this. You don't have to pick up after us.

FATHER: He's out of control. He won't listen to a word I say.

MOTHER: That's normal behavior for his age. It's not a problem. You expect too much of him for his age.

CHILD: The other kids don't like me and won't let me play with them.

PARENT: Don't worry. Let's go out and play together.

Although you may not see an issue as a problem, your child or partner may do so. Therefore, in the interest of good family relations, you need to address the situation and cooperate to help resolve it. Active listening and validation will help you if you are tempted to discount the problem and allow you to better understand the speaker's point of view.

Focus on Realistic Changes

Statements such as, "Nothing works," "She's just like her dad and he's no good," "He'll never change," "I'll try but it won't do any good," communicate a hopeless message that all efforts toward change are futile. The same message can also be communicated by subtle cues, such as one- or two-word replies. "I don't know," "I guess," or "Whatever," spoken in a passive, depressed voice, indicate lack of hope as well as implying a lack of interest. Hopelessness can even be indicated nonverbally by deep sighs or eye rolling.

If you and your family feel a sense of hopelessness when tackling a problem, you need to focus on what changes you can realistically make. You may need to lower your expectations and try to handle the problem one step at a time. And if it cannot be resolved, set it aside for a while. You can return to it later when emotions have calmed down. Although no major problem can be resolved in one discussion, each one has a workable solution. This is an important attitude to convey. For instance, you might communicate hope by saying: "Okay, we're going to have to be patient. The kids need time to adjust to the new baby. Let's talk about what behavior we want to help them with first."

Ask What the Other Person Is Thinking and Feeling

Some people mind-read, believing they know another person's motives or opinions without first checking them out. They may fall into the habit of talking for someone else and then become angry when the person whose mind they think they've read disagrees with their interpretation.

If you find yourself making assumptions about what a quiet family member is thinking or feeling, encourage him or her to talk. You can often do this by discussing things that are of interest to him. Sharing your own experiences can also be helpful. You might tell your quiet child about your childhood experience of getting lost in the woods or learning to ride a bike. As you try to get a reluctant family member to communicate, it's important to put yourself in that person's shoes. Thinking about how your child or partner might see the issue will help you find the questions most likely to elicit a response. Then, be sure to validate the feelings that are finally expressed. You might say, "I can see how that must have hurt your feelings," "That would have made me cross too," or "Yes, my boss makes me feel frustrated by doing the same thing."

Be Calm and Stop Action

Some people wait until they're angry to discuss a problem. However, an angry person is more likely to criticize, be negative and blame others, and less able to think clearly. This leads to ineffective communication.

Try to identify angry thoughts when they first occur. If you find yourself becoming furious, it's best to call a stop action and get away for a while. A short walk, relaxation exercises or deep breathing may help you to become calmer and approach a problem in a more rational manner. Then the first thing to do is ask yourself whether the issue is really worth starting a fight about. If not, hold your tongue. If it is, think about how you can say what you want to say politely and positively. Once you edit your complaints, you will be ready to discuss the problem you want to tackle.

If you are beginning to "see red," take a cooling off period.

Announce Your Filter and Get Feedback

People become defensive when they feel they're being blamed, whether or not they actually are being accused and whether or not they really are to blame. They may react by becoming angry or argumentative, making excuses, becoming distraught and crying or withdrawing and refusing to participate in further discussion.

MOTHER: I can't handle these kids all day long, every day. I need to get a babysitter to help.

FATHER: (He thinks she's saying he doesn't help with the kids.) You don't have the kids all day. They're in school part of the day.

Studies have shown that there are two filters whenever two people are talking. One affects how a person communicates and the other affects how the message is received. It is important to be aware of these filters and how they affect the way you talk to others and the way others hear what you say to them. For instance, if you feel you are being blamed or criticized, it's a good idea to stop the discussion and get feedback about what the speaker meant. The father in the above example could attempt to clarify what his wife meant by asking a question.

FATHER: I may be defensive because I had a rough day at work, but are you saying you don't think I help enough with the kids?

or

Are you angry with me?

Edit Complaints and Make Positive Recommendations
There are two common ways that people often overlook other people's viewpoints. One is "yes-butting" and the other is counter-complaining. Yes-butting occurs when every attempt to make a suggestion or state a point of view is discounted because something is wrong with it. The speaker gets the feeling, "I'm wrong again. Nothing I say is acceptable." This results in, "What's the use of trying to help?" The person who yes-buts is often unaware of rejecting the other person's views.

FATHER: I think we should get a tutor for Andrea to help her with her English homework.

MOTHER: Yes, that's a good idea, but it would never work. You know she wouldn't pay any attention. And besides, she's too busy in the evenings for extra studying.

FATHER: I think it would make a big difference and help her to get better grades.

MOTHER: It would be great if she got better marks, but I think a tutor would be a waste of money.

Counter-complaining occurs when each complaint is met with a complaint.

MOTHER: I made this lovely dinner for you. Instead of being pleased, you're cranky.

FATHER: Well, you know we can't afford to buy a roast. Why don't you get a job?

MOTHER: How can I feel like a good cook if I can't even make a simple roast?

or

CHILD: All we ever have for dinner is meat and potatoes. You never make what I like.

FATHER: You never eat what I cook anyway. You always complain.

In these examples each person summarizes his or her own complaints instead of trying to understand the other person's viewpoint.

Remember to stick to one issue at a time, edit complaints, listen actively and validate the other person's point of view. Another way to handle these problems is to turn a negative complaint into a positive recommendation for dealing with the situation. For instance, instead of saying, "I want you to stop criticizing my meals," you could say, "I'd appreciate it if you paid me more compliments about my cooking."

Strive for Consistent Messages

Sometimes a parent unintentionally gives a child contradictory messages. Mixed messages occur when the content and the feeling of a message do not match. For example, a mother smiles while criticizing her daughter for leaving her room in such a mess. Or a father tells his son, "I always have time for you," and then immediately picks up the phone. Part of the parent's behavior communicates pleasure and approval while another part conveys the opposite. Another example of a mixed message is a positive statement that incorporates a sting. For instance, a mother grins as she says, "I don't believe it! You came to the table the first time I asked!"

Be aware of filters that interfere with communication.

Adults do this with each other as well. A husband says to his wife who calls to ask if she may stay late at work, "Sure, go ahead and leave me alone with the kids. I don't care!" Then, if she comes home instead of working, he says, "I never said you couldn't stay!" Or a compliment may be given in a sarcastic tone of voice, "You're sure a big help." Inconsistent verbal and nonverbal messages result in the confused child or adult becoming suspicious and hostile. Research indicates that when there is a discrepancy, the listener tends to take the nonverbal or feeling messages as truer.

It is very important to be clear, which means that the content and feeling of your messages should match and so should your verbal and nonverbal messages. Otherwise, people may not know how to respond.

Give Positive Requests and Commands

One of the most important communication transactions is that of asking someone to do something. These are known as requests and commands. Ineffective commands are those that are vague, disguised, stated as questions, or delivered in a negative tone—a surly shout of "Take out the garbage!" or a querulous "Why don't you take out the garbage?" or "Why don't you do the dishes?" In relationships where ongoing conflict exists, commands can be particularly troublesome. A command or direct request for a specific behavior may be perceived as authoritarian. Compliance might then be felt to be an acceptance of the hierarchy rather than simple cooperation. People in such relationships find themselves arguing over the specific request when the real issue is the power struggle over who is in control.

There *are* effective ways of giving commands or making requests.

- *Be positive.* State what you want, not what you don't want."Please clean up the kitchen," instead of "Don't make a mess."
- *Be specific.* "Please be home by 10 p.m." instead of "Don't be late."
- *Use "I" language.* "I would like you home by 9 o'clock," instead of "You always come home late."
- *Ask* how *and* what, *not* why. If questions are required for clarification, what and how will focus on getting the problem solved, whereas why may lead to accusations and defensiveness. "What would make it easier for you to clean the bathroom?" instead of "Why didn't you clean up the bathroom?"
- *Look for compliance and reward it.* This is probably the most important step in the process.

Remember, learning new communication techniques is like learning to drive. It will feel awkward and maybe even a little frightening at first, but with practice it will come to feel natural.

To Sum Up...
- Don't interrupt, argue, give advice; listen attentively and validate.
- Don't store up grievances; speak up clearly with "I" messages.
- Express feelings.
- Stick to the point and avoid unloading multiple gripes.
- Edit: be polite and positive.
- Focus on fixing the problem and avoid blaming.
- Recognize another's problem.
- Take one step at a time.
- Don't mind-read.
- Get and give feedback.
- Don't attack angrily.
- Stop and call Time Out if anger mounts.
- Announce your "filter."
- Make positive recommendations.
- Encourage conversation.
- Give consistent verbal and nonverbal messages.
- Give positive rather than negative commands.

CHAPTER FOURTEEN

Problem Solving Between Adults

All families face conflict occasionally and all children have behavior problems. One of the hallmarks of a successful family is the ability to resolve disputes in a way that is satisfactory to everyone. Families that can solve problems by making necessary changes are likely to maintain satisfying relationships and survive even difficult transitional periods. Those that are rigid and unable to respond to the need for change that is the inevitable consequence of children's development will have significant problems. All long-term relationships require sacrifice, adaptability and restriction on personal freedom. In order to grow as a family, collaboration, compromise and problem solving skills are essential. This chapter focuses on problem solving skills that can help you to cope with the conflicts inevitable in all relationships.

Problem solving is not like any other type of interaction. It is neither spontaneous, nor natural, nor relaxing. Rather, it involves a specific set of methods that enhance one's ability to think effectively about conflict. However, this does not mean that it must be dull or even unpleasant. On the contrary, many families report it to be an enjoyable time that brings them together by encouraging flexibility and collaboration.

Problem solving skills incorporate the communication and self-control skills discussed in previous chapters. Uncontrolled feelings of anger cause a narrowing of vision that blocks the ability to perceive options. They also may fuel the belief that other people have deliberately caused a problem or that action must be taken immediately. Extreme feelings of depression can cause withdrawal or a passive attitude towards problems and create a "do nothing" response. You must have control over feelings of intense anger or depression before effective problem solving can begin.

Six Steps to Effective Problem Solving

STEP ONE: Set aside a time and place and decide on an agenda

Don't try to resolve conflicts at the scene of the crime. At such a time, most people are too emotionally aroused to problem solve in a rational manner. Discussing a problem at a *neutral* time makes it much more likely that it will be resolved effectively. In order to prepare for problem solving, determine a specific time and place to have discussions. You may decide to meet at the same time each week. Often this will be at night after the children are in bed, but if the children are over five and the problem involves them, you may choose to include them in the meeting. It is advisable to take the phone off the hook, turn off the television and eliminate as many other distractions as possible. Begin by determining the agenda. Only one or two problems should be discussed at a meeting and no more than 30 minutes should be spent on each one.

STEP TWO: State and define the problem

A problem needs to be defined *clearly* and *positively* using the principles of effective communication discussed in the previous chapter. Avoid put-downs, exaggerations, vague labels or blaming. For instance, a problem stated negatively can sound blaming. A statement such as "I feel you're not involved enough with parenting our children," may force the listener into a defensive position. On the other hand, "I know work has been stressful lately and has taken up a lot of your time, but I would appreciate your spending more time with me and the children if that is possible," recognizes the other person's positive qualities and can increase the desire to collaborate by reducing defensiveness. A well-formulated problem includes the following:

Situation
What is the problem?
Who is involved?
What is done or not done that bothers you?
How often does it happen? (per day, per week)
Where and when does it happen?
How does it happen? What sets it off or follows its occurrence?
What happened last time?
Why do you think it is happening or what reasons do others give?

Response
How do you feel when the problem is occurring?
What do you do and say while it's occurring?

How do you feel afterwards?
Why do you respond that way?

It is important to have a collaborative attitude and to share responsibility for the problem. Although you might feel that you're the victim of a situation and that the other person is the cause of the problem, these feelings need to be put aside as you encourage a sense of working together. Difficult as it is, you must listen carefully to the other person's concerns. Even if only one person in the family considers a situation to be a problem, it's critical that the family address it as a *mutual* problem and be willing to resolve it. This contributes to the well-being of the entire family. For example, "I know that things are kind of chaotic at home and I may criticize you for not helping, but it would be nice if we could do something about this because I would like the children and me to have more time with you."

Finally, the problem should be defined relatively *briefly* in a statement oriented toward change desired in the future rather than focusing on the past. Only one problem should be dealt with at a time. Don't bring up other ones out of defensiveness or anger. Responses such as "I don't come home because I don't agree with how you discipline the children," make problem solving impossible. If one person does sidetrack in this manner, the other can say, "I think we are supposed to be discussing when you come home, not my discipline techniques."

STEP THREE: Summarize goals and expectations

Once the problem has been defined by one family member, the other family members should paraphrase or summarize it to be sure they have understood it correctly. If there is agreement, then it is important to state the desired goal. For instance, "I would like more time with you," or "I would like him to be able to share better." These goals should then be assessed to be sure they are realistic and acceptable. Expecting a tax accountant to be home by seven o'clock during tax season, for instance, isn't realistic.

STEP FOUR: Brainstorm solutions

Once the exact problem and goals have been agreed upon, the next step is to generate possible solutions. No further discussion of the past or of the problem should occur. Generate as many solutions as possible by brainstorming. The focus here is on creativity and productivity, so criticisms and judgments about the solutions should be avoided at this stage. The more imaginative the ideas, the better, but avoid getting bogged down in details. Try to introduce fun and humor into the process. The

Brainstorming—use humor and creativity.

object is to get out of mental ruts and come up with new solutions. Also, the more ideas you come up with, the better the chance that there will be several good ones.

STEP FIVE: Make a plan

The fifth step is to go through the list of ideas to eliminate ridiculous ones and combine any that naturally go together. Then the advantages and disadvantages of each suggestion should be discussed in detail. Each one should be looked at, keeping in mind the following:

- Can it be done realistically?
- What are the best and worst possible outcomes?
- Are the best outcomes short or long term?
- How well do the outcomes match the goal?

Then an agreement should be formulated. This may combine several ideas from the list and should state clearly what each person is going to do and who is responsible for what. The agreement should be written down, signed by family members, and posted for all the family to see. This avoids the necessity of relying on memory, forces each person to take responsibility and minimizes the possibility of any ambiguities in communication. A follow-up meeting should be scheduled to review how the agreement is working and determine any necessary revisions.

Note: All of these problem solving steps can be used either with a partner, with a child or when thinking alone about a problem. Some adaptations of this are made in the chapter for teaching children to problem solve.

STEP SIX: Evaluation of outcome
At a follow-up meeting the solutions should be evaluated by answering several questions. First, was the strategy carried out as planned? If the plan was that Dad would be home by 7:00 p.m. three nights each week and spend Saturday mornings with the family, was this done consistently? If not, what made it hard to implement? Second, if the plan was designed to improve a behavior, how was the behavior affected? For instance, if the goal was to have your child in bed by nine o'clock by using stickers, then some record should be kept to see if this method was successful. Finally, do the goals and observed outcomes match? Do the changes actually create the desired outcome? If not, then a new strategy may have to be developed.

Do those six steps sound easy? The following section discusses some possible pitfalls and suggests ways to make the process go more smoothly.

Defining The Problem
Collaboration
Sometimes when parents begin to discuss a problem with their partner or children they find themselves arguing about who caused the problem. For example, a mother may say to her husband, "If you didn't spend so much time watching TV, you'd have more time to help Evan with his homework." Her husband might respond with, "You never think about my needs and you never listen to me." Such accusing and blaming usually escalate bickering and undermine the problem solving process.

In undertaking a discussion to solve a problem it's important that family members maintain an attitude of collaboration. Each person must share responsibility for the resolution of the problem. Although it's often easy to feel victimized or self-righteous and to wait until the other person changes before you give any ground, this attitude will defeat the problem solving process. Such feelings need to be put aside. In the previous example, Evan's mother might say, "I know you need some time after work to relax and I realize that it doesn't help when I nag you to pay attention to Evan's homework. Let's see how we can solve this problem." The goal is not to decide who is at fault, but to define the nature of the problem and decide how to solve it.

Be Positive

Sometimes when parents problem solve they find themselves becoming very cross with each other and quick to criticize. This may occur because they set up their meeting too soon after the conflict or because they've been storing up a lot of resentment and anger. Whatever the reason, criticism and anger are highly destructive to a problem solving session.

It's important to have a positive attitude and to believe that collaborating will result in solving the problem. One of the first things you can do is to state the problem in a way that recognizes a positive quality of the other person involved. This will increase collaboration and reduce defensiveness. Whereas you might be tempted to begin with, "I feel you don't do enough around the house," a more constructive statement would be, "I know you've had to work a lot of overtime recently, but I would like you to do more of the chores around the house." State the problem clearly and positively without attacking or belittling the other person.

Be Specific and Clear

When discussing a problem, many people fail to state it clearly. Examples of vague problem statements include, "I'm kind of irritated with the way you've been behaving," "Carl isn't behaving properly," "Patrick is always trying to make me mad," "Leanne is lazy," and "You're so wishy-washy." These statements contribute to the other person feeling attacked or blamed. Sometimes when people define a problem, they exaggerate it. For instance, a husband might say, "You'll never learn to do the shopping efficiently," or a mother laments, "He's impossible. He'll never change. He'll become a delinquent." These gloomy forecasts prevent any positive efforts to problem solve.

It's a good idea to take several minutes before a problem solving session to decide exactly what is troubling you and how best to communicate it. Make sure you are clear in your own mind who is involved; what is said and done (or what is not said or done) that bothers you; how the problem occurs; where and when it usually happens; how long it continues. Then, instead of saying "Charlene is not a good worker," you will be able to say, "I'm annoyed because Charlene has forgotten to put out the garbage every Wednesday for the past three weeks."

Express Your Feelings

People are often reluctant to express their feelings when discussing a problem. They may not take the time to evaluate what they are feeling and why or they may fear their emotions are exaggerated or reflect a weakness of their own. Unfortunately, not revealing feelings can contribute to an escalation of anger and resentment that may culminate in angry outbursts that terminate effective problem solving.

When you are defining a problem, it's important to explain how you feel when the problem occurs. Feelings are neither right nor wrong, they simply *are*. If you experience negative feelings in the midst of a particular situation, they serve as a signal that something needs to change. When you explain your feelings, it's a good idea to state them in terms of "I" rather than "you" statements. For instance, a father might say, "I feel lonely when you don't come home until late," or "I get angry when you don't help me discipline Jerry." The alternatives, "You don't care about me because you don't come home," or "You aren't interested in helping me discipline Jerry," create defensiveness and undermine collaboration by their blaming tone.

Be Future-oriented

When parents try to solve problems regarding their children's behavior, they sometimes bog down in rehashing past problems. If you're trying to deal with your son's impertinence, it won't help to talk about how difficult he was as a baby, the problems you had with weaning, toilet training or feeding, and all the efforts you put into handling these various situations. Quite the opposite: reliving past problems is likely to increase your level of anger and frustration and reduce your confidence in being able to effect changes in the future.

Make a point of always looking to the future and focusing on what actions you want to take to change circumstances. You could say, "I know we've had a lot of difficulty managing Irene's behavior in the past, but what we want to think about it now is what we can do to help her in the future. I'm sure that if we work together we can come up with some good solutions." It is important to anticipate a positive future. Gloom and doom prophecies are all too often self-fulfilling.

Be Brief and Keep to One Problem at a Time

It's not always easy to focus when you start discussing problems. Unless you do so, however, you may spend an excessive amount of time itemizing all the problems that exist—or have ever existed—in the family. This can overwhelm your ability to come up with constructive solutions because you end up trying to consider too many things at once.

Only one, or at most, two problems should be discussed in any one problem solving session. Thirty minutes is ample time to discuss a problem and come up with some solutions. If you don't limit yourself in this manner you're likely to become exhausted and frustrated. If someone strays to other problems, an effective response would be, "I think we're supposed to be discussing how to get Lisa to do her homework and not how much time Craig spends watching TV." One person might be assigned to watch for sidetracking and bring the family back on track. For the sake of efficiency, avoid giving four or five examples of the same problem that simply occur in different situations. For instance, instead of describing how your child has temper tantrums in your home, at school, in movie theaters, and on the bus, provide one brief example that illustrates the problem. This will be sufficient and minimize the likelihood that participants will become negative and angry.

Goals And Expectations

Reflect and Summarize

Once parents have finished defining a problem they may rush on to brainstorming without summarizing it. This can lead to misconceptions and misunderstandings. If the problem has not been well defined, summarized and clearly understood by everyone in the session, brainstorming will be ineffective.

When all participants feel that the problem has been adequately discussed and defined, one person should provide a summary. For instance, one parent might summarize the problem with their three-year-old son by saying, "I think Joshua is frustrated because his baby sister is getting into his toys now that she's walking, and he doesn't know how to handle her without hitting her." Other effective summaries include, "I think that you and I are in conflict because we have different expectations about what time the children should go to bed," "The problem is that I'll have to give up my evening classes if I have to help Carl with his homework." Once the problem has been summarized, the other person or people in the session should correct it or indicate agreement that this is an accurate summary.

State the Goal and Desired Behaviors

Another problem occurs when family members spend a great deal of time discussing the negative aspects of the problem, but don't state what they want instead. A wife might mention that her husband comes home too late at night, but never clearly say when she would like him to be home. Or a father who raises the problem that his daughter is too aggressive might not state that his objective is to help her learn to share.

It's important to state a desired goal. This may be to have others participate in household chores, to get a child to go to bed on time, or to get more participation and support from one's partner. Whatever it is, it needs to be stated explicitly. If it's not, the family can't know what to look for as evidence that the problem has been solved.

Brainstorming Solutions

Be Open

As one participant is brainstorming possible solutions, another may bring up reasons why those solutions won't work, saying things like, "There's no point in saying you'll be home at six because it's not realistic. You've never been home that early," or "What's the use of suggesting we try to praise him when he shares? We've tried that and it didn't work." Criticizing solutions and the person who suggests them hinders creativity and undermines the idea of working together that is crucial to effective problem solving.

When brainstorming, the main idea is to be open to as many suggestions as possible, even if you think that they're wild and crazy and totally unrealistic. Allow everyone— yourself included—to generate solutions without judging them. If you can maintain this kind of open attitude, many more new and interesting ideas will be suggested.

Postpone Details

Sometimes during brainstorming, participants get bogged down in the details of how a suggestion will be carried out. A parent might say, "Well, it's impossible for us to reward her every time she shares because we're only around three hours a day," "I don't see how I can help him with his homework because I'm too busy during the school year," or "I don't see how I can monitor them every time they're with their friends because I have to get some work done around here." Focusing on the details is often one variation of criticism and, in the same way, reduces the generation of good solutions. Postpone discussing the details of how a solution will be carried out. The first objective of the brainstorming process is to come up with many ideas. Later, the specific details can be worked out.

Be Creative and Innovative

One of the common mistakes that people make when problem solving is that of restricting the number of solutions they generate. They come up with one or two good ideas and then think that they've done enough. This narrow approach keeps them in the same mental rut, focusing on the same solutions, instead of discussing new and different ways of looking at a problem.

When problem solving, try to think to yourself, "The crazier the idea the better!" This will facilitate free-wheeling discussions that are humorous, even ridiculous, and exciting. This attitude helps to make the sessions more fun. Most important of all, it gets you and your family out of mental ruts and helps you to come up with new ideas. Don't stop brainstorming until you have a long list. And don't be discouraged if it is difficult at first. Practice makes perfect.

Making A Plan

Review Your List

Sometimes when parents are problem solving they come up with one solution that they both like and decide to focus on implementing it. They don't go back over the list to evaluate all the solutions in a systematic way and may miss some other good ideas.

It is important to go through your entire list to eliminate the ridiculous ideas and combine the good ones. Sometimes two average ideas put together will create one excellent solution. After this review, you will have a list of possible solutions that can be discussed at greater length. The advantages and disadvantages of each one can be discussed in more detail at this point.

Evaluating Ideas

Once the more outrageous and impossible ideas have been eliminated, each remaining item on the list should be evaluated in terms of whether it is realistic or not, whether it is a short- or long-term solution, and what the consequences might be. Failing to do this usually leads to choosing an ineffective solution or to failure in implementing the idea chosen.

It's very important to evaluate in terms of whether or not the idea is realistic. Wanting your child to keep the bathroom tidy might be unrealistic if he is four but quite appropriate for an eight-year-old. To expect that you can help your child get A's when she's been getting F's is setting yourself and her up for failure. Ideas should be evaluated not only in terms of whether they are realistic goals for your children to achieve, but also whether they can be realistically carried out by you. Deciding that you're going to reinforce them each time they share may not be realistic for you if you don't have the time for all that monitoring. A second aspect of evaluating is to consider whether it is a short-term or a long-term solution. In the short term, it may be helpful to spank your children every time they don't comply. This may help them to be more compliant, but in the long term it may result in more aggressive behavior and a fearful relationship with you. Another aspect of evaluating a solution is to determine the consequences. What are the best and worst possible outcomes? You might say, "The best outcome would be that the children begin to share more often. The worst would be that they don't learn to share and we have to come up with another strategy."

Identify Barriers and Possible Ways to Overcome Them

In addition to selecting a solution based on how realistic it is and an assessment of possible consequences, also think about whether there are any barriers to following through with the solution. For example, you have decided that you are going to spend more time with your son coaching and supporting him while he does his homework. However, you realize that often you don't know what the teacher's expectations are regarding homework or even what homework your child has. Your child tells you there is no homework, but you are not sure this is the case. Once you realize there is a barrier to following through with the solution you have chosen, the next step is to consider some ways to overcome that barrier. In this case you might decide to talk with your child's teacher to find out what homework is given out each week and how you can be informed of nights there is an assignment due. Perhaps the teacher might agree to put the daily homework on her voice mail, or on her web site so you can check in each day on her expectations. Identifying and understanding potential barriers to your solutions and some possible strategies to coping with them will help you to be successful with your plan.

Write the Plan Down

Sometimes family members decide on a plan but fail to write it down and post it where it can be seen. This often results in ambiguity and people having different recollections about exactly what the plan was. Failure to follow through is more likely to result from such confusion.

Once an agreement has been reached, write it down and post it. This avoids the necessity of relying on memory. Most importantly, by reducing ambiguities in communication it forces everyone to be more precise and clear about the plan. People are more likely to cooperate with an agreement when they know precisely what is expected of them.

Schedule the Next Meeting

Unless you have established a regular problem solving time, it is important for you and your family to schedule your next meeting at the end of the problem solving meeting. The purpose is to monitor whether you have followed through with the chosen strategies, how successful you have been in implementing them, and how you feel about the results. Even good strategies may have flaws. If re-evaluation is not part of the plan, effective methods may be perceived as useless when, in fact, minor revision could have led to successful achievement of goals. At subsequent meetings further problem solving can be carried out. The agreement can be changed, if necessary, to be more realistic or more precise, and any ambiguities or difficulties can be cleared up.

Praise Your Efforts

Sometimes families spend a lot of energy on their problem solving sessions yet fail to reinforce their efforts. This can result in a perception that problem solving is tedious and unrewarding. People who feel this way will be reluctant to participate in future meetings.

To minimize this kind of reaction, remember to praise everyone's efforts, including those you and your partner make in problem solving and your children's efforts in complying with solutions. One session is not going to resolve all the problems in your family. But even if only one small step is made in the desired direction, reinforcing this is critical. Such positive feedback will set the stage for future sessions and for all family members to grow together. If you and your family can successfully problem solve together, you are more likely to maintain flexible, satisfying relationships over a long period of time.

Focus on one problem at a time.

To Sum Up...

Defining the Problem
- Schedule a meeting to problem solve.
- Focus on one problem at a time.
- Collaborate, discussing problems mutually.
- State problem clearly.
- Express feelings but don't criticize or blame.
- Admit role in problem.
- Be future-oriented.
- Be brief.
- State desired behavior.
- Make "I" statements.

Stating the Goal
- Summarize the problem.
- State the goal in realistic terms.

Brainstorming
- Remain open—don't judge or criticize suggestions.
- Encourage imaginative suggestions—as many as possible.
- Be future-oriented.
- Postpone details.

Making Plans
- Review your list.
- Evaluate each solution realistically.
- Identify any barriers to following through with your solutions and ways to overcome them.
- Write down your plan.
- Schedule next meeting to evaluate success and refine if necessary.
- Praise your efforts.

CHAPTER FIFTEEN

Working with Teachers
to Prevent Problems

A parent goes directly to the principal and demands her son be put in a different class. She says the teacher dislikes her 7-year-old son and is singling him out as a behavior problem. She says her child is hyperactive and somewhat impulsive and believes that her child's teacher doesn't have the skills to manage children with these kinds of problems.

For the past few weeks, 4-year-old Jenny has complained that she hates preschool and doesn't want to go. She says she feels left out and has no friends. She says her teacher doesn't like her.

Why Should You Form a Partnership with Your Child's Teacher?
The evidence is now beyond dispute. If parents want their children to be successful in school, the most important thing they can do is to collaborate with their preschool or elementary grade teachers (or day care provider) and strive to maintain regular and effective communication.

However, this is easier said than done. Teachers are often so stressed by large classroom demands that they don't have much time to be involved with parents. Parents, in turn, may be working long hours, or so overwhelmed by stress in their daily lives that they have little energy for school involvement. Sometimes parents feel intimidated by teachers, uncertain how to be involved in their child's education, or unsure about how to communicate with their child's teacher. Moreover, parents whose children are struggling at school and have difficulties with hyperactivity and disruptive behavior often feel a sense of personal failure which makes it uncomfortable to bring up issues with a teacher. However, this investment in your child's future academic success will be well worth the time and effort. Successful partnerships with your child's teachers

Let your child know you are partners with his teacher.

will result in an educational program for your child that is based on your teacher understanding your child's individual emotional and academic needs. Home-school collaboration also provides an opportunity for you and your child's teacher to support each other, resulting in less stress for both of you. In this chapter, we will discuss ways you can become involved in partnering with your child's teacher to support your child's academic, social and emotional competence.

Start Connections with Teachers Right Away

You need to start your involvement efforts even before school starts. Find out about your child's school and teacher. Go to the school orientation meetings to discern your teacher's philosophy of discipline, daily schedule, homework requirements and scheduled parent meetings. Introduce yourself and take some time to get to know your child's teacher so that she or he will know how invested you are in your child's learning. Once you have established a positive relationship and s/he understands your commitment and support, it will be easier to bring up future issues should they occur. If your child has struggled in preschool in the past, now is a good time to let the teacher know about this and to share strategies that have worked in other classrooms or day care settings. Sometimes parents are reluctant to share this information with a new teacher because they are afraid that it will set the teacher up to look for problems. However, this approach lays the ground work for a good working relationship between you and the teacher and will prepare him/her for the most effective ways to work with your child.

Work to Maintain Regular Communication
Be sure to let your child's teacher know (through notes or phone calls or in person) about family matters that might impact your child's school behavior. For example, if there is a new baby, a death in the family, a divorce, or some other trauma in your family, it is important that your child's teacher know about this, so s/he can provide extra support and understand your child's emotional needs.

Let your child's teacher know how your child is responding to school by sending friendly notes about a creative classroom activity that your child particularly enjoyed, or a book your child liked. Even if you work long hours, you can give your child's teacher positive feedback in the form of notes, phone calls, e-mails, and other small surprises such as a gift certificate for a cup of coffee, a book for your child's classroom, or a thank you card. Do not air grievances in notes, as this can result in miscommunication and damage your relationship. These should be discussed in person.

Have a Parent Involvement Plan
In addition to attending the "back to school" nights at the beginning of the year and the regularly scheduled parent-teacher conferences to review your child's progress, it is also important to talk informally with teachers about your child's progress. When you are picking your child up from school, you might go a few minutes early to check in briefly. Ask teachers when the best time of day is for you to make contact with them in person, or by phone, or e-mail. Invite teachers to contact you throughout the year with regard to your child's progress and let them know where you can be reached and times you will be near a phone. If you have a day off work or a little extra time one day, ask your child's teacher how you might help out in the classroom. Perhaps you can help with an art activity, read to some children or help out on a field trip.

Set Up a Study Routine at Home
You can also support your child's school achievement by planning a schedule for daily homework. If your child is too young for homework yet, establish a regular time each day that you read with your child or provide some stimulating play activity. Have a special place to do homework or read together that is free of distractions. Go through your child's backpack each day and check for notices from the teacher or homework. Set limits with your child about the amount of TV, computer, or video game time he can watch, and only allow their use *after* homework or reading is completed first. *Remember it is not the homework per se that*

makes your child successful, but rather the importance that you as a family place on school, reading, and homework. The earlier you start expecting that reading or homework be done and encouraged by you each night, the easier it will be to keep that routine going.

Forecast positive outcomes for your children instead of making threatening comments. For example, positive statements such as "I know you can finish up this page of math before dinner. Then we can look at it together and you can help me finish cooking." Or, "You are really reading well now! Maybe we can have some fun, you read a page and I will read a page," will be more motivating than negative comments such as "You will flunk out if you don't do your homework." Express your faith in your child's abilities and send messages showing that both you and your child's teacher believe in his/her ability to achieve. Praise persistence and patience with the learning process. For example, you might say, "If you keep practicing your reading with me each night, I bet before long you will be able to read a whole page by yourself."

Join Parent Education Groups
In some schools teachers are joining with school counselors, nurses, and psychologists to offer parent education classes. These classes are an opportunity for you to develop joint plans with teachers regarding your child's needs. In these classes you can learn the ways you can support your children's education by working with your children at home. Parent groups are also another way for you to get to know teachers and to let them know your concerns and what family situations may be influencing your children's emotional, social and academic learning. When parent groups involve teachers as co-leaders, long-lasting partnerships are developed which serve to empower each other as well as the children. Moreover, in parent classes you can make friends with other parents and form support networks. It will be important to get to know the parents of the children in your child's classroom. When this happens you can set up playdates and encourage your child's friendships.

Recognize the Value of a Teacher-Parent Partnership Model
Recognize that you and your child's teacher are *both* deeply invested in your child's education and that you have mutual goals. The ideal relationship between the teacher and parent is based on a collaborative partnership. Each brings to the partnership a valuable perspective. The teacher is knowledgeable about teaching principles, curriculum and your child's learning needs, and also has the opportunity to see how your

child behaves in a group context of similar aged children. You, on the other hand, have insights into your child's temperament, likes and dislikes, emotional needs, and what has worked in previous school settings. Accepting the notion of complementary expertise creates a relationship between parents and teachers that is mutually respectful and supportive.

Having A Successful School Conference Meeting

The key to successful conferences with teachers is the parent's use of effective communication and problem solving skills. The following example of a "get acquainted" meeting at the beginning of the school year offers some insights into ways to promote a successful partnership with teachers. You might even want to practice this dialogue before you go to your first teacher conference. Notice the questions this parent asks the teacher.

Sample Teacher-Parent
"Get Acquainted Meeting" in September

TEACHER: Hello, Ms. Jones, I'm Ms. Parks, thanks for taking the time to come in and get acquainted. I've enjoyed working with Takisha these first two weeks of school.

PARENT: It's nice to meet you early in the year. Takisha's been telling me about how much she likes circle time. She's so excited about circle time that I don't hear about the rest of the day. I'd love to know what else is on the schedule so I can ask her questions about the rest of her day. (*Makes a positive comment and asks about daily schedule*)

TEACHER: Well, circle time is the way we start the day. It's a good opportunity for kids to talk about themselves. We also do calendar and talk about the weather.

PARENT: Is Takisha sitting still in the circle? She's a very active little girl, and in preschool, she didn't stay in one place very long.

TEACHER: That's good for me to know. At the beginning of the year, I don't expect any of the children to sit very long, but I do notice that Takisha is restless unless we are up singing and moving. I like to do a lot of movement in the group, so it hasn't been a problem yet.

PARENT: I'm glad to hear that. She also really liked to be a helper when she was in preschool and the teacher sometimes let her help if she stayed sitting in the circle. (*Shows interest and involvement*)

TEACHER: That sounds like a good plan. If it seems like she needs that, I can give that a try too. You know, circle time is just a few minutes of our day at this point in the year. After circle time, the kids get to choose their first center. All of the centers have pre-reading or pre-math themes and the children do hands-on activities that help them learn.

PARENT: I'm wondering, what center does Takisha usually choose? She doesn't really know any math and she can't read. Does she participate? (*Asks about child's interests and participation*)

TEACHER: Oh, she is very involved during this time, and many children this age don't read and do math yet. I've noticed she loves the manipulatives table. That's a center where there are boxes of coins or stones or blocks and the children can make patterns or count or sort the pieces. It looks like they're just playing, but actually what they're doing is getting comfortable with the concept of numbers which is a premath activity. After their first center activity, they all switch, and the children have a chance to work at one of the other centers. Then we have a snack and a 20 minute outdoor recess.

PARENT: You know, sometimes Takisha doesn't play well with other children her age. She gets along better with younger children. Is she making friends here during free play and recess? (*Asks about peer relationships*)

TEACHER: I haven't noticed any problems but thanks for alerting me. I'll keep an eye out for how things are going for her. If she has any trouble I'll let you know, and we can talk about how to help her. For now she seems to be joining in well with the others.

PARENT: That's great, you can always reach me at this number in the evenings. What can I do to help Takisha do well this year? (*Makes known her availability and eagerness to support her child's education at home*)

TEACHER: Next week I'll be sending home a list of books for parents to read with their kids. It would be great if you and Takisha could read together for 10 minutes every night. I have the books in the classroom if you'd like to borrow them, or I know most of them are available at the library. By reading together, I mean you reading to her or just looking at pictures together and talking about what might be going on in the pictures. You don't have to get her to sound out the words. Just let it be a fun, enjoyable time for you both.

PARENT: That will be easy, she loves looking at picture books. Thanks for taking the time to meet with me. If there's anything I can do to help or if there's anything I should know about Takisha's progress, please call me. If I need to talk with you, is there a time of day that is best to call you? Do you mind if I send you email? (*Shows involvement and clarifies how she can communicate with the teacher in the future*)

TEACHER: It is best to reach me by phone at 3:30 after the children have left. Also emailing me is good too, but I only check my email every other day so if it is urgent calling is best. It was great meeting you. I know you work full time, but if you ever have a chance to come and observe or help out in the class, I'd love to have you. I think Takisha's going to have a good kindergarten year.

In this first meeting the parent and teacher have successfully begun their partnership. They have each clarified their methods for open communication and signaled their willingness to work as partners. The parent was prepared for the meeting and had thought about her goals. She was successful in finding out about her child's academic schedule and letting the teacher be aware of possible behavioral and social concerns. This working together sets the stage for consistency between home and school and creates an atmosphere of support—all of which benefits the children.

Other Questions You can Ask Your Child's Teacher
• How well does my child get along with other children? Who does he play with most?
• Does my child participate in circle time discussions?
• What does he particularly like to do in class?
• Have you noticed any changes in my child's behavior or mood?
• Is my child delayed in his reading or language or writing abilities? Should I have him tested?
• Is my child making friends in the classroom and interacting with the other children?
• How much homework should he be doing at home?
• How can I help him or tutor him at home with school related activities?
• What is the best way to communicate with you about any concerns?
• Are there times I can visit the class?
• Even though I work, are there things I can do evenings or weekends that would be helpful to you?

Some Communication Guidelines for Conferencing About a Problem in the Classroom

All children will have academic or social problems at school from time to time. It is important to have a conference meeting with the teacher to talk about the problem as soon as you recognize it. While you may feel guilty or partially to blame for the problem and be unsure how to solve it, or even have doubts about the teacher's ability to handle the problem, it is important that you go into this meeting with a sense of working together to fix the problem—and not to fix the blame. Using the following effective communication skills will help assure a positive tone and outcome.

Address Problems Early On—They are Easier to Solve

You need to contact the teacher as soon as you are aware your child has an academic, learning or behavioral problem, even if it is the first week of school! This is at the core of successful collaboration. You might be tempted to avoid telling the teacher about your child's problems because you don't want to "label" your child, or set up a self-fulfilling prophesy. You might hope that your child will eventually improve or outgrow the problem. However, this avoidance of talking about the problems can delay your child from getting the extra services or support that will help him to be successful in school.

Sometimes teachers don't speak up about problems with parents because they fear being criticized for not being a competent teacher. They may think it is a sign of inadequacy to admit to a parent that they need their help in managing a child's problems. They may believe in the "good teacher" myth, that good teachers should handle all of their students' problems on their own without the help of parents. Rather, just the reverse is true. It is the most competent teachers who will involve parents from the outset in collaborative planning regarding a student's difficulties.

However, discussions about a child's problems should not be dealt with "on the fly," but rather an appointment should be set up at a mutually agreed upon time to talk. This will permit a more thoughtful meeting and a high likelihood of a workable solution.

Speaking Up About Your Concerns

Prepare for your meeting by clarifying your concerns ahead of time, and thinking about what you want to accomplish with the teacher. Consider how your child's teacher might see the problem and think about your common goals.

Begin with a statement of appreciation: Start your meetings by thanking the teacher for agreeing to meet with you and letting her know that you appreciate what she is doing to help teach your child and the rest of the class. Your introductory statement expressing appreciation will set the tone for the entire conversation.

Briefly describe your concern and express your goals. Next briefly describe your concern and your goals or what you want to accomplish in the meeting. Avoid focusing on the negative, or what you don't want. Avoid recounting multiple episodes of your child's problems or the school's failures to prove your point.

> PARENT: The situation is unacceptable. You don't answer my calls. You don't seem to understand my child or care about his learning. He says you don't like him. Have you ever worked with children with attention deficit disorder before?

In this example, the parent starts by blaming the teacher for her child's problems. This approach is likely to result in defensiveness from the teacher, rather than solutions to the problem. State your concern positively and briefly.

> PARENT: I am concerned that Timmy is unhappy at school. He tells me he doesn't like school. I know he is inattentive and must be difficult to teach. I wonder if there is a way we can work together to help encourage him to learn and get his work completed?

Here the parent has described her concern clearly and briefly and has focused on the positive outcome that is desired. Avoid describing your child's problems with vague statements such as, "She's not behaving," or "Her attitude isn't good" and avoid judgmental comments.

Use "I" messages instead of "You" messages. As described in the Communication chapter, "I" messages communicate what you want or feel. They're a way to be clear about an issue without having a destructive effect. I messages focus on your feelings and your desire for change.

> PARENT: I am having a frustrating time reading with Billy. He gets mad when I correct him and doesn't seem to want me to read with him.

or

PARENT: I'm worried about Billy. He doesn't seem to have any friends. He never gets invited to other children's houses. He tells me he is lonely.

Ask for feedback. Sometimes you may not be sure if the teacher has understood your point of view. If this happens, you can ask, "Am I making sense?" This is much more effective than rambling on and on, and it assures the teacher that you believe his or her comprehension of the situation is important.

Be respectful of the time constraints on your child's teacher. Speaking up does not mean you should be indiscriminate about where, when, or how you express your feelings. First of all, it is important to ask yourself: "Do I have a legitimate concern or am I in a bad mood?" "Am I overreacting?" "What am I really interested in solving?" Determine ahead of time the length of time for your meeting and be respectful of time constraints on the teacher, avoid rambling or talking too much.

Describe steps you have taken to solve problem. It is important for your child's teacher to recognize that you have already thought about the problem and have taken appropriate action to deal with the situation; that you're not calling them to solve the problem themselves. For example, you might say, "I am working at home with Scott's problem of disobedience and swearing. I am giving him extra attention and praise for polite talk and am rewarding him for following directions. But I would also like your input and to coordinate a plan with you at school if that is possible?"

Obtaining Teacher Input

A frequently voiced complaint by teachers is that they don't feel listened to and respected by parents. (Parents often feel the same way about teachers!) Unfortunately, instead of listening and allowing teachers to provide their insights into the child's problem, parents sometimes respond defensively to teacher's concerns with arguments, anger and denial. Some teachers report they feel criticized by parents for their failure to control their children in the classroom. When a person doesn't feel listened to, it is likely that he or she will withdraw totally from the relationship and avoid problem solving. Listening fully to your child's teacher's perspective, and even to his complaints, will show that you value his opinion and is a powerful tool for beginning the process of working together. Review Chapter Thirteen for more tips on Active Listening.

It's important to put yourself in the other person's shoes. Think about how the teacher might feel about the issue, then validate this feeling. You might say, "I can see how that must have disrupted your whole class," "That would have made me cross too," or "Yes, I feel frustrated when my son does the same thing at home." In these instances, the teacher's feelings are validated as the parent tries to see the problem from the teacher's point of view. This approach can help reduce the gap that might exist between the parent and teacher.

Be Polite and Positive and Edit Your Complaints

As you listen, you may feel some frustration or defensiveness with a teacher's assessment of your child or you may disagree with his or her interpretation. Even so, it is essential to remain positive and avoid criticisms of the teacher. Put-downs will evoke anger, resentment, defensiveness, guilt, or depression, and undermine effective communication and problem solving.

Focus on Fixing the Problem

Sometimes effective communication is hindered by blaming. This occurs when people place the responsibility for a problem with someone else. They may directly accuse others of creating the problem or they may do this more subtly. Following meetings, parents and teachers often report that they felt blamed for the children's behavior problems. Here are some common examples of blaming as reported by parents and teachers.

TEACHER: Your daughter gets her own way and you never discipline her. That's why she's such a behavior problem. You're not tough enough.

TEACHER: Your child is the most aggressive child I have ever seen. He is really out of control. I've handled tough kids before, but not like your child.

PARENT: He didn't have any problems with the teacher last year. You must not like him and he senses that from you.

PARENT: You yell a lot at him in class and he doesn't want to come to school anymore.

Blaming sets people against each other in battle rather than uniting them to solve a problem. However once you remember that you and the teacher share a common goal to solve the child's problems, you can form a good working partnership. For instance, you might say to the teacher, "The problem seems to be that Gillian is overly aggressive. Let's decide how we both want to handle these problems in the future so that we can be consistent with each other. I know if we work together we can help her be more cooperative." This approach emphasizes collaboration and consistency is more likely to lead to a successful outcome for your child.

Continue to Advocate for Your Child

You might bring up an issue, only to have it dismissed by the teacher as not being a serious problem. For instance, perhaps you are concerned that your child is acting aggressively at home or is overly anxious about school work. However, the teacher may not see a problem in the classroom and therefore might not see the value of discussing it. It may be reassuring to you to find out that the problem isn't happening at school, but it is also important for you to be able to express your concerns and enlist the teacher's help. Asking for the teacher's advice about how to handle the problem at home can be a good approach. "I'm relieved to hear that Chris is getting along well with other children on the playground. I'm concerned about how aggressive he is with friends in the neighborhood. Do you have any suggestions for how to work on this issue at home?"

Express Hope

Although no major problem can be resolved in one meeting, each one does have a workable solution. This is an important attitude to convey. For instance, you might communicate an attitude of hope by saying: "Okay, it is so helpful to work with you and get your ideas. I know we are going to have to be patient with him as it takes time to change. He's been through a lot but I'm confident that by working together we can help him. Can we talk about what are the most important behaviors to focus on first?"

Agree on Mutual Goals and Brainstorm Solutions

Once the issue or problem has been discussed and both you and the teacher feel your views have been expressed and been listened to, the next step is for you to agree upon common goals and to brainstorm possible solutions. You can ask the teacher if s/he has any suggestions for how to solve the problem. Share your ideas for what you have already tried and what you think will be helpful to your child given the new information from the teacher. After brainstorming together, work out a plan of exactly what the teacher will do at school and what you will do at home. For example, the teacher might say, "Here's what I will do at school. I will set up a sticker program to help him remember to listen and not blurt out in class. Then I will send home a note each day to let you know how many stickers he has earned that day." The parent might say, "That sounds good. I will keep track of the

stickers that he earns at school, and when he
has earned 25 of them, I'll plan a surprise at
home." The behavior plan should be written
down and a phone check-in scheduled to be
sure it is working.

HEY, LET'S TELL THE TEACHER ABOUT HOW WE SOLVED THAT PROBLEM ON THE PLAYGROUND.

Express Confidence in Teacher
Whenever there is a problem with your child,
you will probably feel anxious. However,
you need to let the teacher know you have
confidence in her ability to handle the situation and to work in partnership with you to
help your child learn new behaviors.

Plan Follow Up
It is important to plan a follow-up meeting or phone call to review the
success of the planned intervention. The follow-up plan is vital to reaf-
firm each person's commitment to the plan.

**Sample Parent-Teacher Meeting
to Discuss a Problem**

TEACHER: It's good to see you again Ms. Parks. You said you wanted
to talk about a problem.

PARENT: Yes, I'm concerned because Jonathan is impulsive and aggressive and he never listens to me. I'm trying to discipline him
but I'd like to know if this is a problem for you as well in
the classroom and if so, if we can work together to help
him be more cooperative. (*clear description*)

TEACHER: Yes he is very active and impulsive at times. He also has
trouble focusing on his work. I'm glad you came to talk to
me about this. I would like to coordinate with you.

PARENT: Yes I can imagine then that this will be frustrating for you
because you have 25 other students as well. I would like to
be supportive in whatever way I can. (*acknowledges teacher's
feelings*)

TEACHER: He is a delightful child in many ways, and I enjoy working
with him. I don't expect to change his temperament but perhaps together we can help him learn to follow directions more
often and also help him learn some social skills so he can

make friends. His impulsive and aggressive behavior sometimes results in other kids isolating him, and I don't want that
to happen. He will enjoy school more when he has friends.

PARENT: I'm glad you understand children like this and I agree that
it is good idea to work on his social skills and cooperation.
You know I put him on a sticker chart at home, and he
seems to have responded to that. Every time he does what
I ask him to do, I give him a sticker for his chart. When
he gets 10 stickers, he gets to pick out some baseball cards
and he is really eager to add to his collection. Perhaps
something similar to that might work in the classroom?
(listens to teacher, validates her idea, and suggests an idea)

TEACHER: That's a great idea. I could put a little chart on his desk and
keep track of his cooperative behaviors. He could earn a
stamp on his chart for doing what I ask and for every time
I see him sharing with other children. I could send home a
note each day telling you how many stamps he has earned
and you could add these to his total sticker chart to earn
baseball cards. Maybe I could even have some other incentive at school for earning a certain number of stamps. What
do you think he likes at school?

PARENT: That's a great plan. I think that would help Jonathan. You
know he is a good reader and loves books about dinosaurs.
Maybe when he earns a certain number of stamps he could
read a book about dinosaurs to the class. I could get the book
at the library if you don't have any in class. What do you
think? *(Offers a suggestion and asks for teacher feedback)*

TEACHER: That's a great idea because it would also help the other kids
to see something that he does really well and would help
us work on his image problem. At circle time I could also
work with the kids to understand that everyone has different
strengths and areas to work on. I am also going to have a
class rule about "no exclusion", that is, no one is allowed
to exclude another child from a game. By the way, he plays
well with Michael, who is very easy going and accepting; do
you think you might set up some supervised play dates to
encourage that friendship?

PARENT: I like that idea, and I wasn't sure who is friends were so that
is helpful. Then I could praise him and give him stickers
for his sharing at home when Michael comes over. *(Agrees
with teacher's suggestion)*

TEACHER: Okay so I think that is a good start, should we plan to talk again in 2 weeks?

PARENT: Yes I would like that. You can always call me at work if you want to talk before then. When is a good time to reach you? Thank you very much for taking the time to meet with me. I feel better now that I know what our goals are. (*plan follow up discussion*)

TEACHER: Could I call you in the evening? It's hard for me to call during the school day.

PARENT: Yes, any time after 6:30 would be fine. I feel very supported by you and know how much this will mean to Jonathan. (*Express confidence and support*)

When to Involve School Counselor or Principal

Your first step is always to try to work out the problem directly with your child's teacher. This will likely result in the most benefit for your child. However, if you feel for some reason you are reaching an impasse, then you might consider bringing in the school counselor or principal to help you find a solution.

Adopt a Unified, Productive Approach In Front of Children

There will always be times when you disagree with a teacher or feel the classroom or teacher chemistry isn't quite right for your child. However, you should never voice your negative thoughts about teachers in front of your children. If children sense you don't respect their teacher, this will undermine the teacher's authority and ability to teach your child. Unified parent-teacher partnerships are key to children's achievement. When your children see you working with their teacher together to resolve conflicts, it gives them the message that school is important and that both parties care about their success.

Take a Long Term Perspective

If your child is experiencing some behavior problems due to a family crisis (death or divorce or abuse), it will take a commitment from the parent and teacher to work closely together over the entire year and perhaps future years. Likewise for children who are hyperactive or impulsive or developmentally delayed, it will also take ongoing meetings to plan target behaviors and coordinate incentive programs and academic needs. Keep a positive attitude and take one step at a time while continuing to encourage your child, your child's teacher, and yourself for your progress.

To Sum Up...

Working with teachers and becoming involved in your child's education is a process that is demanding and time-consuming, sometimes frustrating, and often rewarding. For busy parents and overworked teachers it can seem difficult to know how to carve out any extra time for this collaboration work. However, the value of this approach for your children's social and academic growth cannot be underestimated. In the long run, this commitment on your part to work together with your teacher may actually save time, for it can lead to more support for you and the teacher. For the child it will make all the difference.

Remember:
- Make a plan for parent involvement before school starts.
- Send your teacher positive notes or emails.
- Set up informal and formal mechanisms to communicate with your child's teachers.
- Don't store up grievances; call a meeting with your child's teacher if your child is having problems.
- Be brief, clear and concise when describing your child's problem.
- Listen and ask for teacher feedback and suggestions for solutions.
- Be polite and positive.
- Focus on fixing the problem and avoid blaming.
- Recognize the teacher's point of view.
- Make positive recommendations.
- Plan a follow-up with teacher.
- Encourage ongoing conversation.

PART THREE

Coping with Common Behavior Problems

Taking Control of Your Child's "Screen Time"

Sally is exhausted. She was up three times last night with her newborn baby and now her four-year-old son, Henry, is running around demanding her attention and messing up each room just as she gets things picked up. She finally thinks to herself, "I need a break!" So she turns to her son and says, "Henry, why don't you watch TV or play a computer game for a while?" He willingly turns on the television and sits mesmerized in front of it for the next hour watching cartoons, all his energy suddenly gone. Quiet reigns in the house and Sally begins to make dinner, unaware of what he is watching.

Does this sound familiar? Television viewing and computer games can be addictive, not only for young children but also for their parents, since it may be the only time in the day when parents can have some peace and quiet or get chores done. Television can become a convenient and regular baby sitter. In fact, research indicates that children as young as 18 months see an average of 14 hours of TV a week, preschoolers about 23 hours a week, and school-age children 25 to 30 hours a week. By the age of 18, the average child will probably have seen 15,000 hours of TV. Furthermore, it appears that greater access to home computers rapidly adds to children's total "screen time," that is, time spent using a computer, playing video games, and watching TV combined. More than 20% of all children between ages of 8 and 18 report having a computer in their bedrooms, suggesting that the computer may often be used in social isolation. In a national survey, parents reported that children with computer access spent an average of 5 hours per day engaged in screen time (excluding use of computer for homework). Moreover, children's daily use of computers is increasing each year. As the amount of time children spend involved with these various media increases, the amount of time they can spend participating in organized sports, social inter-actions, and playing outside decreases. This interferes with children's development of friendships and also impacts their physical fitness. Another startling fact is that less than 25 percent of this viewing time is spent watching programs designed for young children's developmental needs. They will see over 18,000 murders and over 350,000 commer-cials—two-thirds of which are for sugar products. A study carried out by Temple University surveyed 2,279 children between the ages of seven and 11. Over 50 percent of them reported that they were allowed to watch television or play computer games *whenever* they wanted, and 30 percent were allowed to watch *whatever* they wanted or play whatever games they wanted.

Why Be Concerned About What Television Programs or Computer Games Your Child is Exposed To?

Over the past 25 years there has been considerable research evaluating the effects of television on children. Educational TV programs such as *Mr. Rogers' Neighborhood,* which was geared to a young child's cogni-tive and emotional developmental level, have been shown to promote positive behaviors and increase cooperative and imaginative play. Educational computer software focused on reading, math and science concepts, have been shown to enhance children's ability to read, do mathematics and generally to improve academic performance. However, these educational television and computer programs are the exception. The amount of aggression and violence has increased with each new generation of games. A content analysis of recent popular Nintendo and Sega Genesis computer games found that nearly 80% of the games had aggression or violence as an objective. Yet parents are often unaware of even the most popular violent titles (e.g., Duke Nukem), despite the rating system from the Educational Software Ratings Board (ESRB). Many tele-vision and computer programs are not developmentally appropriate for young children and can result in negative consequences. Here are some of the harmful effects that have been reported.

Violent Television and Computer Programs Increase Children's Aggressive Play and Fights with Others

Numerous studies have shown that excessive viewing of violent computer games and television programs increases children's aggressive behavior and hostility. Children are likely to imitate and learn new forms of aggression by watching violent characters on television or on computer games. Moreover, children's attitudes to aggressive behaviors are changed by a heavy diet of such viewing. Those who watch such programs are more likely to become emotionally insensitive to others' suffering or aggressive behavior in real life. Television and computer violence seems to numb their sense of sympathy for victims. In fact, they learn to see aggression as an appropriate problem-solving strategy. If a "good guy" on television or a computer game wins by shooting a "bad guy," many young watchers come to believe that violence is permissible as long as you think you are a "good guy." (At least since the 1980's, US and British military have used violent video games for training, reportedly to desensitize soldiers to the suffering of their targets.) In particular, young children have difficulty distinguishing between real and artificial life when playing computer simulation games. This can lead to confusion concerning what it means to be "alive."

Too Much Violent Television or Computer Time Can Foster Bad Cognitive Habits

The typical television and computer programs emphasize fast-paced, brief events, or plenty of action with constant cuts, interruptions and special effects. Changes occur at least every two minutes. This rapid succession of material is designed to sustain the viewer's attention. However, the price of this approach is that children are not given time to look away or to reflect on what they have seen. In fact, the rapidity of many programs probably interferes with their rehearsal and retention of new material. The only way they can have any control over the information presented is to shut it off completely. A book provides the opportunity to go back and forth over a sentence until it is learned and understood. After reading a line, children can stop, think about what they have read, elaborate upon it in their minds, or develop some visual image of what is going on. This kind of learning process is not possible while watching television. Because they are not given time to interact cognitively with such fast-paced content, children learn to sit back and passively absorb what is presented to them.

Not only does television promote bad cognitive habits, it also encourages children to expect that parents, teachers, and other adults will be highly entertaining in their teaching. Those who watch a great deal of TV or engage in many hours of computer games find it difficult to sustain their attention through long explanations. Less entertaining approaches to teaching leave them bored, and bored children may increase their activity level. Some studies have suggested that hyperactive children are heavier television viewers than other youngsters. On the other hand, research by Jerome Singer, from the Yale Institute on Television, has shown that children who watched the slow-paced *Mr. Rogers' Neighborhood* for several weeks were more imaginative and cooperative than those who watched fast-paced programs during the same period. Fast-paced shows do not allow children time to develop thinking strategies or time to reflect. These skills are much more important to true learning than the rote memorization of numbers and letters.

Television Watching Fosters Passivity and Discourages Other Learning Activities

Excessive time spent watching television and playing computer games means less time for playing with peers, reading, thinking or imaginative play. Connections have been shown between heavy television viewing and reduced school performance, poor reading ability, attention span and imagination, decreased enthusiasm for school, and increased hyper-activity. Researchers theorize that the reduced school performance and reading ability occur because television and computer games interfere with or replace studying, thinking, writing and time spent reading. Time spent alone on the computer in the bedroom or watching TV also means less time for playing with other children and less physical activity. There is some evidence that excessive use of screen time including heavy Internet usage is associated with increases in children's reports of loneliness and depression.

Television and Computer Games Interfere with Conversation and Discussion

Watching television and playing computer games can reduce family dialogues between adults as well as between parents and their children. A pattern can develop where children wake up in the morning and immediately turn on the set. They go to school and return home to watch TV or continue their computer game. They may even be joined by their parents to eat dinner in front of the set, and then watch until bedtime.

Television and Computer Games Discourage Physical Play

Physical activity is essential for children's normal social, emotional, cognitive, and physical development. They learn by doing, by manipulating objects and by active involvement in fantasies and play. Since television renders children passive, they have less interest in active learning. As viewing increases, time and interest for more creative, active play decreases. There is some evidence that extensive screen time is contributing to children's obesity.

Television and Computer Advertising Teaches Poor Eating Habits and Increases Children's Demands for Material Possessions
Most commercials that are shown within children's programs emphasize sugar cereals, candy, toys and other tempting products in a way that encourages youngsters to pressure their parents to buy them. In some cases, the whole cartoon is actually an advertisement for the product. Children's pleas for advertised products often create conflict with their parents, who cannot and should not meet all these requests. Youngsters are extremely vulnerable to commercials because they are easily influenced by the special effects. Naive and trusting consumers, most assume that advertisements provide accurate information, and can't understand their parents' objections to purchasing such wonderful products.

Television and Computer Games Foster a Poor Reality Base in Young Children
Up to eight years of age, children have difficulty separating fantasy from reality. Fantasy and imagination are an extremely fun and an important part of children's emotional and social development and, in the right context, can be wonderful. Fairy tales, games of pretend, and imaginative play are ways for children to explore experiences outside of their immediate reality and to experience the point of view of others. However, television and computer games that are not geared towards their developmental levels can be confusing or anxiety producing. Violent or scary scenes or characters may seem real to them. For example, watching a program with ghosts or monsters may contribute to fears of going to bed at night. News programs depicting war scenes or volcanoes erupting can also be very distressing. Children may begin to view the world as a hostile, frightening and an unpredictable place, and start to demonstrate fears clearly related to program content. This kind of scary adult content is particularly problematic for children if they see it without parental monitoring. If parents are present, they can watch for their child's reaction and can help to explain what is real and what is

The TV addict.

imaginary and can reassure them that they will keep them safe. Parents can also make a judgment about what program content is inappropriate according to their child's developmental level.

Television Reflects Prejudice and Stereotypes of Human Beings that Children Learn to Imitate

Television does not accurately reflect the world we live in. In particular, women, minority groups, the elderly and working class people are often under-represented, presented in a negative or prejudiced fashion, or appear only in stereotypical roles. Male-female relationships progress rapidly to sexual involvement. Many lead characters smoke or drink heavily, disrespect adults, or use swear words. Research demonstrates that children imitate the stereotypical behaviors of adults as presented on television. This is of particular concern because so many of these adults are inappropriate role models.

Getting the Most Out of Television and Computers

Benefits of TV and Computer Games

Many studies suggest that moderate use of age appropriate computer games and television programs has no significant impact on children's friendships and family relationships, and can even enhance certain visual intelligence skills, such as ability to read and recognize visualize images, and can serve as a building block to computer literacy. Television and computer technology can be a window to a world of events and ideas that you and your family would not otherwise experience. It can take you to concerts, ballets and other artistic events. You can travel to Africa, through underwater worlds, and into scientific laboratories. You can see how others solve personal problems or deal with difficult issues such as crime, poverty, drugs, old age, or death. Your children can learn to read, do math, play the piano, or become more cooperative with educational programs. Television and computers can be an important educational experience for your children if you take active control of them rather than allowing yourself or them to be addicted to them. Here are some ways you can help to maximize the positive effects and minimize the negative effects of media in your children's lives.

What To Do

Set limits on extent of exposure: The research indicates that it is the "excessive use" of screen technologies that place children at risk for harmful effects on their physical, social and psychological development.

To ensure healthy and appropriate use of TV and computer games, limit the amount of time spent by your children on these activities. One hour daily is plenty, especially for preschoolers. If your children are having problems at school, homework should be completed before they're allowed to watch TV or play computer games. Or, you might decide to limit your family to weekend watching. Be firm and consistent about your household rule. If you don't take it seriously, neither will your children. However, be reasonable about the limit you set, and if there is a special program on that you all want to watch allow your children to take advantage of this opportunity. With older children, you may want each family member to keep a chart of the number of hours spent viewing and programs seen for a week. Then you can review this and decide whether or not your family is watching too much television or spending too much time playing computer games.

Supervise and monitor the type of programs watched: In addition to limiting the amount of time your children spend with the screen, carefully select the type of program watched. Teach your children which programs or games are forbidden. Don't let them watch evening news, violent programs or R-rated films and select computer games carefully by checking out the Entertainment Software Ratings of age appropriateness. Research has shown that children who see a lot of violent programs have increased nightmares and fears. Programs should be ones that have been specifically designed for children. Computer programs for young children that teach reading and science concepts and reinforce characters for cooperative behavior have been shown to have considerable educational and social value. Substitute these games for aggressive computer games. By being discriminating yourself, teach your children to be selective in their viewing. Encourage them to schedule ahead of time what to watch rather than simply turning on the TV and randomly choosing. The advent of cable television means that you must monitor your children's viewing habits even more closely than in previous years because they have far greater access to programs that were not intended for them. Use filters for your TV and computer to prevent children from accessing inappropriate Internet sites or television programs.

Encourage other physical and social activities and reading: Turn off the television and computer. Play with your children, take a walk, go to a zoo, or science center. Encourage sports, hobbies, and music by participating in them yourself rather than being a "couch potato." Read to your children as often as possible. Invite one of your child's friends over to play and plan an interactive activity such cooking together, building a fort, playing ball, or engaging in an art activity. These experiences give your children opportunities to interact with others and to learn social skills and problem solving as well as make friends.

Set a bedtime that is not altered by television programs or computer games: Don't put TVs or computers in the bedrooms of young children, or they may stay up late watching programs. Moreover, if you place them in a public place or family room, you can easily monitor what they are viewing.

Praise your children for good viewing habits: Praise your children for turning off the television at the end of a show, or for watching an educational program or for stopping a computer game to help with setting the table.

Watch television and computer games with your children to mitigate their effects: Watch programs with your children and talk about the characters who are caring and sensitive. Use programs to bring up discussions about topics such as trust, sharing, and cooperation. For older children, you can use shows as a catalyst to discuss the effects of drinking and drugs, sexual activity, violence, stereotypes, prejudice and death. For instance, you might point out how violence hurts people and their families and talk about alternatives to violence. Ask your children to rewrite plots in order to come up with a different solution instead of a shootout. Talk about commercials and show them how products are presented in a manner designed to sell. Discuss the factors advertisements ignore; for example, that sugared cereal and candy promote tooth decay. Watch the news with older children and discuss the role of editors and reporters. Ask them to compare what's in the newspaper with what is shown on TV, and to notice how topics can be presented from different viewpoints. When watching dramatic shows, talk about how different characters handle conflict, treat each other, and whether or not they communicate their feelings. With preschoolers, you can help them understand the difference between the world of fantasy, or make-believe, and the real world. Explain how dramatic stories differ from news programs, or how commercials differ from other programs. If your children see a program they like, encourage them to go to the library and read about the topic. While passive viewing doesn't seem to increase a child's social or academic learning, research indicates that discussions with parents or teachers about programs can help to integrate the viewing experience into learning about new ideas.

Set a good example: Few people realize that they watch as much television as they do. Try to be honest with yourself. You may not want to admit that you watch too much. However, remember that your children will model and learn from your viewing habits. If you watch hours of TV each day, you can be sure that your children will learn to do the same. Take a hard look at your own viewing habits, and if you feel you spend too much time in front of the TV or playing computer games, encourage yourself to read more, play with your children, take time for hobbies, exercise and other constructive activities.

Strive for a balance: Computer games and television programs can not only be relaxing and fun but also provide rich learning experiences for children. What is important is that you take control over what your children are watching and how much they are watching. Help your children achieve a balance between screen time activities and other activities involving social interactions and friendship making, sports and reading.

Behavior in Public Places

"I took our four-year-old son to a nice restaurant with his grand-parents. It was a disaster. He kept getting up from his chair and crawling under the table. He spilled his milk and didn't eat a thing. I was so embarrassed. I'll never do that again!"

Why Do Behavior Problems Occur in Public Places?
Taking children to grocery stores, the doctor's office, movie theaters and restaurants can be an exasperating experience for just about every parent. Who hasn't seen a youngster in a grocery store throw a tantrum when a favorite box of breakfast cereal was denied? Children's behavior can deteriorate in public places for a variety of reasons. Sometimes parents are so busy talking to each other while eating out or reviewing a shopping list at the market that they ignore their quiet, well-behaved children. Not until the children misbehave do they get noticed. Parents who pay attention to misbehavior while ignoring good behavior teach their children that misbehaving earns more of a payoff than behaving appropriately.

A second reason that children misbehave in public is that visits to restaurants, the doctor's office or movie theaters usually last too long for them. The expectation that a child of four or five will be able to stay quiet, cooperative and compliant for one or two hours is unrealistic. Misbehavior may occur because most children have had relatively few learning experiences in public. Unsure about what to expect and how to behave appropriately, they become anxious and misbehave. These behavior problems will likely escalate if parents respond differently than they would at home, hoping to avoid a scene. Youngsters are quick to get the message that their parents will give in at the mere threat of a public tantrum. They therefore need to learn that not only are tantrums unsuccessful at home, they are also unsuccessful in public. Of course, another problem with stores and restaurants is that they provide children with hundreds of inviting temptations that require limit-setting on the part of their parents. It is usually necessary to say no to them more often in public than at home. Finally, when young children are in settings such as parks with lots of other children, they can become very excited, especially if they haven't had much experience with other children. They may misbehave in order to see what kind of a reaction they can get or in an effort to show off. Often this occurs simply because they don't know any appropriate techniques for interacting in such situations.

What To Do

Set up learning experiences: Because excursions to public places provide temptations for misbehavior, they also offer opportunities for you to teach your children new behaviors. The trick is to rethink these situations as teaching opportunities. For instance, if your child has had a bad experience in a doctor's office or store, it's important not to avoid that place in the future. Instead, return as soon as possible but set up the experience so that your child will succeed. This can be done in a number of ways.

Say your daughter has difficulty in a grocery store. You will need to set up trial runs, or training trips, by taking her to the store with no intention of shopping. The goal is to teach appropriate grocery store behaviors. Stay in the store only five to ten minutes so that she has an opportunity to be successful. During this brief training time praise appropriate behaviors, such as staying by your side and not picking things off the shelves or climbing on the cart. Be sure to choose a time when there are few people in the store so that if you have to discipline her, you won't have many onlookers.

On the other hand, if restaurant behavior is a problem, you could take training trips to inexpensive places. Instead of ordering an entire meal, have a drink or snack so your stay can be brief. During these visits, reinforce appropriate mealtime and restaurant behaviors. Another approach is to practice at home: have the family dress up as if you are going out to dinner and practice your best manners. During these meals, your children should be praised every time they display appropriate behaviors.

State the rules: Be sure that you are clear about the rules for behavior in public places. For instance, here is how you might matter-of-factly remind your children of the rules for the bank: "Remember, in the bank you must stay by my side and speak quietly." Similarly, when going to a library, you might want to remind your children, "In the library, you must read or talk quietly and not run around making lots of noise."

Time Out: Be prepared to discipline your children in public places. For example, if your son has a tantrum in a bank, you may be able to ignore

Handling misbehavior in public places.

his misbehavior as long as other adults are not reinforcing it with their attention. If you can't ignore the tantrum, it may be necessary to leave the bank and have him do a short Time Out just outside. Once it has been completed you can give him another chance to be successful. Sometimes you have no choice but to take your screaming youngster to your car to calm down. It's important that your children learn that the rules that apply at home also apply in other settings. Don't give in to tantrums because if you do you can expect them to be repeated on future trips.

If your child runs away when you visit grocery stores, explain that it will cost him or her one minute in a shopping cart. You could say, "Each time you run away from my side, I'm going to put you in the cart for a minute so that you learn to stay by me." Once you establish the rule, be sure to enforce it. When you have to discipline your children in public, try not to worry about what other people are thinking. Concentrate on helping your children get their behavior under control and on maintaining your own calm. It is far better to do this when they are age four that when they are 15.

Reinforcement programs: Set up tangible reinforcement programs for misbehaviors in public. For example, Randy had a problem with four-year-old Tanya running away from his side in the grocery store. He set up a tangible reward program to help get this behavior under control. He told Tanya, "If you stay by my side until we get to the end of an aisle you'll get a sticker. When we're done, you can trade your stickers in for something you want. If you go down all six aisles by my side, you could earn six stickers. Then you can get a bag of pretzels or popcorn if you like. Would you like that?" It would also be important for Randy to praise his daughter for staying by his side as soon as he gets in the store. In fact, he'll need to praise her every 15 or 20 feet at first.

Be realistic and teach gradually: Expecting your children to behave well for prolonged periods of time in restaurants, churches or stores is unrealistic. Sometimes it's better to enjoy shopping or eating out with other adults and leave your children at home with a baby sitter. On the other hand, if you wait until they're eight or ten before you take them to a restaurant or church service, they won't know how to behave in these situations. All children, regardless of age, need learning experiences. So whenever you start, be sure to set up brief learning trips and gradually lengthen the time. The idea is to allow your children to have successful experiences, so be sure you can leave before they misbehave.

Involve your child if possible: Try to involve your children in conversations in public places. At the dentist's office you might say to the doctor, "Reggie wants to show you his clean teeth. He's been brushing them every day." Or in the grocery store you could say to your daughter, "Will you please hand me the can of tomato sauce over there?" You can use these experiences to teach all kinds of things, such as where pineapples grow, how much things cost, the use of freezers and so on. The more involved your children are in helping you, cooperating and talking, the less likely they are to misbehave.

Dawdling

Tom walks into his five-year-old daughter's bedroom one morning to see Lisa still in her pajamas, playing on the floor with her toys. "Lisa, you're not dressed yet!" he exclaims. "Hurry up! I'll be late for work!" He leaves the room to make school lunches. Five minutes later he returns to find her with only one sock on. He's getting really cross and says, "Hurry up! Or do I have to dress you like a baby?" He storms out of the room. Ten minutes later, Lisa is only wearing socks and a T-shirt. He yells, "You're impossible! You'll never learn to dress yourself!"

Why Does Dawdling Occur?

Does this scene sound familiar? One of the most frequent complaints from parents is that their children dawdle. They dawdle while dressing in the mornings, during meals, while going to bed, and when doing their chores. Dawdling occurs for many reasons. Sometimes the problem is more in the adult's perception than in the child's behavior. Parents often have unrealistic expectations for their children. They may expect their four-year-old to get dressed without any parental guidance or reinforcement and they may not allow enough time to complete the process. It's important to remember that young children don't understand the concept of time. Until ten years of age, most children can't plan ahead because they don't understand the passage of time. Therefore, it's unrealistic to expect them to be punctual without adult help. Individual temperamental differences also affect their activity level and concept of time. Some are just naturally slower, more lethargic, and easily distracted. They may daydream and forget all about a request. In other instances, children dawdle in order to avoid some unpleasant experience, such as going to school, separating from parents, or doing a chore.

Once dawdling begins, it can become habitual by creating a power struggle between parents and children. In the example above, the more Tom tried to hurry Lisa, the more she slowed down. Children soon discover that through dawdling they can assert their independence and power, rendering their parents helpless and frustrated. Lisa realized that she could gain more attention for not dressing than for dressing. Thus, parental attention, albeit negative, inadvertently reinforced her dawdling and perpetuated the power struggle.

What To Do

Praise and reward programs: Positive attention should be given for any effort your children make to behave well. In the example above, Lisa should have been praised for putting on one sock and then for every small step toward getting dressed. To overcome dawdling, her father would need to go into her room every minute or two to praise her efforts. Eventually, he would be able to leave the room for longer and longer periods of time. Another approach is to set up a tangible reinforcement program such as playing "beat the clock." For instance, challenge your child to be dressed or finished with dinner before the buzzer goes off, and then he or she can earn a sticker. These stickers can be turned in for a particular reward on a reinforcement menu, such as reading an extra story or playing a game with you.

Ignore stalling: The trick to moving a dawdler along is to turn the situation around so that attention is not given for dawdling. Don't criticize your children for what they can't do well. This negative attention actually reinforces not getting dressed, not eating, and other stalling behaviors. Pay lavish attention to what they can do and ignore what they can't do.

Make up games: Unlikely as it sounds, you can help your children speed up by playing games. For instance, some children like their parents to count out loud and see how fast they can get dressed. You might say, "I wonder if you can be dressed by the time I count to 20." Others respond well to rocket warnings, such as, "Five minutes left to go...Two minutes left...One minute left...And now we're taking off." Some children like marching music to help them dress, get ready for bed or do their chores more quickly. Music also encourages a cheerful mood. Whether it involves marching to bed or playing follow-the-leader to the car in the morning, these games not only speed things up, but they are fun.

Natural and logical consequences: Let your children experience the natural consequences of dawdling. These can include having to get dressed in the car on the way to school or not having time for breakfast before going to school; no bedtime snack unless they are in their pajamas by the time the timer goes off; no dessert if they can't beat the clock eating dinner; no television until they are dressed and have eaten breakfast. However, if you decide to use this approach, you should explain the consequences in detail to your children ahead of time. It's important that they be told what will happen if they're not dressed or ready on time. Usually, experiencing consequences once or twice will put an end to dawdling.

Time Out: For the highly oppositional children, reinforcement programs and games may fail to move them along more quickly—if this is the case, it may be necessary to add a Time Out consequence. Tell them that if they aren't ready or haven't completed their chores when a timer goes off, they'll have a three-minute Time Out. It might seem that this technique would reinforce dawdling since it will actually make things take longer, but it does just the opposite. Since dawdling is a way in which children do not comply with parental requests, Time Out ensures that they do comply and adds to the impact of parental requests in the future. Be sure to combine Time Out with a reinforcement program where they are praised and reinforced for their efforts to do things more quickly. Motivating good behavior at the same time you use discipline for the misbehavior is crucial.

Give plenty of warning and lead time: Young children need plenty of time to make transitions. Some have particular difficulty waking up in the mornings. They may be grumpy, irritable or weepy. Such children may need to be woken up an hour or even two before they're expected to leave the house so that there's time for their negative mood to pass. Most young children need regular reminders as well—"In ten minutes it will be time to go," or "In five minutes, when the alarm goes off, it will be time to put the toys away and go to bed." These warnings help them make the transitions and are especially important for intense youngsters who have difficulty switching from one activity to another.

Establish a routine: Whether it is going to bed or getting up in the morning, predictable routines help children feel secure and learn behaviors more quickly. Plan what your morning and evening routine will be. Your children may get up at 7 a.m., go to the bathroom, get dressed, eat breakfast, brush teeth, and then play or go to school. Specific rules should be established about dressing in the bedroom, no television or breakfast until completely dressed, no evening snack until in pajamas and so on. Clarifying procedures this way encourages children to get the task done.

Self-talk: You can show your children how to use self-talk by saying things aloud to yourself about speeding things up and promoting cheerfulness. You might say, "Well, it's a beautiful morning. I'm going to enjoy work today. I'll start by getting ready quickly." Or, "It feels good getting ready faster in the mornings. I have more time to relax."

Have appropriate expectations: Be sure your expectations are appropriate for the age and developmental stage of your children. Don't expect them to succeed in dressing independently until they have demonstrated that they have the skills to do so. Few children can be expected to completely dress themselves until they are four or five. It can help to choose their clothes the night before and to lay them out. Moreover, preschoolers need at least 30 minutes to complete dressing. Remember, learning to dress starts at two or three and takes two to three years to complete, so try to be patient and make it fun. If you have a three-year-old who's just learning, make sure clothes are big and easy to pull on. You can help by pulling up pants and letting him or her finish the process. Then, gradually, you can step back and watch your child do more and more. However, each step of the way you must supply encouragement, support and praise.

What's the Hurry?
Finally, it's important to ask yourself from time to time, "What's the hurry?" We are a hurried and a hurrying society, obsessed by time and schedules. We may be rushing our children in the same way we rush ourselves, speeding to the bank or the office, running them off to preschool. The important question is are we being unnecessarily impatient with our children, hurrying them from one achievement to the next without allowing them the time to enjoy a sense of accomplishment? Too much hurrying can create stress in a child's life and can disrupt normal social and emotional development. Slow down and give both your children and yourself time to learn and explore.

Sibling Rivalry and Fights Between Children

SALLY: He started it, he hit me.
DONALD: You're a brat. I hate you.
MOM: Donald, don't talk to your sister that way.
DONALD: You always take her side.

Bickering, arguing and fights between sisters and brothers are a normal part of growing up. Parents often feel disappointed about this because they believe it reflects unhappy relationships. However, through the experience of disagreeing with each other, children learn how to stand up for their rights, defend themselves and express their feelings. Mild teasing may even be a way to communicate affection and playful fun. Parents who rush to mediate arguments or resolve disputes are inadvertently denying their children opportunities to learn these communication and conflict resolution skills. Of course, if sibling rivalry or peer arguments become excessive or destructive, parents must intervene. Physical fights should never be allowed under any circumstances. There is a growing recognition of the need to control child and spouse abuse, yet sibling abuse can also be a serious problem. Parents should take excessive sibling rivalry seriously and protect their children from psychological and verbal abuse from older siblings as well as physical abuse.

Why Does It Occur?
Excessive sibling rivalry may develop for a number of reasons. Parents may exhibit favoritism toward one child and this may spark resentment. Sometimes older siblings resent the attention that parents give to younger ones. In other families, brothers or sisters may act out parents' unconscious dislike or rejection of a child who is hyperactive, difficult

or less intelligent than siblings. Problems can also occur if one sibling is clearly less talented than a brother or sister close in age or of the same sex. (Rivalry tends to be greatest between two children of the same sex.) Sometimes children fight with each other because they're imitating conflicts that occur between their parents. Such children may also fight in an attempt to divert their parents from marital problems. They hope that their misbehavior will draw their parents together, that if they can make their parents focus on them, the marital problems will diminish.

What To Do

Ignore minor squabbles: If your children are fairly evenly matched it may be possible to let them settle minor squabbles on their own, as long as they don't hurt each other or behave destructively. Resolving their own disagreements teaches them to fight their own battles without depending on adults. Undoubtedly there'll be times when you'll be called in to settle disputes, and sometimes you can get out of it by saying, "Settle it yourselves."

Beware of tattlers: You need to be careful not to reinforce tattling behavior. For instance, at the start of an argument, one child may rush to you and whine about another child, saying that she or he started a fight or, perhaps one sibling tattles to you about some trouble his brother got into at school. In the case of a sibling argument, you can respond somewhat indifferently so as not to reinforce or give satisfaction to the tattler. A good response is to say that you are sure they can find a solution on their own. For example, "Come and tell me when you've figured out a solution to this problem." On the other hand, sometimes a tattler tells you about something that cannot be ignored, such as hitting or destroying toys. In this case, the trick is to help the tattler think about how he could solve the problem in ways other than tattling.

Teach problem-solving skills: You can teach your children ways to resolve conflict by having discussions when they're not fighting. You might make up stories or use puppets to illustrate problems that they have. For instance, Cathy is concerned that her two children squabble constantly over toys. She helps them by telling them a story using puppets to role-play. One puppet, Bert, keeps grabbing toys from the other puppet, Ernie. Cathy asks the children, "What should Ernie do when Bert takes his toys?" She then encourages them to come up with possible solutions. They suggest telling Bert to give back the toy, hitting Bert, ignoring Bert or finding another toy to play with. Then she reverses the story and says, "Bert really wants Ernie's toy, and Ernie has had it for a long, long time. What could Bert do?" Again she encourages them to think of ideas. Eventually, they have quite a list, including hitting Ernie to make him give up the toy, offering to share another toy or to trade toys, asking nicely to play with the toy together, or going away and waiting until Ernie gets tired of the toy. Once her children offer their solutions, Cathy helps them think about the consequences of each solution. She might ask, "What would happen if Bert hit Ernie?" After exploring the possible outcomes of hitting, she goes on to ask what the consequences of the next idea on the list would be. In this way she is teaching them problem-solving strategies, ways to get what they want without yelling, hitting or complaining. As we have pointed out in the Problem Solving Chapter, many children hit simply because they don't know any other strategies for getting what they want.

Once you've taught your children how to problem solve, then when a real conflict occurs, they can begin to use the skill. For example, four-year-old Anna and six-year-old Nigel want to play with the computer. Both shout, "I want the computer first!" Anna says, "Nigel, you had it first last time," and her brother retorts, "No, you did." In this case, their father might say, "Okay, we have a problem here. There is only one computer and you both want to use it. Do you have any ideas about what to do?" They might then come up with solutions such as flipping a coin or sharing or taking turns. Once a decision is reached, the child who has

Children sometimes need parents as referees.

to wait her turn may still feel upset, but they have both begun to learn how to handle conflict. At this point the parent can praise the child who has to wait for staying calm and waiting patiently.

Set up a reward program: Establish a reward program by explaining to your children that if they don't bicker or fight for a certain amount of time, they'll each get a sticker. Tell them they'll also earn a sticker every time you see them sharing or cooperating with each other. Their stickers can then be turned in for rewards that they choose from a reinforcement menu. You must then remember to watch for when they play quietly together and provide praise as well as the stickers.

Use Time Out and natural and logical consequences: Children need to learn that there will be consequences if they hit each other or break something while arguing. It is important for them to recognize that they'll be held responsible for their behavior. Whenever hitting occurs, immediately call a Time Out for both children because they need to learn that they are equally responsible for starting a fight. Don't talk about the fight or try to determine who started it. Most fighting between siblings has long and tangled roots. It is just as important that the victim learn to avoid the aggressor as it is for the aggressor to learn self-control. (In some families, the victim may use subtle but effective tactics for inciting the aggressor, who then gets blamed.) Time Outs for fights should include children's guests as well as siblings. However, it is always a good idea to let the parents of your children's friends know that that is how you handle physical fights. If they object or if guests balk at Time Out, you can always send the children home. Over time, imposing Time Outs will not only reduce physical conflict but will help motivate your children to learn skills such as negotiating, problem solving and self-control to avoid fights.

Natural or Logical Consequences can also be an effective discipline approach for sibling arguments. If your children are arguing over a toy, the logical consequence would be to take it away until they decide who will play with it first. If they're fighting over television programs, the logical consequence would be to turn off the set until they decide which program to watch first. Or say you hear giggling from the kitchen and find food and milk all over the floor. If you ask, "Who did this?" the result will usually be a chorus of, "He did it," "No, she did it," "No, he did it!" and a fight about who is to blame. Rather than trying to identify the guilty party, all the children should pitch in to tidy up. This is the natural consequence of joint mischief.

Hold family meetings: With school-age children, it can be helpful to set up weekly family meetings. At a specified time each week, the whole family meets for discussion, sharing, griping and planning. Your children can be encouraged to express their feelings and ideas and be assured that each person will get a chance to talk. If they use the opportunity to blame or abuse a family member—as no doubt they occasionally will—stop them immediately and encourage them to focus on how to solve problems.

Love uniquely rather than equally: Sometimes parents try to treat and love each of their children in exactly the same way. They give them the same clothes, toys, amount of time each day, enroll them in the same activities. This regimented approach is more likely to create competitiveness than to decrease it. Try to treat each child as a unique and special person with his or her own talents and needs. Difficult as it may be, avoid comparing one child with another. Avoid statements like "Well, your brother could read this when he was your age, so I'm sure you could too if you'd only try a little harder," or "Linda takes better care of her belongings than you do and her room is so neat." Such an approach produces anger and resentment in the undervalued child and hostility towards both the sibling who is held up as a model and the parents. Instead, focus on each child's particular strengths. By appreciating the uniqueness and different abilities of each one, you are more likely to make them all feel special and to decrease jealousy and competitiveness between them.

Another way to demonstrate unique feelings for each child is to give them special privileges that are appropriate for their age. An older child might be allowed to go overnight to Scout or Guide camp, or cycle to a neighborhood park. Other treats would be given to a younger child, such as having a friend stay overnight and lunch out with you. When you buy things for your children, make need rather than fairness the basis for your decisions. The fact that an older child needs a pair of pants for school doesn't mean you have to give a pair to a younger child who doesn't. Don't feel that each child must receive exactly the same things or that you need to spend the same amount on each.

Avoid favoritism: Most parents, at some time, will feel favoritism for one of their children or disappointment with one who seems to create a lot of trouble. Be aware of periods when this happens and try to avoid expressing this favoritism as it will produce or increase bickering and rivalry. Instead, be aware of your feelings and try to protect the less favored child by focusing on his or her special abilities. Although this can be a difficult task, it is important to prevent a temporary difficult period from becoming a way of life for your child.

A parent's preference for one child and disappointment with another won't always be temporary. One may be outstanding intellectually, athletically or socially while the other is not. Or one may be easier to relate to for some undefinable reason. On the other hand, there may be a temperament clash between a parent and one particular child, or a resemblance between a child and a former spouse that brings back bad memories. In such cases, wise parents will strive to accept the child, focus on his or her individual strengths and not demonstrate the preference openly. It is important to do everything possible to make all your children feel loved, cherished, appreciated, admired and important to you. However, beware of over-compensating due to feelings of guilt concerning a less favored youngster.

Prepare children for new family members: When a new baby is expected, let siblings help with preparations and give them the feeling that the baby belongs to them as well as to you. Gifts should be bought for all youngsters in the family, not just for the baby. Remember that children will probably show some initial resentment towards a new family member. They may also display increased aggressive behavior as the baby becomes more mobile and more entertaining. With support and reassurance, these misbehaviors will disappear over time.

Give each child time alone with you: If possible, try to spend some uninterrupted time alone with each child. Take one out to lunch or to a special event. Even a trip to the playground alone with you can be a real treat. It isn't necessary to give each child exactly the same amount of time each day. Instead, give your time according to their needs. Often, a youngster who is sick or celebrating a birthday or having trouble at school will need extra time and attention. The ups and downs of life ensure that each of your children will have special need of you at particular times.

Encourage separate spaces: Usually a younger child will want to tag along with an older brother or sister. This can be difficult for the older child, who may resent the intrusion especially if it results in the disruption of an activity or plan. Imagine the outcome if a child playing Monopoly with friends has a preschool brother or sister who keeps turning over the board or taking too many turns. Understandably the older child becomes frustrated and angry and may push the younger sibling away, resulting in tears. How should you respond? Force the child to include the preschooler in the interests of fairness, niceness and caring, and to teach a sense of responsibility? Or should you separate older and younger children when friends come over?

In general, it is prudent to encourage your children to have some separate experiences and pursuits as well as different companions. Forcing an older sibling to always include a younger one may backfire and result in increased rivalry and resentment. It's ironic that when you push closeness, you often get the opposite result, but if you promote separateness you may find that siblings will become friends. A certain amount of physical separation fosters the development of separate identities and helps reduce friction.

On the other hand, there are times when separate spaces or companions can't be arranged, and older siblings should be encouraged to develop empathy and patience for a youngster's needs and abilities. A father might say to his older son, "You know slamming the door on Dennis makes him cross because he thinks so much of you and your friends. Do you suppose there's some way you could include him in what you're doing?" or "I'm sure it's frustrating for you because Dennis isn't old enough to understand the rules, but maybe there's some way he can play without wrecking the game." When the older boy includes Dennis, his father might say, "You're really patient with Dennis. He's lucky to have such a kind big brother." Taking a balanced approach that fosters separateness when feasible but also uses strategies to promote acceptance and understanding between siblings is more likely to lead to long-term friendships than either approach alone.

Teach property rights: Young children are naturally selfish. They grow out of it slowly, but first they need to feel secure about themselves. Even then, they should not be expected to share all their belongings with one another. Adult or child, we all need some special objects of our own. Moreover, if you try to force sharing too early you may trigger even more selfishness. Encourage your children to respect each other's belongings and to ask permission to use them.

Avoid overprotecting a younger child: Don't be too protective of a younger child when there are arguments or fights with an older sibling. Research has shown that it's more often a younger sibling who triggers aggressive behaviors than an older one. However, it is usually the older child who is blamed. In such a situation, both children must learn to control their contribution to the conflict.

Avoid placing too much responsibility on older children: Parents may inadvertently give too much responsibility to their older children. This is particularly true of older girls, who may be expected to babysit siblings, wash dishes, set the table and so on. This imbalance can contribute to older children resenting younger ones who seem to get off easily. At the same time, younger ones may become jealous of older siblings' increased responsibilities. So it is important for you to be sensitive to the amount of responsibility given to each child. Give them tasks that are appropriate for their age and developmental ability. For instance, a preschooler can be taught to set the table while an older child can clean up after a meal. You should also be aware of differing expectations you might have for your sons and daughters. Do the boys have the same number of chores as the girls? Do the chores tend to differ by sex? If a girl always has to clean the bathrooms while her brother gets to putter on the car with his father, this may build resentment and sibling rivalry.

Managing games: Four-year-old Ben and his brother Peter, aged seven, are playing checkers. Suddenly their mother hears: "That's not fair. You cheated!" "No, I didn't." "Yes, you did. I saw you." Sometimes parents need to act as referees and help enforce rules and other times they may need to support a younger child. Ben may not understand rigid adherence to rules, while Peter is fixated by them. Their mother may want to dilute this confrontation and competition by encouraging other people to play with them. This takes the edge off the win-or-lose situation that arouses jealousy. It also helps to buy games that focus on chance and luck rather than skill to win.

Remember that fights between siblings are normal: Be realistic about the amount of family harmony you expect. A great deal of quarreling goes on in normal households, and if you can accept this, you can approach parenting in a more objective fashion. Don't moan loudly in your children's presence that they fight all the time. Keep your anxieties to yourself or your children just may live up to your complaint.

Child Disobedience

It's 8:30 in the evening and time for four-year-old Lee to go to bed. Her parents are in the living room talking to friends while Lee plays with blocks on the floor. Her father says, "Honey, it's time to go to bed." She continues to play as if she hasn't heard him. He repeats his request a little more firmly, "It's already past your bedtime. Please go to bed now." "No, I'm not tired," she says. "I don't want to go to bed!" He begins to feel helpless and says to himself, "If I push her, she'll have a tantrum. Perhaps I should just let her stay up until our friends leave." Instead, he decides to reason with her. "You know you'll be tired tomorrow if you don't go to bed now. Come on, be a good girl and go get ready." Lee says, "I'm not tired. I'm not going!" Then her mother says crossly, "If you don't go to bed right now, you'll be in big trouble!" And she thinks to herself, "If only Raymond wouldn't give in to Lee all the time. What she needs is someone to show her who's boss." Meanwhile, Lee, who is feeling stubborn and sleepy, cries, "But I'm not tired. I don't want to go to sleep."

Lee's day is filled with similar power struggles with her parents. They occur in regard to all kinds of simple transitions, such as turning off the TV, getting ready for preschool, putting on her socks and shoes to go outside, or leaving a park. By mid-afternoon, Raymond is usually exhausted and alternates between giving in to her demands and punishing her, depending on his energy level. Lee's mother, who is usually only home an hour or two daily before her daughter goes to bed, doesn't understand why he won't follow through with consequences for Lee's disobedient behavior. Her criticism compounds the situation by making him feel even more angry, unsupported and inadequate.

Why Does It Occur?
Not complying, or disobeying, basically refers to refusing to respond to a request or command made by another person. Such behavior is common

and part of the normal development of children. They all disobey at times and refuse to follow reasonable rules set by their parents. Not complying reaches a peak during the "terrible twos" and usually decreases over the next years. However, research shows that normal children aged four to five obey only about two-thirds of parental requests. Therefore, not complying some of the time should be seen as a healthy indication that a child is seeking independence, rather than as a reflection of parental incompetence or deliberate manipulation by children. Too often, however, occasional disobedience results in long battles and power struggles that may teach children to resist most adult requests.

Some children who persist in disobeying live in families where there are few rules. Their parents may be highly permissive, dislike having to say no and fail to follow through with any requests they do make. On the other hand, disobeying can increase in families with too many rules or commands and unduly harsh discipline. In such homes, children receive about one command per minute from their parents, most of them unnecessary, and there is little follow-through. Still other situations where not complying becomes a problem involve parents who vacillate between giving in to a child who resists and digging in their heels, so to speak. In the example above, Lee's father took a permissive approach while her mother countered with excessive force. Either of these approaches alone will result in increased disobedience. In combination, they make it even more difficult for a child to learn to cooperate.

What To Do
Reduce your commands to those that are most important: Decide ahead of time which of your commands are really necessary. Choose your battles. When you decide to give a command, be sure you're prepared to follow through until your children do as they're told. Moreover, make sure your rules, commands or expectations are realistic and appropriate for the age of your children. Avoid nagging since it teaches them that you don't expect prompt compliance.

Give clear, specific, positive commands: State your commands clearly and respectfully, and detail exactly what positive behaviors you want to see. Good examples include: "Walk slowly," "Please go to bed," "Talk in a quiet voice," and "Please keep the felt pens on the paper." These Do commands specify the behaviors you expect from your children.

Avoid giving vague, negative and critical commands such as, "Be good," "Simmer down," "Sit still for once in your life," "Stop eating like a pig," and "Shut up." If your children are made to feel incompetent or defensive, they are less likely to heed you. Also avoid question-commands such as, "Wouldn't you like to go to bed now?" or "Why don't you take the garbage out?" that imply an option and usually result in children not complying. Try to give commands with alternatives or choices attached to them: "You may not watch TV but you may help me make bread," or "Play quietly inside or go outside to play." And remember to state your commands in a positive manner as if you are confident that your children will obey. When this message is communicated, they are more likely to want to cooperate.

Give lead time if possible: Some parents expect instant obedience from their children. However, just like adults, youngsters find it difficult to disengage abruptly from an interesting activity. If you bark a request at your son who is happily engrossed in a project, he will probably protest and feel unhappy. A reminder or warning given prior to a command helps your children make transitions. For instance, you might say, "In five more minutes it will be time to go to bed," or "When you finish reading that page it will be time to set the table."

Praise compliance: Don't take compliance for granted and ignore it. Whenever you give a command, pause for five seconds and watch for a response. If your children do as requested, express pleasure and approval. Typically parents pay attention when children do not comply and ignore them when they do. The trick is to turn this around so that your children experience more benefits for obeying than for disobeying.

Set up reinforcement programs: You can help your children to be more compliant by setting up a reinforcement program where they receive points or stickers each time they comply to a request. These points or stickers can be collected and traded in for items from a reinforcement menu. You may want to choose a specific time of day to conduct the program, such as between five and eight in the evening when you have the time to monitor their behavior, or you may want to establish a program for compliance in a specific situation, such as going to bed or picking up toys.

Use Time Out consequences: Time Out is an effective method for teaching children—especially highly oppositional children between the ages of four and eight—to be more compliant. First, explain to your children exactly what misbehaviors will result in Time Out. For example, Lee's parents could introduce a program as follows:

> *"Lee, you do a lot of nice things at home, but there is one thing we have problems with; you often don't do what we tell you to. We're going to help you learn how to obey by putting you in Time Out every time you don't obey. You'll have to go to Time Out in the chair in the corner of the room for four minutes. And you'll have to be quiet for at least two minutes before you can get off the chair. We're also going to give you a sticker every time you do what we ask you to do. Then you can turn stickers in for something you want."*

In such a program, parents will need to recognize when their children are not complying with requests and then be prepared to carry out a Time Out consequence. Suppose you are Lee's mother or father. Begin by giving a clear, positive command, and then pausing for five seconds to see whether she complies. If she does, praise her and give her a sticker. If she doesn't, repeat the command and warn her that she will have to go to Time Out if she doesn't comply. Wait another five seconds to see how she responds. If she obeys, reinforce her compliance with praise and a sticker. If she disobeys, take her to Time Out. Once Time Out is completed, *repeat the initial command.* If she complies this time, praise her and give her a sticker. If she doesn't comply, repeat the entire sequence.

Expect testing: Remember, it is common for children to test their parents' commands and rules especially if these have been enforced inconsistently in the past. It's a normal part of seeking independence and self-direction. So expect some defiance and try to ignore minor protests or you may get trapped in counter-arguments. Allow your children to grumble when they're obeying a rule they find unpleasant. Although you can help them to learn to do what they're asked, you shouldn't expect them to always be happy about doing it.

Model compliance with other adults and with your children: The key to fostering a cooperative attitude in children is for parents to avoid being too permissive or too authoritarian. Don't be afraid to set necessary rules, give commands and follow through in a respectful manner. Of course, rules and commands should be balanced by warmth, praise and sensitivity to your children's special needs. In the scene at the beginning of this chapter, Raymond needs to recognize when to give commands, how to avoid nagging and how to follow through when Lee doesn't comply. On the other hand, his wife needs to realize that not complying is part of a normal developmental process rather than a sign of her husband's inadequacy. This could help her be less punitive and less demanding of immediate compliance. Both parents need to be more supportive of each other and to recognize when it is appropriate to attend to their child's requests. Remember, modeling the behavior you want is one of your most effective teaching strategies. For instance, if a mother calls the family to dinner and her husband doesn't come because he wants to finish fixing something, then he is modeling noncompliance. Or if a father tells the family to help him rake the leaves in the backyard and his wife says she'll come in a minute and never does, she is not complying. If one parent ignores the other's requests, the children will learn to do so too. So it is important that you model compliance with your partner and children, and set the tone for compliance to requests within your family.

Accept your child's temperament: Some children are more willful, stubborn and intense than others. Some children are inattentive and easily distractible and more likely to forget the parent's request than others. Such children can cause parents to feel helpless and powerless at times. However, they may grow up to be especially creative, energetic and committed adults. If you have children like this, you need to be sure you get away often, take personal Time Out, and refuel yourself so you have the energy to better meet their extra needs.

Resistance to Going to Bed
The Jack-in-the-Box Syndrome

Three-year-old Andrew starts his evening ritual by putting on his pajamas, eating a snack, brushing his teeth; then his mother reads three stories, and finally she kisses him and turns out his bedroom light. Just as she starts to relax, she hears a voice, "Mommy, I need a drink." She gets him a glass of water and then sits down in the living room to read. A few minutes later a voice cries out, "Mommy, I can't get to sleep." Now she's feeling cross and she says, "Be quiet and go to sleep."

Does this scenario sound familiar? Perhaps it's reassuring to know that almost all children resist going to bed at some point or another. This is a natural reaction because bedtime signals the end of a fun day. Studies have shown that 30 to 40 percent of normal children have trouble going to sleep and develop strategies to postpone going to bed.

Why Does It Occur?
Between the ages of one and two and a half or so, children resist sleep because they fear separation from their parents. Toddlers between 18 months and three years worry about what will happen to their parents when they go to sleep. On the other hand, children aged four to six are often afraid to go to sleep because they imagine monsters in the dark and have nightmares. They also worry about catastrophes that might occur while they're asleep—a fire breaking out or robbers hurting their parents. School-age children say they have trouble going to sleep because of worries, noises heard in the dark or physical pains. Sometimes, children can't get to sleep because they've been overstimulated just before bedtime or because afternoon naps have left them wide awake at bedtime. Consequently, they are bored and are looking for an interesting diversion.

What To Do

Decide on a bedtime: First, decide on a bedtime for your children, keeping in mind their needs for sleep as well as their ages. Then inform your children. If they can't tell time, draw a picture of a clock with their bedtime on it and place it near a clock. Older children can be given a clock or watch to remind them when they have to go to bed. Be as consistent as you can about enforcing this bedtime or your children will constantly test it. Of course there will be occasions—a very special program on television, a visitor from out of town—when being inflexible would only foster feelings of resentment and unfairness in your children. However, you should make it clear that a late bedtime is a special privilege. One word of caution: be sure resistance is not due to a child being put to bed too early. Some children need less sleep than others, so consider whether you may need to eliminate an afternoon nap or establish a later bedtime.

Establish a winding-down routine: About an hour before bedtime start a winding-down routine. This should be consistent and ritualistic, including relaxing events such as a warm bath, stories, listening to music, quiet play and a snack, all in a predictable order. Bedtime rituals seem to be reassuring and soothing for children, and have been shown to reduce resistance to falling asleep as well as to calm separation fears. It is also important to avoid roughhousing, scary TV programs, and foods or drinks that contain caffeine prior to bedtime as they will overstimulate most youngsters and make it hard for them to fall asleep.

Give a warning: Ten to 15 minutes before bedtime give your child a warning. You might say, "In ten minutes when the alarm goes off it will be time to go to bed," or "After this story is finished it will be time to go to bed." Telling them suddenly, "Go to bed" only invites resistance. You can also play beat the clock, where they race a timer to their bedrooms, or make a train to get to their rooms quickly. Sometimes playing a low-key game of hide-and-seek about half an hour before bedtime will help them cope with their separation anxiety and make going to bed somewhat easier.

Be firm and ignore protests: After they've had their snack and brushed their teeth, make it clear that this is your final good-night kiss and the end of the day. Be confident and convey the message that you know they can stay in their room. If they call out, whine or cry after you leave, ignore them unless they're sick. In the beginning, protests may last five minutes to an hour, but after a few nights of consistent ignoring they'll disappear. Don't insist that your children go to sleep right away. Let

Resistance to going to bed—the jack-in-the-box syndrome.

them know that if they are not sleepy they can listen to a tape played at a low volume, read stories or play quietly. Most children take about half an hour to go to sleep, so it's important for them to learn how to amuse themselves while waiting to fall asleep. These are habits that will stand them in good stead when they're older.

Check-in: If your children often call out after you leave their bedrooms, you can make an agreement with them. If they don't call you, you'll check in on them in five to 10 minutes to see how they're doing and to make sure everything is okay. Most children will rarely be awake by the second check, but telling them that you'll come back prevents them from becoming frustrated and angry or keeping themselves awake by repeatedly crying out to you.

Night lights and security objects: A special blanket or stuffed animal can give children a sense of security while going to sleep. A soft night light can help to dispel fear of the dark. Don't worry about them becoming so attached to a night light or security object that they'll need it for the rest of their lives. They usually only need such things for a short time to help them through a difficult period.

Set up a reinforcement program: Set up a sticker program to encourage your children to go to bed readily and stay in their rooms without a fuss. Each morning they have been successful, they can be praised and given a sticker. You might say something like, "You stayed in your room last night. That was great. You are really growing up! And now you have earned enough stickers to pick your favorite snack."

Return your child to his or her room: If you have young children who wander in and out of their rooms, it is best to put them back immediately without any discussion or scolding. If children over four come out of their rooms, there are two different approaches you might take. The first, which works best with preschoolers, is to tell them that if they come out of their bedrooms they'll have to go for three minutes of Time Out. This should be done calmly without scolding or lecturing. Once Time Out is over, take them quietly back to bed. The second approach, which works better for school-age children, is that for every minute they are out of their rooms, they have to go to bed a minute earlier the next night. Research has shown that with the consistent use of Time Out, a reinforcement program and clear limit-setting, most children can learn to stay in their rooms within three weeks.

A final point to remember is that you should never lock your children in their rooms at night. Not only is it not safe in the event of an emergency, but it can increase their fears and sense of helplessness.

Model good bedtime behavior for your children: Parents who fall asleep on the couch in front of the TV are setting a bad example and tend to have children with poor bedtime routines. Work on establishing your own routines for getting ready for bed. Also, be sure that the television and radio are turned down low and noises in the rest of the house are reduced once your children go to bed.

Nighttime Awakenings
Nighttime—Ghosts, Lions and Witches

Five-year-old Emma wakes up in the middle of the night and goes into her parents' bed insisting that she has seen a ghost in her room. They willingly comfort and cuddle her until they all fall asleep. A few weeks later Emma is in the habit of coming to sleep with her parents every night. They've lost their privacy and now never get an uninterrupted night's sleep. Their efforts to return her to her room have only resulted in tears, scenes when she come back to their bed, and even less sleep. It seems as though the only way to get enough sleep is to just let her stay in their bed.

Why Does It Occur?

Night wakenings and coming into parents' beds is a common occurrence in young children. In fact, 30 to 40 percent of children aged two to five get up at night on a regular basis. Moreover, research indicates that children go in and out of four or five periods of deep sleep during the night. As they come out of deep sleep cycles, dreams occur and they may awaken. Coming into their parents' room is usually due to fear of being alone in the dark, concern about what has happened to their parents, or fear of ghosts, robbers or scary animals in their rooms. For toddlers, needing their parents at night is usually associated with separation anxiety, while for children between the ages of four and six it is associated with nightmares or ghosts. Although nearly all youngsters have mildly unpleasant dreams, nightmares reach a peak in four- to six-year-olds. By the time they are six to 12 years of age, only 28 percent still have nightmares. As you can see from the number of reasons that cause children to wake at night, your approach to this problem will depend in part on your assessment of the cause of the wakening.

What To Do

Provide a night light: If your children are afraid of the dark or think they see ghosts in their rooms, give them a night light or flashlight to put under their pillow. If a night light is not bright enough, you may want to use a dimmer so that you can gradually turn the light down each night.

Reassure your child: If your children come into your room at night because they're worried about whether you're there, reassure them that you will always be there. This fear can be a particular problem in families where there is a separation or divorce in progress. Children become concerned that since one parent has left home, the other will abandon them as well. They need constant reassurance that the remaining parent will stay there through the night.

If you are planning to go out after your children are asleep, tell them in advance where you're going, who will babysit them and when you'll be back. You might say, "I'm going to a movie tonight and I won't be leaving until after you are asleep. Sonia will be here to babysit you while I'm gone. But when you wake up in the morning, I'll be here."

Be understanding: When your children have nightmares, go to their room to hold and cuddle them, don't take them to your bed. Turn on the light to show them how familiar everything is in their room, and talk to them soothingly and reassuringly. Explain that everyone has scary dreams at times and that these are not real monsters or ghosts but dreams. Reassure them that you are nearby and will not let anything bad happen. Don't say the dreams are silly or ridiculous because they seem very real and need to be treated respectfully. Let your children talk about them if they like and reiterate that nothing bad will happen.

Return your child to bed: If your children come to your room, return them immediately to their own bed and comfort them there. Let them know that you believe they can handle their worries in their own bed and that you'll be nearby if they need you. Return them to bed as many times as is necessary. It's not a good idea to sleep with your children when they're frightened because this makes them feel they can't manage their fears on their own. It often results in them believing that your presence is essential to get through the night.

Confront dreams and think about something good: If your children are afraid of ghosts, tell them to say, "Go away!" to any ghosts they think they see. If they have nightmares, tell them that they can help to control their dreams so that everything turns out fine. You can encourage them to come up with a good ending for a bad dream, one where they courageously overcome something fearful. You can also help them learn to cope by telling them to think of something that makes them feel good, such as a fun holiday or swimming at the beach. Let them know that part of growing up is learning how to handle and control fears and nightmares, and being able to get through the night without help from you.

Ignore crying: After comforting and reassuring your children until they calm down, leave their room. They may cry in protest, but if you're sure that they are not ill or wet it is best to leave them alone. If getting up at night, crying and staying in your bed has become a habit, they may cry for up to one or even two hours the first night you insist they stay in their own room. However, with a consistent ignoring approach the time will gradually be reduced each night. If they come out of their room again, return them to bed without discussion.

Set up a reinforcement program: A program that rewards your children with a sticker for each time they manage to sleep through the night without coming into your room will help to encourage them. These stickers can then be traded in for something special from a reinforcement menu. You might say, "We're going to help you learn to stay in your bed at night. If you forget and get up, we'll take you back to your room. And if you stay in bed all night, you'll get a sticker. When you get enough stickers, you can choose something you want." If your children are afraid of the dark, a program can be set up for sleeping through the night with progressively less light in the room. By installing a dimmer switch, you can turn the light down a little bit each night. If they make it through the night with that amount of light, they should be praised in the morning and given a sticker.

Help your child feel safe and loved during the day: During the day, give your children approval and reassurance so that they feel secure and well loved. Never threaten to abandon them for misbehaving or say that a bogeyman or monster will get them if they are bad. You may have to repeat again and again that dreams are not real and what to do when a bad dream wakes them up. Remember that children need constant reassurance and messages about how they can cope with fear in their lives, and that dreams are the first expressions of their fears.

Stealing

One day Terri found a toy in her son's pockets that she didn't recognize. It was the third time this had happened. When she asked him where it came from he said, "I borrowed it from a friend." A father discovered that some money was missing from his wallet and realized that his six-year-old was the only one who could have taken it. In another family, a mother noticed after going grocery shopping that her seven-year-old daughter had a candy bar in her pocket. Each parent thought, "Can my child be stealing?"

Of all behavior problems, stealing probably worries parents the most. It's shocking to discover one's own child stealing and it brings on visions of them becoming criminals. There's a natural tendency to want to deny that it can possibly be true. Since stealing happens infrequently at first, parents, who usually don't see the theft happen and thus can't prove it, may ignore their suspicions. This approach can add to the problem because stealing is reinforced when children are allowed to keep a stolen object.

Why Does Stealing Occur?

All children try to steal something at some point in their lives. Taking something away from another child without asking begins when they are two or three and peaks when they are between the ages of five and eight. By the age of 10 most normal youngsters have stopped stealing. If they haven't, they need professional help. Preschoolers may take things because they have no concept of private ownership or because they don't understand the difference between borrowing and stealing. If they don't realize that there's anything wrong with taking a friend's toy, it's meaningless to label this as stealing or try to get them to understand the concept. The best response for very young children is to say, "We don't take other people's belongings. Let's take the toy back to Jimmy."

Older children may steal for a variety of reasons. Some do it to see if they can get away with it. Others steal because they feel deprived and want to have the things that their peers have. In fact, they may feel that these things will help make them more popular. Some children steal to get even with their parents. The message seems to be, "How does it feel when you force me to steal what you won't buy for me?" Still others do it because they are depressed, unhappy or angry. They want to get attention from their parents or are trying to replace something that is missing in their lives, such as love and affection.

What To Do

Remain calm: React calmly. Try to remember that all youngsters steal at times and that your job is to teach your children more self-control. You can do this best by remaining in control yourself. Don't overreact or take this episode as a personal attack on your parenting ability or a sign that they will become delinquents. Don't shame, criticize, or force them to confess. Remember that what a troubled child needs most is affection and encouragement in learning to handle problems.

Confront your child: In the opening example, the mother whose child took a candy bar should say, "I know you took a candy bar from the store. You must have really wanted it and didn't know how else to get it. But stealing is not allowed. Next time, if you want something, ask me and we'll talk about it. I think you can do that because I know you want to be honest. Now let's see how we can solve this problem..." She confronts her daughter in a straightforward way and labels the act as stealing but does not humiliate her. She expresses her understanding of the motive for taking the candy bar and ends with positive expectations for the future. It's helpful to encourage children to try to understand the feelings of other people towards those who steal. Asking questions such as, "How would you feel if someone took something of yours?" encourages them to look at their actions from a different perspective.

Enforce a consequence: The most reasonable, natural consequence of stealing is to have a child return what was taken. In the previous example, the mother should take her daughter back to the store and make her return the candy bar with an apology. If the stolen object is lost, damaged or eaten, the child should be required to repay it from her allowance or by doing chores. If the child lied about stealing then there should be a punishment for lying as well as for stealing. For instance, loss of TV privileges in addition to paying for the stolen object would be appropriate. You must enforce consequences immediately even if your children apologize and promise never to do it again. It is essential to hold them responsible for stealing at the time it occurs. If they get away with it, they will be reinforced and more likely to try it again.

One of the problems with stealing is that you may be quite sure a child has stolen something but have no proof. If one of your children has a habit of stealing, you need to redefine stealing. Tell your child that he or she will be responsible for any new object found or anything missing from the house or school. The expectation is that new objects will not appear. New purchases must be accompanied by sales receipts and an account of where the money came from to buy them. This way, you will no longer have to prove that your child is stealing; it is up to him or her to avoid trouble.

Monitoring: Research has shown that many children who steal are left unsupervised for long periods of time. They may wander off after school to explore stores or stay at home alone for hours. While older children need some freedom to investigate their environment, they should be held responsible for telling their parents exactly where they are, what they are doing and when they will be home. Children who habitually steal need close monitoring by their parents so that there is a high probability that this misbehavior will be detected if it occurs. Since people cheat, lie and steal less frequently if the risk of detection is high, youngsters who steal need regular pocket emptying and room searching until the problem is corrected. In other words, they have sacrificed their right to privacy.

Provide reassurance and praise: Some children steal in reaction to divorce, a new baby, lack of attention or feelings of deprivation. In such cases, parents will need to provide extra love, praise and reassurance in addition to following the above courses of action.

Lying

John walks into the kitchen and sees a broken plate on the floor. He says to his daughter, "Jane, did you break that?" She shakes her head. "No, I didn't. Tommy did." The following day Jane, who has been having problems at school, comes home from school and says to her father, "I got all happy faces on my report card, but I lost it on the way home."

Most parents become upset when their children lie because they place a high value on honesty. Moreover, they may be unsure how to handle lying, vacillating between lecturing and demanding confessions and ignoring it altogether in the hope that it won't happen again. Neither of these approaches will solve the problem. First, you need to look at why lying occurs and then you must learn effective ways to deal with it.

Why Does Lying Occur?
All children lie from time to time. At first, they may tell exploratory lies in order to test the limits of what they can get away with and to see what will happen if they break rules. In a sense this is one of their first steps towards independence. Another type of lie is a deliberate attempt to conceal something that they have done wrong in order to avoid punishment. A third type is a whopper that involves extreme bragging or exaggeration about a family member or an experience. The fantasy lie, a fourth type, occurs when children use their imagination, perhaps claiming that an imaginary friend broke something or caused the problem. Since preschoolers have particular difficulty separating fantasy from reality, they are more likely to exaggerate, deny or exhibit wishful thinking. School-age children are more likely to tell a deliberate lie in order to avoid trouble or gain an advantage over someone else.

What To Do

Don't panic: The first step is to respond to your children's lies calmly. Like any other common behavior problem, lying represents another opportunity to help them learn. Avoid trying to scare or force them to confess because most people, even adults, will lie when asked to incriminate themselves. If you know one of your children broke a plate, don't ask, "Did you break it?" This invites the child to lie. Instead, state matter-of-factly, "I see you broke a plate. What should we do about that?" Avoid lectures, moralizing, and criticism since this negative attention is likely to lead to power struggles and may encourage defensiveness, rebellion and more lying. Sometimes you may find it difficult to be calm with teenagers who lie because they're old enough to know the rules. However, remaining calm is important with children of all ages who lie.

Confront your child in a positive way: If you have a preschooler who tells a story about something that isn't true, calmly respond that you know it is make-believe. For instance, if your son says, "My dad's getting me a dog," you might say, "I know you really want a dog and wish you could get one, so you were imagining your own dog." Or if he says, "A ghost came in and messed my room up," you might respond, "That's an interesting make-believe story. Now tell me what the true story is." You can confront an older child who lies to avoid punishment or to conceal something by saying, "I know that isn't true. It doesn't help to lie. Let's see how we can solve this problem." The idea is to point out the truth in a way that doesn't make the child feel defensive. Never call your child a liar, for such a negative label reduces self-esteem.

Try to understand the reason for the lie: It is important to assess why your child feels the need to lie. For instance, suppose your daughter told a series of whoppers such as, "I got all A's" or, "I'm the best hitter on the team" when, in fact, she is having problems at school or is clumsy at baseball. It is important to figure out whether she is under too much pressure from you or her peers and lying helps her to compensate for feelings of inadequacy. You can help such a self-image problem by explaining, "I know you're working really hard on your homework and it's difficult for you. I'll spend some extra time helping you tonight if you like." Or "I know how much you'd like to be good at baseball. Let's practice batting after dinner." If, on the other hand, lies are told to avoid punishment, you need to be sure that your discipline is not so fearful or painful that your child would rather not tell the truth than get in trouble with you. While consequences should be enforced for lying and for the misbehavior that led to it, it is important to remember that consequences are designed to teach, not to inflict physical or emotional pain.

Follow through with discipline where appropriate: When school-age children lie in a deliberate attempt to cover up some problem, they should be held accountable both for not telling the truth and for the misdeed. This may result in a double punishment or the loss of two privileges. For instance, Jamila says to her eight-year-old son:

> *"Tyler, I want you to be honest with me. If I discover that you've done something wrong and lied about it, the punishment will be twice what it would have been if you'd told me the truth. If you tell the truth, I'll be proud of you. For example, let's say you broke a window and you told me about it. I'd be proud of you for telling me the truth and we'd probably work out an arrangement for you to pay for the window. But if you broke a window and lied about it, you would have two punishments. You'd have to pay for replacing the window and you'd lose one privilege for lying, such as no television for a few nights."*

Using this approach will help your children to understand that the next time they do something wrong, they'll receive less punishment for telling the truth than risking a lie. This sort of explanation also emphasizes how strongly you value honesty. Remember, punishment should not be severe or they will learn to lie as a means of self-protection.

Model honesty: Adults sometimes model dishonesty by telling white lies. A father may say to his child, "Let's tell Mommy that this cost $10," when it really cost $40. Or a mother may tell her child who is answering the phone, "If that's Mary for me, tell her I'm not home." You need to establish the same standards of honesty for yourself that you set for your children.

Misplaced honesty: Of course, there is such a thing as misplaced honesty; that is, saying truthful things that are better left unsaid. For instance, a child telling another child, "You're a lousy soccer player," or "Your grandma is fat and ugly," only serves to hurt feelings. As your children grow old enough to understand, you should explain that although saying such things is honest, it's nonetheless better not to say them.

Praise and reward honesty: When possible, praise your children for being honest about their mistakes and difficulties. Teach them about honesty and how dishonesty is destructive to themselves and others. Remind them of the boy who "cried wolf" so often that no one believed he was telling the truth when he was really in trouble.

If one of your children has a problem with frequent lying, it is helpful to set up a reinforcement program where he or she gets a sticker or token for each day without lying. These stickers or tokens can then be traded in for various privileges such as games, treats and special time with you.

Mealtime Problems

It's 6:15 p.m. and the Mehta family is just sitting down to dinner. The adults begin to discuss plans for remodeling the kitchen when they notice that four-year-old Jasmine is pushing her spaghetti around on her plate. "Don't play with your food, dear. Eat it," her mother says. Jasmine continues to play with her food. "Eat it," her mother says more firmly. "I hate spaghetti!" Jasmine wails. Since spaghetti is one of the few foods she routinely eats, her mother is puzzled. "Sweetie, you love spaghetti," her mother says gently. "Now take four bites and you can have dessert." Jasmine looks at her and says, "I'll take two bites." "Jasmine," her father says sharply, "if you don't eat everything on your plate right now you'll go to bed." "But I'm not hungry," she cries.

Why Does It Occur?

Almost every child becomes picky about food at some time or another. At some ages, this is simply a matter of disliking certain tastes or textures or being more interested in exploring and talking than eating. However, some children learn to be picky after observing other family members who are finicky. Another reason is that just as language or motor development progresses in stops and starts, so do growth, weight gain and appetite. At certain ages, children have less need for calories. Between the ages of one and five, most children gain four to five pounds a year but many will go three to four months without any weight gain at all, resulting in a decline in appetite. Finally, some youngsters refuse to eat as a declaration of their increasing independence, a way to begin making decisions on their own.

Too often a child's lack of interest in eating turns into a power struggle regardless of the reason for it. Sometimes parents worry that poor eating habits will lead to illness, malnutrition, weight loss and life-long problems. Or they may work hard to prepare a nutritious meal and be offended and angry when their children seem ungrateful. Either of these situations can result in pleading, urging, criticizing, threatening or punishing children for not eating. Unfortunately, children may learn that this is a way of controlling or getting even with their parents. And when eating becomes a battle of wills, parents can't win by forcing their children to eat. Force will only aggravate the problem and children may even choose to endanger their health rather than give in.

What To Do

Relax: Take some time to disengage yourself from the power struggle and think about why you are so upset about your children's eating habits. Are you worried about nutrition or health? Are you cross that yet another simple event is a struggle? Do you feel that their response is another example of them not appreciating all the work you do? Is the behavior similar to that of a family member who grew up to have an eating disorder? By understanding your own emotional response, you will be able to control your reactions and deal with the problem more effectively.

Consider your child's hunger level: Although most adults have been socialized to believe that meals should occur three times daily, that is often not the schedule that best suits young children. Most need four to five small meals a day: morning, mid-morning, noontime, mid-afternoon and evening. If your children have a snack at 3:30, they may not have a big appetite at six o'clock. Some mealtime battles can be eliminated by accepting that they do not have the same appetite that you do. If they eat nutritious snacks mid-morning and mid-afternoon, you don't need to be concerned about them having a big dinner. However, if you have concerns about their health, check with your pediatrician to ensure that their weight-for-height is within normal limits. Remember not to judge adequate nutrition by how much is eaten since there are wide differences in the amount of food individuals need.

Eliminate constant snacking and junk food: On the other hand, don't let your children nibble all day long or they will learn poor eating habits. If they eat constantly, they never have the opportunity to read their body's hunger cues. Limit their access to food to no more than five times daily, at regular times. This teaches them that opportunities to eat are limited. The logical consequence of this is that if they skip a meal or snack, they will feel hungry. Ultimately, you want them to learn to eat when they are hungry and not eat when they aren't.

Encourage your children to avoid junk foods—salted chips, soft drinks, and highly sweetened snacks. Not only do these foods spoil mealtime appetites, their intense, artificial flavorings can become almost addictive, decreasing interest in more nutritious but less exciting foods such as fruits and vegetables.

Have time-limited meals: Some children drag mealtimes out by eating slowly, complaining at every mouthful and playing with their food. Instead of letting meals drag on and on, determine a reasonable amount of time in which you will expect your children to finish eating, perhaps 20 to 30 minutes. Explain ahead of time that when a timer goes off, their plates will be removed. Don't nag or plead if they don't eat, and resist the urge to say, "Only ten more minutes..., only eight more minutes...." Of course youngsters who can't judge time may need one or two reminders. When the timer does go off, calmly remove their plates. You might say, "I guess you're not hungry today" if they haven't eaten much. The goal is to make them feel responsible for their own eating. This may involve allowing them to go hungry after several uncompleted meals. Once they realize that time is limited and experience the consequences of not eating, they may become more interested in eating at mealtimes rather than trying to get your attention by not eating.

The time-limited approach may also be useful if your children find it difficult to remain seated at the table throughout a meal. Youngsters don't have much tolerance for the adult concept of meals, where people sit for long periods, eating slowly and chatting. They can learn to endure and even enjoy the process, but this comes slowly. Initially, you must accept that they won't want to stay at the table once they've finished eating. Decide how long you can reasonably expect them to pay attention to their food and remain seated. For a two-year-old, this may be only 10 minutes. Whatever you decide, set a timer for this interval. When it goes off, remove your children's plates and tell them they may leave the table. This will greatly reduce fidgeting and complaining during meals.

Offer limited choices: If your children are picky eaters, refusing to eat much of the usual family fare, give them an option. Allow them to eat what the family eats or, instead, one type of nutritious food that they like, such as a peanut butter sandwich. The choice should be made well before each meal, so that the cook is not forced into last-minute preparations. Providing such an option diminishes the power struggle that results when you try to force them to eat a particular food. By offering an alternative, you give them a face-saving way out of the conflict. They don't have to win by refusing food altogether. It also introduces the idea of compromise, a concept that is useful in resolving all types of conflict. Offering choices indicates that you're willing to give them some room to negotiate. Finally, when you offer an alternative you know they like you don't have to worry that they will starve. Peanut butter sandwiches may not be your idea of a perfect meal, but they are nutritious and this diet won't last forever. In time, when your children realize that mealtimes are not battlegrounds for control, they'll be more interested in trying new foods.

Mealtime problems.

Serve small portions: Often, parents base the size of the portions on what they think their children should eat, rather than their actual needs or appetites. Children may not be hungry and resent having food forced upon them. Allow them to serve their own portions when possible. Having some control over the food that goes on their plates may reduce the struggle over the food that goes into their mouth. For very young children, offer small portions—less than you think they will eat—for this will lead to a sense of accomplishment. Sandwiches can be cut in quarters and glasses filled only halfway. It's very pleasant to have them ask for more instead of complaining about too much.

Ignore picky eating and bad table manners: Strange as it may seem, scolding, nagging and criticizing actually reinforce eating problems and escalate power struggles. Children learn that toying with food or eating things they shouldn't with their fingers or refusing to try new foods are powerful ways to get attention. In the example at the beginning of this chapter, Jasmine's fussiness was an effective method of focusing attention on herself. You should try to ignore eating behaviors that are irritating. This means not only refraining from coaxing or threatening, but also controlling your facial expressions and negative comments to other people.

Reward good eating and table manners: If one of your children misbehaves at the table, find opportunities to praise another who is behaving appropriately. For example, praise staying seated, using cutlery carefully, trying a new food and talking quietly. If one child is eating mashed potatoes with his or her fingers, turn to a well-behaved sibling to say, "You're doing such a good job of eating your dinner with your fork," or "It's really nice that you can eat your food in such a grown-up way." When you pay attention to good manners rather than bad, your children will learn that there is little payoff for misbehaving. You may want to establish a tangible reward system that involves a number of mealtime behaviors, such as staying seated until the timer rings, talking quietly and finishing before a timer rings. At first, you may find it most effective to reward behaviors other than eating. Removing the focus from eating emphasizes that food is not a source of conflict between you and your children. Therefore, what goes into their mouth is now their own choice.

Use natural or logical consequences: Although you can't force your children to eat at mealtimes, you can have control over what they eat between meals. Hunger is a natural consequence of not eating so use it to your advantage. Explain to your children, "If you don't eat your lunch by the time the timer rings, I'll take away your plate and there won't be any snacks until dinner." If you regularly serve dessert, the logical consequence of not eating the main course is to miss out on dessert. Don't make children sit at the table after other family members have left, however, for this will lead to negative associations with mealtimes.

Use Time Out for disruptive behaviors: If your children have extremely inappropriate table behaviors, such as spitting or throwing food, call a Time Out as a consequence.

Model good eating habits: If parents snack on chips, candy, cookies and soft drinks throughout the day and then try to cut down on calories by nibbling at mealtimes, their children will learn to do the same. If parents are particular about what they will and will not eat, their children likely will be too. One of the most powerful ways your children learn what and how to eat is by observing you. Therefore, eat nutritious, well-balanced meals and snacks, avoid critical comments about particular foods, and express your enjoyment of food and family meals.

Make eating a fun, relaxed event: Most important, remember that mealtimes and eating can and should be a positive, relatively conflict-free experience. A relaxed, supportive attitude is crucial. Offer new foods in a casual manner without urging your children to try them. Never feed them if they are capable of feeding themselves—usually after 14 months of age. Be sure you're not hurrying meals, especially for toddlers who need time to explore their foods. Clean plates, clean floors and perfect manners should not be seen as a sign of a successful meal.

Preschoolers and older children should be involved in shopping, food selection, preparation and cooking. There are fun ways to present food, slicing cheese to create clown faces or animals, making rice balls or rice triangles, freezing yogurt popsicles, serving fruit milkshakes and raw vegetables with dips. New or disliked foods can be offered with old favorites. Meals can be presented in attractive and colorful ways. And remember to be sure that mealtimes are relaxed and joyful for your family, not conducted in a noisy, confused atmosphere with television or radio blaring or distracting activities going on. Encourage your children to talk about things not related to food as they eat. You'll find that once you allow them to be in control of their own eating, problems will probably disappear in three to four weeks, and you can rest assured that by adolescence their appetites will probably have reached gigantic proportions.

Bed Wetting

It is normal for young toddlers to wet their beds, but children are labeled *enuretics* or *bedwetters* when it doesn't go away at the expected time. Parents have varied expectations for when they think their children should be toilet trained and dry at night. Some parents worry about bedwetting when their children are three and four, but this is too early to be concerned.

Bedwetting beyond the age of five is not an uncommon problem. Data indicate that as many as one out of four children between the ages of 4 and 16 have this problem. Forty percent of children are bedwetters at age three, 30 percent at age four, 20 percent at age five, about 12 percent from ages six to eight, 5 percent at age 10-12, and 2 percent in young adulthood. Twice as many boys as girls are likely to have bedwetting problems.

Why Does it Occur?
There are many theories as to the cause of bedwetting, but none has been conclusively proven. For the majority of bedwetters who have never achieved nighttime dryness, the most likely reason for bedwetting is a development or maturational lag (i.e., slow physiological maturation of bladder control mechanisms). Becoming dry is a natural developmental process like walking and talking, determined by a combination of physical maturation and motivational readiness. There is also a heredity or genetic factor involved: parents of bedwetters are three times more likely to have been bedwetters themselves as children than parents of non-bedwetters. Among families where there is one bedwetter, 70 percent have at least one other bedwetter.

For the child who has been dry at night for a significant period of time—six months or so—then starts nighttime wetting again, the cause may be some external stress. The birth of a new baby, physical illness, divorce, or a move to a new home or school can cause temporary regressive behavior such as bedwetting. Developmentally, the skill a child has most recently learned is the most vulnerable to relapse if there is added stress. This is usually temporary and goes away with added reassurance. Bedwetting should not be seen as a sign of deep-seated emotional disturbance or impaired intellectual development.

Physical causes for bedwetting, such as urinary tract infections, are rare—1-2 percent or less. However, if your child has daytime and night-time wetting beyond the age of five or has painful urination, then the first step would be a doctor's examination.

What To Do For the Four- to Six-Year-Old

Be patient and reassuring: Regardless of the child's age, the most important approach to this problem is to have a positive, supportive and confident attitude about his ability to eventually learn bladder control. Do not pressure, punish, scold, or shame the child for bedwetting as these approaches are likely to make him feel incompetent, anxious and discouraged and the bedwetting problem worse.

While you yourself may be discouraged because of the never-ending laundry, remember that your child is not intentionally or deliberately trying to make life difficult for you. The object is to remove the sense of guilt and shame he may have about bedwetting and instead, promote a feeling of optimism about his eventual ability to control his wetting. Be sure also not to allow siblings to tease the bedwetter.

Set up a chart: Set up a sticker chart with your child for dry nights or dry beds. You might want to give one sticker (accompanied by lots of praise and encouragement, of course) for each dry night. Then when the child earns so many stickers she can trade them in for something from the reward menu. You can keep a calendar with stickers or happy faces on it for dry nights. Such a tangible reward program helps motivate children and gives them a goal to work toward. But remember nothing matches a parent's encouragement, praise and support.

Promote good toilet habits: It can be helpful to set up a regular toilet schedule for children. This might involve going to the bathroom immediately upon wakening, then again after breakfast, lunch and dinner. Many times children get engrossed in play and forget to go to the bathroom—later they get excited and suddenly wet their pants. Gentle reminders to go the bathroom can help prevent some of these accidents. Praise your child for remembering to go to the toilet during the day or nighttime on his own.

Reduce stress: For the child who has been consistently dry and then suddenly starts wetting again, check to see whether there has been a stressful event that might have triggered the regression. If there is some external event such as a new baby or move to a new school, then do what you can to try to alleviate the stressful feelings. This might involve extra attention and support and extra one-to-one playtime. Once the child adjusts to the situation and feels reassured, the symptoms usually go away.

For Six- to Eight-Year-Olds

Limit the Amount of Fluid in the Evening: Sometime it helps to reduce the amount of fluid drinking after the evening meal. If this can be easily accomplished without a power struggle, it's probably worth a try. On the other hand, if you find yourself engaged in battles over drinking at night, it is best to let the child drink something since it hasn't been conclusively proven that the amount of drinking before bed relates to bedwetting per se. Also, the focus of parental attention on drinking can only serve to make the child more sensitive about the bedwetting.

Use logical consequences and promote child's responsibility: For the school-age child, it can be helpful to put a towel (or a folded sheet) over the bottom sheet. Then show him how to pull off the wet towel if he has an accident, replace it with a new one, and get back into bed without waking you. Be sure the child has access to a supply of his own towels and knows where to put wet pajamas and towels. This approach not only gives the child responsibility for his behavior but it minimizes the amount of parental attention he gets for wetting.

Bladder stretching exercises: There is some research to suggest that bedwetters may have smaller bladder capabilities than non-bedwetters. Thus, training the child to hold greater and greater amounts of fluid can increase the bladder capacity. You can do this by getting the child to drink increased amounts of fluid and then hold his urine as long as possible. Then ask him to urinate into a measuring cup and record how much he was able to hold. Each day the child tries to break his record from the day before. If he is successful he should be reinforced. (Bladder capacity of five to seven ounces is normal in the six-year-old.)

Another kind of bladder exercise is to ask your child to "start and stop" the flow of urine while urinating. He can be told he is exercising his muscles and strengthening his bladder valve's ability to stop the bed-wetting. Remember both of these exercises require a motivated child and a big commitment from parents for several months.

Nighttime Wakening: It helps if you can determine what time of night your child is wetting. If she usually wets two hours after going to bed, you can wake her at that time to go to the toilet. Or if she wants, you can put an alarm clock in her room set to go off just before she normally wets. Eventually, she will learn to recognize the signal of a full bladder and will get up on her own.

For Eight- to Twelve-Year-Olds

Buzzer: The new alarms (Wetstop, Nytone, and Night Trainer) have without a doubt been a very successful way of helping older children learn to stay dry at night. However, your child needs to be interested and motivated for this approach to work. The child wears a small lightweight, portable, battery operated buzzer in his pajamas and the alarm goes off at the first tiny drop of urine. He wakes up, stops urinating and goes to the bathroom to finish. Within two to three months, he learns to wake up to the feeling of a full bladder. There is 70 percent initial cure, but a fairly high relapse rate once the alarm is discontinued. Relapses can be prevented, however, by taking some extra steps when phasing out the buzzer alarm system. First, when the child seems dry, start withdrawing the buzzer every third night, and then every other night and so forth. Also, ask the child to drink a lot before going to bed so that he learns how to stay dry even with a full bladder.

Medications: The most popular drug prescribed by physicians for this problem is imipramine, an antidepressant that stops bedwetting for reasons which are unclear. About 25 to 40 percent of children will improve on imipramine after two weeks on the drug. However, there is a high relapse rate once the medication is stopped. Medication should only be used with children over eight years of age and after everything else has been tried first. There are select instances where it might be helpful, such as when a child is going away to camp.

You should not really worry about bedwetting as a problem unless it has begun to seriously interfere with your child's social life. For example, if bedwetting causes your son to be afraid to go to camp or stay at a friend's house overnight, then he will probably be motivated to work with you to do something about it. But remember, bedwetting is not a disease—all children eventually get over it regardless of treatment. So, be patient, reassuring and positive, and you are guaranteed a good outcome with your child's self-esteem intact.

Hyperactivity, Impulsiveness and Short Attention Span

Cory is six years old and his mother often says, "He's so different from his older brother. If I'd had him first I would never have had another child!" Although Cory can sit still to watch television, he is otherwise restless and easily distracted, constantly moving from one thing to another. He talks loudly, gets excited easily in groups and is difficult to put to bed at night. Simple transitions from one activity to another result in battles. His parents feel exhausted from the constant need to monitor his behavior, and they report that discipline techniques that work with their other son don't work with him. In kindergarten, the teacher thinks of him as a troublemaker. She questions how to handle him as he is frequently "hyperactive" and bothers other children. He won't listen to instructions or stay on task with an activity. Recently, his parents have been even more worried because he says "I'm bad," and his usually sunny disposition has been replaced by a defiant attitude. A pediatrician and psychologist have raised the possibility of parenting classes and medication for a possible attention deficit disorder with hyperactivity (ADHD).

Why Does It Occur?

A child's level of activity, impulsiveness and attention span are part of his or her temperament. The difference in temperament can be observed from infancy onward. While some babies are relatively passive and easily soothed, others are active and cry easily. As toddlers, some children are easily distracted and full of energy, while others are more focused and less energetic. However, in general, most two- to three-year-olds are very active and impulsive. They have difficulty listening while someone talks or gives instructions and will probably not stay with any activity for longer than five or 10 minutes without adult guidance. Thus the term "terrible twos" was coined. It is a difficult time for parents. By five or six years of age, however, most children have matured and developed an ability to control their impulsive behavior, activity level and can focus for at least 20 to 25 minutes on activities other than television.

If you have a child between the age of five and six who exhibits some of the following characteristics, you may want to consider evaluation for hyperactivity. The medical term for this is Attention Deficit/Hyperactivity Disorder (ADHD). A child with ADHD shows many of the behaviors listed below, in more than one setting (e.g., at home and at school). (Note: Teachers are very good at detecting when a child is developmentally more active than other children.)

- does not pay attention to details and makes careless mistakes in school work or other projects
- does not listen when someone talks
- does not follow through on instructions and doesn't finish school work, chores, or projects
- has trouble organizing tasks and activities
- may avoid or refuse tasks that require sustained attention (homework or school work)
- frequently loses things
- shows increased motor activity, fidgeting and squirming
- cannot stay seated for long in situations where this is expected (school)
- runs and climbs excessively in situations where this is inappropriate
- has trouble playing quietly
- is "on the go" or acts as if "driven by a motor"
- talks excessively and interrupts or intrudes on others
- blurts out answers
- has difficulty waiting for a turn

ADHD is, in fact, one of the most common developmental disorders, especially in boys (boys are 4 times more likely to be diagnosed with ADHD than girls). ADHD is diagnosed in eight to 10 percent of boys and three percent of girls. Researchers believe that a delay in maturation of the brain or neurological system causes poor self-control and hyperactivity. Because of these deficits, such a child requires external controls by parents and teachers for longer periods of time than do his or her peers. Often, temperament and short attention span are hereditary or genetic. In most cases, the parenting style or environment did not cause these problems. Only a very small percentage of children with ADHD are reacting to a chaotic home environment or abusive discipline.

However, the good news is that parents and teachers can make changes to the home and school environments that will help children with ADHD to function as well as their peers without ADHD. A good outcome can be expected for children with ADHD if parents and teachers are understanding, supportive, and effective in their use of discipline. Such children require extra monitoring, special parenting, and school intervention. While initially the tasks of teaching and managing are extremely challenging, the long-term results can be most rewarding. Many of these youngsters with endless energy grow up to become highly successful and productive members of society. On the other hand, a child with ADHD who is constantly nagged, criticized, and severely punished will develop further problems of poor self-esteem, poor interpersonal skills, poor academic skills, and be discouraged from even trying to complete tasks successfully.

What To Do
Although you can't be sure about the diagnosis of ADHD until your child is five or six, you can help a child who has problems with a short attention span, impulsiveness, and high activity levels as early as 18 months of age. Here are some techniques that are helpful.

Reinforce appropriate behaviors: Research has shown that temperamentally "difficult" and "hyperactive" children receive more critical feedback, negative commands, and less praise than other, less active children. In essence, they train their parents not to praise or reinforce them because they are so exhausting to deal with. However, they need positive feedback even more than typically developing children. Even when praise does occur, children with ADHD are likely not to notice or process it. This means you will have to work hard to give praise for every positive behavior that your child exhibits. Your goal should be to give praise and reinforcement at least 5 times for every correction you need to give your child. It is particularly important to try to praise behaviors involving increased attention span and persistence with tasks, such as sitting still reading, coloring, doing puzzles or playing quietly. Reinforce any productive, calm, purposeful activities. For instance, you might say, "I'm pleased you finished that picture" or "Wow! You're sitting so well at dinner right now!" or "That was great. You calmed yourself down" or "That was terrific. You kept trying even though you were having trouble building that castle because it kept falling down." You can also teach children to reinforce themselves. Teach them to say self-praising statements out loud such as "I did a good job" or

"I sat still very well." This is the beginning of helping them learn how to self-evaluate.

Tangible reward and incentive programs: Tangible reward programs can be set up to encourage behaviors reflecting reduced activity levels and increased attention span. First, determine how long your child usually can play quietly or work on a project. This may only be one to five minutes. Then, each day, schedule a playtime and set a timer for a period of time you feel certain he or she can accomplish, such as three minutes. During this period, praise his or her attention occasionally but be careful not to be a distraction. If your child plays continuously for the specified time, give him or her a reward, such as a sticker or token. This approach can also be used for other situations such as sitting at the dinner table for 5 minutes, complying with a request, finishing a puzzle, reading for 5 minutes, playing cooperatively for 5 minutes with another child, waiting his or her turn, and completing a task. These stickers or tokens can be traded in for toys, extra privileges or special trips from a reinforcement menu. Gradually, after three or four days, you can lengthen the time that you expect your child to remain engaged in the activity. It is helpful to set aside a regular time each day to work with your child to gradually increase persistence and attention. Be sure you don't lengthen the time until he or she is consistently successful with the shorter time.

Clear limit-setting, structure and good organization: With an active, easily distracted child you need to state the household rules clearly and be specific about what behaviors are appropriate. For example, you might say, "You need to sit at the table with us for 5 minutes. When the timer goes off, you may ask to be excused." Consistent limit-setting helps children feel calmer and safer. Whenever possible, try to keep your commands short and to the point. Reduce the number of distractions when you make a request and be sure to maintain eye contact. It may be necessary to touch your child and to squat down so your eyes are on the same level.

Because these children have difficulty with transitions, preparing them ahead of time can help avoid some problems. For instance, before going to the grocery store you might say, "Remember, you cannot touch things while we are in the store, but you can hold this toy." If your child is playing, you might say, "In five minutes we will be leaving for preschool." It also can be helpful to keep a very active child occupied with new toys or special books in situations where he or she may need to sit still for long periods of time, such as at the doctor's offices or on an airplane. At home, it is important to have toys in bedrooms well-organized and labeled. Too many toys overwhelm easily distracted youngsters and can lure them from one object to another. Put toys away in boxes and periodically bring out a "new" one for your child to play with.

Ignore and redirect: Many minor annoying misbehaviors such as fidgeting, wiggling, hanging off the seat, and blurting out are best managed by ignoring, especially if they are not disruptive or hurtful to others or themselves. Often children with ADHD will verbalize their thoughts and take longer to learn to internalize self-talk. This is a self-regulatory strategy and should be ignored. You can combine your ignoring with a redirection. For example, if your child is wiggling and fidgeting at the dinner table, you might ignore her wiggling, but ask her to pass you the salt or get up and get you a clean spoon. This can break up the wiggling cycle and also give you an opportunity to praise her for following your directions. You can help a wiggly child to refocus by redirecting him or her with an appropriate opportunity to move.

Be firm: If you use Time Out calmly and consistently, it can be very effective for behaviors such as not complying, destructiveness, and hitting. Time Out teaches children to calm down and assures that they are not getting attention for misbehavior.

Teach self-control: Very young children normally get what they want frequently and immediately because parents respond quickly to fussing and fretting. However, as children get older, it is appropriate that their ability to wait gradually increase. You can help your child learn to wait by not giving in every time he or she wants something. Praising the ability to wait for longer and longer periods of time is also effective. You can teach your child to use self-statements to wait longer, such as, "I won't eat all of this now. I'll save some for later," "I'm doing a good job finishing this puzzle," "I can wait my turn," or "I want to finish this so I'll pay attention and play later."

Teach problem solving: Impulsive reactions in children often occur because they do not have more effective strategies for getting what they want. They need to be taught problem-solving strategies and how to plan ahead for the consequences of such strategies. The basic idea is to teach your child to generate several possible solutions to a problem. For example, if your son has an ongoing problem of grabbing toys other children are using, you could make up a kind of game by saying, "Let's pretend your friend is riding a bike. What could you do to have a turn on it?" When he has an idea, be encouraging and ask for another. "That's a good idea. What else could you try?" When you are sure that the child has come up with as many solutions as he can think of, then you can help by offering other possible solutions. You might suggest the solution of offering the child to play with a special toy in return for using the bicycle. Then, you can act out these solutions with puppets, dolls, stuffed animals, or just act them out with your own bodies. Next, think together about the consequences of each solution. For example, you can help him to understand that if he hits the friend in order to get the bike, he might be in trouble and his friend might be mad.

Another strategy to teach problem solving is to review a problem situation that has occurred and go over how your child might have handled the situation in a different way. This will be a very worthwhile discussion as long as you do not blame or criticize. Instead, the focus should be on helping you child think of effective ways to solve a problem should it occur again.

Accept your child's limitations: It is important to remember that these behaviors are not intentional nor are they a deliberate attempt to make parenting difficult for you. Accept the fact that your child is intrinsically active, energetic, and has a short attention span. Probably, he or she will always be that way. While you can help a temperamentally difficult or a child with ADHD to manage his or her behavior and help channel energy in a positive direction, you cannot eliminate it. No one can help make a hyperactive child into a quiet, passive one. Such an attempt will not only be frustrating, but harmful to the child. Your tolerance, patience, and acceptance are crucial factors in your active child's adjustment.

Educate other people about your child: Sometimes hyperactive children become the target of negative reactions or labeling by teachers, friends, and neighbors. These adults, not being aware of the problem of ADHD, may inadvertently blame the parents for creating such a problem child. Or they may interpret the child's misbehavior as deliberate manipulation. It is important for you to educate neighbors, teachers, and family members, and enlist their help with your child. If you can help them understand that your child tries hard but has difficulty controlling energy at times, you will probably receive more support. Your child, too, will get a more positive message. Although, at times, you may feel like giving up with such an exhausting child, it is important to constantly give the message he or she is loved and accepted. As long as self-esteem and confidence are high, your child will be able to survive many of the obstacles that he or she has to face academically and socially.

Refuel yourself: Any adult would become exhausted from working with a child with ADHD for 24 hours. So ensure that you take the time to get away, take personal time out, and refuel yourself so that you can better meet your child's extra needs. It is helpful to set up a regular sitter for at least one night a week. Parents who are at home need to have sitters for some afternoons so that they can get away and meet their own needs. Not only will time away help to refresh you, but it will show your child that you know how to take care of yourself and model coping skills that will be important for your child to learn.

Medications: Research suggests that about two-thirds of the children accurately diagnosed as ADHD are helped with medications such as Ritalin. These seem to work by helping them to increase their concentration and their ability to control impulsive responses. In general, medications are not prescribed until children have reached school age. And medication trials should always be preceded by thorough medical and school evaluations. Individual educational plans (IEP) should also be arranged at school. Research shows that prescription drugs without special education and behavior management programs have no long-term benefits. While the medication itself can be helpful, the message parents convey to their children about it must be handled carefully. Sometimes, children are told, directly or indirectly, that when they are well-behaved it is due to the medication. The underlying theme is that they are responsible for their bad behavior but not for good behavior. As you can imagine, this is a very discouraging message. Regardless of whether or not your child is on medication, hold him or her responsible for behavior problems and expect that he or she will be able to learn to change. Also, be sure to give your child, not the medication, credit for success.

Special school programs: Preschool for two to three hours a day two to three times a week for young children can help them learn how to behave in group settings. By the same token, it is important to seek out a classroom setting that will support, rather than frustrate your child. Children with ADHD benefit from small class sizes, quiet study space, tutoring and involvement in classroom tasks, such as erasing the board or handing out papers, in order to help them manage their excess energy. It is important that their teachers recognize their need for movement, adaptations, and extra support. If you feel that your child has ADHD and has not been tested, ask the school special education program to do a thorough evaluation.

Social skills and problem solving training: Children with ADHD often are delayed in their social and emotional skills, although they maybe quite bright academically. Because of their impulsivity, they are less skilled at problem solving and handling conflict with peers and have difficulty making friends. It has been shown that their play skills with other children are significantly delayed compared to typically developing children. For this reason, parents are encouraged to play with their children one-on-one using the child-directed play concepts and emotional and peer coaching outlined in Chapter One. It will be very important for parents to model and reinforce them whenever they observe them sharing, waiting, taking turns, asking for something, following directions and staying calm in a frustrating situation.

Model self-control, problem solving and quiet activities: You can also help your child by modeling calming and positive self-talk statements. For example, if you are having trouble doing a puzzle, you might say out loud, "I better stop and think before I continue." Or if you get lost in the car, you might say, "I think I'm lost. I should stop and think about what to do." Likewise, if you want your child to read more or work quietly on projects, it is important that he or she see you doing the same. As always, it is important to model the kind of behavior you expect your child to exhibit. (See Chapter Eleven for information on using positive self-talk.)

Parenting a child with ADHD can be exhausting, but also extremely rewarding. It's important to remember that you and your child's teachers will make the biggest contribution to your child's success, and with some persistent and hard work, your child will be successful at home and at school. In the midst of this tough parenting job, remember to take the time to enjoy your child's energy and high spirited personality.

Helping Your Children
with Divorce

Divorce is a critical event that affects the entire family. Although it is believed that at least 52 percent of all young children will directly experience the disruption of divorce, few families are really prepared for the trauma and stress it causes. The practical problems of a divorce can create major stress through such things as having to move, reduced housing area and financial loss. The loss of income may force mothers back to working full time, or necessitate a return to school and reliance on full-time child care. Single fathers may face unfamiliar tasks, such as coping with laundry, shopping, preparing meals and cleaning. In the first year, both mothers and fathers will experience more anxiety, depression, anger, feelings of rejection and incompetence, and a kind of identity crisis. They may feel lonely and estranged from their married friends and prior social life.

Children also have strong reactions to divorce. Three- to five-year-olds have an unclear understanding of the events and may respond to the loss of a parent with fears that any routine separation in daily life will result in abandonment. They may become anxious about going to day care or staying with sitters. Many will react to routine separations by clinging, whining, crying and throwing tantrums. Fear of nightmares and other bedtime anxieties may result in pleas to sleep in a parent's bed. Regression in toilet training or a greater need for security blankets are also common reactions to divorce. In general, children seem to develop a neediness and insatiable hunger for affection and nurturing from the important adults in their lives.

Preschoolers also frequently show increases in aggressiveness and other behavior problems. Since they have difficulty separating fantasy from reality, they will often make up stories to explain a parent's departure, especially if the divorce has not been explained to them adequately.

Some children will deny the divorce altogether and create elaborate fantasies that both parents have been restored to the family. Many conclude that the departed parent has rejected them or replaced them with a better family elsewhere. Another common response is a tendency to feel responsible. Because they are naturally self-centered, they have difficulty realizing that a divorce is related to the parents' relationship problems rather than to their own behavior. Such guilt-ridden fantasies are often partially substantiated by arguments that they may have overheard about themselves before the divorce took place.

The more mature intellectual and emotional development of children aged six to eight enables them to better understand the meaning of divorce and some of its implications for them. They're less likely to feel responsible than preschoolers. However, like younger children, they do fear being rejected and left without a family. They often feel lonely, depressed and very sad. Fantasies of being deprived of food, toys or some other important element of their life may pervade their thinking. Studies have shown that children who stayed with their mothers rarely expressed anger toward their father, as if fearful that this anger might cause him to reject them. On the other hand, many expressed considerable anger at their mother, either for causing the divorce or for driving their father away. Most of these children wished for reconciliation between their parents and had recurrent fantasies of them remarrying.

Children between the ages of eight and 12 appear more poised and courageous, and make more efforts to control their feelings than younger ones. Unlike younger children, however, they are ashamed and embarrassed about what has been happening and try to conceal the events from teachers and friends. The most common feature that distinguishes them is intense anger, usually directed toward their mother. They may have significant problems in peer relationships as well as a noticeable decline in school performance. And they may have more headaches, stomachaches and other physical complaints.

Divorce presents a somewhat different threat to the adolescent. The normal developmental task at this age is to separate from parents and develop an independent identity. A divorce disrupts this process, undermining the teenager's view of the family as a safe, predictable place. In fact, the tables are often turned, especially if parents are involved in dating. Preoccupied with their own needs and decisions, they may be unable to concentrate on the needs of their adolescents. Adolescents often feel that they are rushed to achieve independence following a divorce. Because the marital disruption occurred at an age when the normal adolescent is preoccupied with heterosexual relationships and sex, these issues may become centers of anxiety. They may fear that they also will be failures in love and marriage. They will feel a sense of loss and grief and may express intense outrage toward what they see as their parents' betrayal, selfishness and insensitivity. Thus, parents are no longer seen as respected role models. Sometimes during a divorce, one or both parents may turn to an adolescent for support. This can further compound feelings of anger, guilt and depression, and create conflicts related to allegiance and loyalty. Adolescents may react by becoming aloof, distancing themselves as a means of self-protection. They not only feel estranged from their families during the adjustment period after divorce but also have difficulty relating to their peer group. They experience strong feelings of shame and embarrassment at their parents' failure and may not even tell their closest friends about a divorce. Finally, adolescents worry about money, particularly whether their parents will be able to provide for their education.

Impact On Parent/Child Relationships
The divorce process results in parents feeling more stress. Preoccupied with their own troubles, they may show their children less affection. On the other hand, children may react by becoming more aggressive, dependent, disobedient, demanding and unaffectionate. Parents' guilt, lowered self-esteem and fear of their children's anger may cause them to communicate poorly and be less consistent with discipline. Some mothers try to take on what had been the father's role by becoming more of a disciplinarian. This usually involves becoming more restrictive and increasing the use of punishment. Fathers, on the other hand, may become more permissive and indulgent, avoiding discipline for fear of losing their children's love. In this way, the normal parenting process is disrupted, and that may further aggravate behavior problems.

Children's problems can intensify if they are forced to align with one parent and to denounce the other to insure affection. Another disruptive process occurs if the parents mentally associate a child with a former spouse and use the child as scapegoat for hostility felt toward that person. Children, on the other hand, may attempt to deal with the loss of a parent by adopting a real or imagined role. Even at very early ages sons are quick to take on the role of man of the family. And if they identify with the aggressive aspect of their father, they are likely to demonstrate hostility toward their mother, which will further exacerbate the situation. A third potentially hazardous situation occurs if parents treat their children as equals. This happens when they repeatedly turn to their offspring for support, advice and companionship. Children in any of these situations are at risk of becoming depressed or severely troubled.

What To Do

While divorce does change the lives of parents and their children, it does not automatically mean psychological scars or delayed development. What is important for children's overall adjustment is how their parents manage the divorce and its aftermath. They play an essential role in buffering and minimizing both the immediate and the long-term effects on their children's social and emotional development. Here are some ways in which you can help your children learn to adjust to a divorce and the subsequent change in the family structure.

Talk to your child about the divorce: Studies have shown that 80 percent of young children were not provided with either an explanation of the divorce or assurance of continued care by one parent. Many reported that they woke up one morning to find a parent gone! Indeed, divorce was a shock for most children since many were unaware of their parents' unhappiness prior to the separation. These findings indicate that the most important thing that you can do at the outset is to sit down and talk to your children about the impending separation and divorce. This should be done a week or two prior to the actual separation. If the information is given too far ahead, they won't believe it will happen. On the other hand, if it is given only a few days in advance, they won't have sufficient time to adjust or to seek reassurance by asking questions of both you and your spouse. It's important to be as honest and open as possible. The concept should be explained at a level appropriate to their intellectual and psychological development. The explanation should be factual and realistic, taking into account the basic reason for the divorce in terms as emotionally objective as possible. To withhold information regarding the major issues that brought about the divorce will only produce anxiety, insecurity and distrust. But don't burden your children with all the sordid details or engage in blaming or making derogatory remarks. Above all, you should emphasize that the divorce is between you and your spouse and will not affect the love either one of you has for them.

Reassure your children that they will not be abandoned or divorced: It is important to reassure your children that they will continue to have two parents even though they live apart. It helps to make the distinction between married couples' love and parental love. You might say, "Parents don't stop loving their children. I will always love you because you are my children." However, if one parent does not intend to continue parenting and will be absent, this kind of reassurance is unrealistic and sets children up for disappointment. In such cases, it is better to be honest about how involved each parent will be. Children need concrete information about where you and your spouse will be living and how often they will see each of you.

Make your children's world as reliable and predictable as possible: Tell your children where they will live, how they will be cared for and what changes will be made in school or day care. Since divorce causes them to feel that their world is suddenly less reliable and predictable, it's important that you provide them with as much practical information as you can to help them feel more secure.

Create an atmosphere where your children can talk, ask questions and express feelings: Your children may ask the same question repeatedly, so be prepared to go over the reasons for the divorce again and again as this helps them to work through what they have been told. They need opportunities to express sad, hurt and angry feelings. Don't discourage them from crying or expressing their feelings by telling them to "be brave." Open, ongoing communication will be needed for the months and the years that follow the divorce. Be aware, however, that not all children react the same way. In the beginning, some don't want to discuss it and respond with denial. They may be afraid to express their anger, fearing rejection. Or they may withhold their feelings in order to protect parents from further discomfort. It can, in fact, be several months before some children are able to express their grief and anger, finally secure that these thoughts will not hurt anyone.

Do not use your children as spies: Never use your children as spies, messengers or instruments for hurting your ex-spouse. If they are kept in the middle, they will feel guilty and be unable to turn to either parent for support. This can preoccupy them to the detriment of their social, emotional and academic development.

Avoid negativity and anger toward the absent parent: Not only should your children be kept out of the middle, they should be honestly encouraged to love and maintain healthy relationships with both you and your ex-spouse. A child should not be expected to choose sides. Problems concerning finances or custody should not be discussed in the presence of your children. And you should not discuss your personal problems with them even if no one else is available to listen. Hoarding bitter, angry feelings about your ex-spouse prevents the closure of the divorce and keeps the bad feelings alive for your children. Exposing them to a list of grievances about their mother or father does not allow them the chance to move ahead and grow. Moreover, since a part of your children is made up of each parent, putting down your ex-spouse is really putting them down. Remember that your children have fragile self-esteem, particularly in times of stress, and they need help to feel good about themselves.

Give yourself and your child time to work through the process: The process of healing and coping with the stresses that emerge from a divorce takes time and patience. Most parents and children report that they become comfortable with their lives again 12 to 16 months after the divorce.

Be consistent in limit-setting and rules: Avoid excessive spending or overindulgence, and express your love and concern by spending more time with your children. If they respond with negative behaviors such as aggression, follow through with limit-setting, Time Out or logical consequences as appropriate. Your guilt about the divorce should not prevent you from enforcing household rules and appropriate limit-setting. Consistent limit-setting helps provide an orderly, predictable and safe world for an upset child.

Arrange a visitation policy that you and your former spouse support and respect: Studies have shown that in about two-thirds of families, visitations are fraught with parental anger and antagonism. Moreover, research indicates that non-custodial parents (most often fathers) find it very painful to visit their children. They may feel they have lost their children and expect to be rejected by them. Sometimes these parents prefer visiting less frequently rather than enduring weekly psychological trauma. Unless they're careful, they may distance themselves emotionally in order to protect themselves from the pain of separation from their children. Interviews with children indicate that they feel they don't have enough contact with the parent who doesn't have custody.

In setting up visitation arrangements there are several things to keep in mind. First, older children seem to prefer a flexible schedule. They also want to be involved in planning the visits. Younger children usually want a stable visiting schedule they can count on. Conflicts over visitation should be minimized because they burden children with a sense of responsibility for the conflict. It will help a lot if you and your ex-spouse agree that your children can love you both and allow them to talk about the fun they had with one of you to the other. If they're afraid to express their feelings about either of you, mistrust will result. Visitation should meet the needs of the whole family and should reflect parental willingness to adapt to children's changing developmental needs and circumstances. Visitation commitments should always be kept unless there is an emergency. Telephone calls to children are an added way for out-of-home parents to keep in touch and these calls should be frequent and regular. Above all, issues of child support should not be confused with visitation and should not be used to as a way to manipulate advantage in another area.

Fears

Julie is six years old and she complains frequently of stomach aches and head aches. Sometimes she stays home from school or from soccer practices because of these complaints. Her mother has taken her to the doctor several times and he says he can find no medical reason for her symptoms. The mother thinks that her daughter is anxious because her grandmother is terminally ill. She wonders if she should let her stay home more.

Alex is four years old and has recently started preschool. His teacher notices that he usually plays alone and avoids contact with other children. He is very shy and seems withdrawn. When his mother brings him to school, he clings to her, crying, and tantrums when she leaves. She says he is also afraid of the dark and has nightmares. His mother sometimes stays with him in the classroom and frequently lets him say home. She asks if he is too young for preschool.

Why Do Fears Occur?

Fears and worries are a normal part of growing up and are experienced by all young children. In fact, there is a peak in the occurrence of nightmares (especially of monsters or bad guys that chase them) in children during the preschool age period. Because young children often cannot express their anxieties with words, they sometimes express them through physical symptoms such as stomach aches or head aches. Other times they respond to the fear by tantrumming, withdrawal, or avoidance of the feared situation. There are many theories as to the cause of fears. Sometimes parents are aware of an incident that precipitated the fear. For example a child who was attacked by a dog and became afraid of dogs, or a child who had a scary dunking in a pool and became afraid of the water. Often times the cause of the fear is not so apparent. For example, a child who previously slept alone in her bedroom at night

might one night say that she is scared to go into her bedroom, but is not be able to tell her parents why she is scared. Once children are fearful of something, for example going swimming or going to sleep alone, they may experience aversive physiological arousal such as increased heart rate, tense muscles, or stomach tightness when faced with the feared situation. Avoiding the feared situation (swimming or going to sleep alone) reduces the negative physical arousal, and brings relief to the child by preventing the frightening consequence the child has imagined. Because avoidance is doubly rewarded, through reduced arousal and a perception that the feared outcome has been prevented, it is very likely that the child will continue to try to avoid the feared situation again in the future.

Although children are not conscious of this, their physical symptoms or behavioral responses may result in their avoidance of a particular feared situation and thereby reinforce the symptom. For example, Julie is afraid to leave her grandmother who she is very attached to. When she has stomach aches, she gets to stay home with her grandmother, so she may begin to experience more frequent stomach aches. This happens because she has experienced that stomach aches work to avoid her fear of leaving her grandmother alone. Alex, who is an only child, has had very few experiences with other children, and is worried about leaving his mother to go to school. Sometimes his tantrums are so violent that his mother allows him to stay home from school, or she stays with him in the classroom. In this case his tantrums and clinging behavior leads to not being separated from him mother: a very reinforcing outcome for him. Or, perhaps the child who is afraid to sleep alone in her bedroom gets to sleep in her parents' bed: again a very reinforcing outcome.

What To Do

In all cases, the strategies for helping your child cope with their fears involve facing the situation, not avoiding it. Avoiding dogs, swimming pools, sleeping alone, or keeping your child home will only make the problem worse.

Be patient and reassuring: The most important approach to your child's expression of any kind of fear, be they social or school fears, fears of separating from parents, or physical symptoms (stomach and headaches) is to have a positive and confident attitude about your child's ability to handle the situation. Do not pressure, punish, scold, or shame the child for these fears, as these approaches are likely to make your child feel incompetent and more anxious.

First, you will want to reassure yourself and your child that the situation really is not dangerous. For physical symptoms, it is helpful to have your child see a pediatrician for a check up. For school related fears, you might check with the child's teacher to make sure that she is supportive and nurturing of your child at school and that your child is not being bullied or hurt by other children. After you are reassured of these things yourself, you should express a feeling of optimism to your child about his or her ability to cope with the situation.

For example, you might say to your child, "I know school is scary right now, but I am sure you can be brave and that it will get easier for you to go every day. I bet you will even start to make some friends very soon" or, "Grandmother will be fine when you are gone. She wants you to enjoy school. You can tell her what you learned when you get home, and she will love to hear about that."

Praise your child's brave behavior: Whenever your child separates from you at school easily or faces an uncomfortable situation, praise her courage or braveness. For example, "You are really developing 'growing up muscles' that are getting stronger now. You were very brave at the doctor's office today. I am proud of you." Think of yourself as a kind of "coach" for your child and that your job as parent is to encourage your child's "growing up" behaviors. This means praising them for taking a risk, or trying something new, or making a new friend, or doing something independently.

Set up a sticker chart: You might want to set up a sticker chart with your child for particularly brave behaviors such as for going to preschool and separating from you without a fuss. If your child is withdrawing from social contact in the classroom, you can work with your child's teacher to set up a system whereby your child is praised and reinforced for interacting with other children. This will encourage more social interactions and making friends. Likewise, you could set up sticker charts for staying in his own bed all night, or, going to swimming lessons or, staying overnight at a friend's house.

Ignore tantrums and minimize attention to psychosomatic expression of fears: Sometimes tantrums and expression of physical symptoms get a lot of attention from adults and this attention can inadvertently reinforce their occurrence. So strike a balance between being supportive and not giving these expressions of fear too much focus. For example, as you are leaving your child at school you might express confidence by saying, "I know you are going to have fun today with your friend (child begins to tantrum). Look at Billy over there. He has that truck you like (distract). I will be back at twelve o'clock, to pick you up and find out what you did today." After reassuring your child confidently of your return, walk away without giving the tantrum any further attention. This can be very hard for parents to do, but remember, if you stay at school and try to talk your child through the tantrum, he or she is learning that tantrums work to keep you from leaving. The same principles apply to a child who has a stomach ache each morning before school. In this case, the parent might say, "I'm sorry your stomach hurts. Let's make sure you have a good snack to eat later at school. That usually makes my stomach feel better." After that, ignore other talk about the stomach ache, and help your child finish getting ready for school. Fear of going to bed at night can be handled in the same way. After finishing a bedtime routine with your child, you can tuck him or her in and then say, "I'm going to leave the night light on and go downstairs now. I know you can be brave and stay in your bed and fall asleep." If your child whines or cries, you should still leave the room and ignore the crying.

Provide predictable separation and reunion routines for children with separation anxiety: It is quite normal for young children to react adversely with clinging and crying behavior when you leave them at school, when you leave them at home with a babysitter, or when you tuck them into bed at night. One way to separate from children is to have a predictable routine involving the following steps:

- express confidence and happiness about the classroom or the experience the child is about to have.
- let them know calmly and clearly that you will be leaving. For example, "In a few minutes I will be leaving for work," or, "leaving to go out for dinner." (Don't sneak away without saying goodbye.)
- if possible, stay a few minutes in the classroom playing before leaving.
- remind your child of when you will return. For example, " I will be back at noon to pick you up." Or, " I will back when you are asleep but I will see you in the morning."

Similarly establish a predictable routine for your reunion after leaving your child for awhile. This should involve the following:

- return when you say you will. Don't lie to children about the length of time you will be gone.
- look excited about seeing your child. You may be distracted by work or other stressful events that may have occurred while you were gone, but your child will be looking for your expression of joy when you return. He will not understand if you seem sad or anxious and may interpret these feelings as having something to do with him.
- if possible, spend a few minutes at the end of the day talking to the teacher, other children or parents (or babysitter) so that your child can see that you are comfortable in that setting and with the people that he or she has been interacting with.

Model nonfearful behavior: Think about whether you are modeling fearful behaviors and remember that children learn by observing others. If you are expressing fears of social events, animals, insects, particular situations, or your children going to school, then your children will absorb these fears as well. Even if you are nervous about these situations, try to act confident in front of your children.

Monitor parental conflict, anxiety and depression: High levels of conflict and criticism between marital partners or in a family can fuel a child's sense of insecurity. Monitor your level of conflict in front of young children and have these difficult conversations when children are not present. Model positive family interactions and family harmony.

Likewise monitor your own expression of anxiety and depression because children will model your behaviors and thinking styles. If you find your anxiety or conflict is interfering with your ability to effectively parent consider finding treatment to alleviate your symptoms.

Reinforce exposure: If your child is afraid of a particular situation or activity (e.g., dogs or swimming) try to face these situations in small doses and reinforce your children for doing so. For example, first you might read books about dogs with your child. This will provide information and mild exposure to dogs in a non-threatening way. Then stop with your child to watch other children pat a dog and make positive comments about how much fun they are having. Don't require your child to actually pat the dog, just start by watching positive models of other children enjoying dogs. Your child will begin to realize that the other children don't experience the same fear of the dog. He or she will see that, in fact, others even enjoy the experience and will begin to change his/her anticipated fear to something more positive. Enlist the help of a friend with a very gentle dog and gradually increase how close you get to the dog until you are patting the dog yourself. Praise your child for getting closer despite her fear.

Teach positive self-talk: Teach your child some self-statements that he or she can use to confront fear. First model these statements so that your child will begin to learn and eventually memorize them. For example you might teach him/her to say, "I am brave and I can do it!" The child who is afraid of the dark might be coached by you to say, "I am a brave girl, I can take care of myself in the dark. I am safe here in my room."

"I can be brave. I'll think of my happy place and fall asleep."

Or, the child who is afraid to stay at school might be coached to say, "I can be brave. I will play in the block area first and mom will be back at lunch time to pick me up." The emphasis is on the power that children have to make themselves feel better.

Positive imagery and relaxation exercises: Another way to help children learn to cope with fears is to teach them some relaxation and positive imagery exercises. First, teach your child to slow his or her breathing down and to clenching and relaxing each muscle in his or her body starting with the feet and moving up to the face. Next you can teach your child to use positive imagery by thinking of a relaxing or pleasant scene, such as going to the beach. You can practice these exercises with your child each day. Doing these before your child goes to bed can be a soothing way to end the day and will also be helpful for the child who is afraid of the dark or is scared to go to sleep.

Problem solving: As you have seen in the problem solving chapter, one of the first steps in problem solving is to be aware of the uncomfortable feeling. Once children can identify that they are feeling afraid or sad or worried, then they learn to use some of the solutions. You can help them remember the variety of solutions they can use including: take 3 deep breaths, do a tense-relax exercise, think of your happy place, tell yourself to be brave, give yourself a reward for trying and so forth. (See Chapter on Problem Solving.)

Teach social skills: Invite friends over for play dates and coach your child's social skills and friendly interactions. Social competence and close friendships can serve as a protective factor or buffer against fears and sadness.

I AM GOING TO RELAX AND IMAGINE I AM IN MY TURTLE SHELL AND TAKE DEEP BREATHS.

Remember your behavior management strategies: The management principles outlined in Part One of this book are helpful for children with fears or sadness. The child-directed play ideas will help your child feel confident and valued in their relationship with you. Creating predictable environments with clear expectations, ongoing monitoring and consistent consequences makes it more likely children will feel safe and secure in their attachment to you.

You should not really worry about expression of fears from your children since they are a natural product of growing up. Fears of facing new situations, separating from parents and coping with stressful life events are quite natural. It is important that you remain calm and confident about your child's ability to cope with these situations and that you not encourage a child's avoidance of the feared situation. Children who are allowed to repeatedly avoid a feared situation may develop fears that seriously interfere with their life and functioning. But remember, with support from their parents, most children eventually grow out of their fears. So, be patient, reassuring, and positive, and minimize the amount of attention and worry you give to your child's fears. This will guaranteed a good outcome and will boost your child's self-confidence.

Remember to...
- Have predictable routines for leaving and picking up children.
- Always return when you say you will.
- Express confidence in your child's ability to cope with fearful situations.
- Minimize attention to separation tantrums and somatic symptoms such as stomach aches once your physician has ruled out any medical disorder.
- Teach your child brave self-talk for facing fearful situations.
- Teach your child positive imagery and relaxation strategies to use in fearful situations.
- Confront fears gradually and consistently.
- Provide positive role models of other children who are not afraid of the situation or object.
- Reinforce brave or courageous behavior with your praise and encouragement.
- Set up an incentive system to get your child started in the steps needed to face the feared situation.

"Reading with Care" to Promote Your Child's Reading Skills

Cory is six years old and his mother is worried about his inability to read, "He's not reading any words and most of the other kids in his class can read sentences. He thinks he is dumb because he can't read." His mother explains she tries to read with him at home but it usually ends up with him frustrated and in tears.

Reading Development Varies

Just as toddlers learn to walk and talk at different developmental rates, not all children learn to read on the same schedule. Some children can read single words or even sentences at age four while others cannot do this until they are seven years old. There is a wide variation in ability to learn to read and write and development plays a large role in acquiring this skill. Nonetheless, there are quite a few things that parents can do to encourage their children's reading readiness and to set the stage for reading to progress.

Most parents understand the importance of reading to young children to help prepare them for school success. However, did you know that how you read to your children is as important as how frequently you read to them? The traditional way many of us have experienced reading is having the parent read while the child listens passively. The problem with this approach is that young children have difficulty sustaining their attention and understanding the verbal language when they are not actively involved in the process.

In this chapter you will learn ways to enhance your child's learning and love of reading by using an "interactive reading" approach that encourages your child to be active, to practice, and to be the teller of the story. Using this approach, especially in the pre-reading years (ages 3-7), has been shown to build the foundation for formal reading. Interactive reading is enjoyable and important for promoting your child's school readiness skills and will also foster social, emotional, and academic skills. Reading with your children helps build life-long language expression and problem-solving skills.

What To Do

Here are the four key reading with CARE building blocks for helping your child learn to read.

C *Building Block C: Commenting, connecting and describing the pictures on the page*

As you look at picture books with your child, name the objects and describe the story depicted on the pages. Comment on what you see on the page while pointing to each picture as you describe it or word as you read it. For example, *"There is the red roof and a small bird sitting on under the porch. And here is a big brown horse galloping in the field and a happy boy is sitting on top of the horse."* You can name the pictures and describe the action as well as the colors and sizes of things. This is an important pre-reading step for children to associate the written word, or in this case, the picture representation, with the verbal word. Using prepositions such as *under, on top of, beside, next to,* and *inside* as you describe the pictures also helps children to understand the meaning of these prepositions. This is an important school readiness skill.

Try commenting or describing the feelings of the characters in the story as well. For example, you might say, "He looks frustrated because he is having trouble learning to ride that bike" or "He is happy when he is patting his cat." By labeling emotions, you help your child learn feeling vocabulary and also to consider the feelings or point of view of the characters in the story. This is the beginning of your child learning perspective taking or empathy skills. This approach is especially helpful for young children with few language skills and will build their vocabulary as well as their reading skills. To practice this, start with picture books that have few or no words.

Another way to comment is to make a statement that connects the story to another story your child knows. For example, you might point out how a character in a story is similar to another character you have read about. "That boy is nervous about learning to ride that bike. That is kind of like the story we read where the boy was afraid to go to camp. Do you remember how that boy solved his problem?"

A *Building Block A: Ask open-ended questions and predict what comes next*

Ask your child what she thinks is happening on the page of pictures? This will encourage your child to make up a story and increases language fluency. Before turning the page, see if your child can guess what picture might come next, or what will happen next in the story. This has the effect of helping your child to imagine or make up his own story and to become actively involved in the story telling. You can have fun taking turns predicting what might be shown or happen on the next page. Or, you can guess what the character in the story is feeling and why he or she might be feeling that way. This reading approach makes a magical game out of the story reading, which will be enjoyable for you and your child.

Building Block R: Respond to your child's responses with praise and encouragement

Praise will increase your child's self-confidence and motivation to read. Praise any attempt to read or name the pictures. Praise your child's interest in the book as well as his patience with trying to read. Praise with enthusiasm and positive affect in your voice and show interest in his ideas. This will contribute to your child's continuing motivation to read and sustained attention.

Encourage your child to tell you what she is thinking or feeling about the story or to ask you questions. Remember one of the most encouraging things you can do is to listen to your child when she reads. As you listen remember your reactions are important. Listen without interrupting and be enthusiastic in your response. Give your child time to figure out difficult words.

Building Block E: Expand on what your child says

You can expand on what your child says by simply repeating his or her words and by adding an extra descriptor to her comment. For example you might say, "Yes you are right, that is a tractor, and it is a big, red tractor." You are praising your child's knowledge of the word or object (tractor) and then adding to her knowledge by providing descriptors (red, big).

A second way you can expand is by following your child's lead into his imaginary world. For example, perhaps your child is reading a book about dinosaurs who are playing together. You join into the child's imagination by talking about how much fun the dinosaurs are having playing soccer or eating ice cream.

It is also expanding your child's understanding when you relate his comment to some other meaningful event in their life. For example you might say, "Yes that is a red tractor and it reminds me of Uncle Ralph's tractor on his farm. You like to ride that tractor don't you?" This reading strategy will further strengthen your child's interest in books.

A fourth way to expand for an older and more articulate child is to ask if she agrees or disagrees with the author, and why.

Other Suggestions

Choose books with topics of interest to your child: Another way of engaging children's interest in books is to let them choose the book they want to read or pick out books from the library on topics that are of interest to them. For example if your child likes dinosaurs, space objects, or baseball, you can check out books on these topics. Ask your child about the kinds of books he or she would like to read. Try to select books that are not too difficult. Don't worry if the books selected are a little easier than those that come home from school.

Set up a predictable reading time daily: Try to establish a time when you read together each day. Perhaps it is before your child goes to bed at night or after dinner. Make this a quiet relaxing time by turning off the TV and taking the phone off the hook. Choose a comfortable place to sit. Have a reading shelf or basket where you keep your child's books. Once you establish this habit you will find your children will continue with these learning habits for years to come.

Encourage your child to act out stories: When asking your child to "think ahead" or predict what happens next, you might ask your child to act out what they think will happen next using puppets. You can each take a role in the story and act out the plot. This will make stories fun and come alive for the children as well as build language and develop children's imaginations.

Or, at the end of reading a story, you could act out the story plot with your child. This will help you to see how much your child understood from the story and encourage rehearsal of the vocabulary learned in the story.

Make reading fun: Perhaps the most important aspect of reading with CARE is to engage your children by having fun. You can do this by being playful, using an enthusiastic voice, following your child's lead and interests, pausing to explore pictures before diving into reading a page, taking turns reading and connecting stories and pictures to real life experiences. Sing songs such as the alphabet song and recite nursery rhymes and encourage your child to join in. Read with drama and excitement. Use different voices for the characters in the story. When you make reading fun, your children will be motivated and interested in reading for the rest of their lives.

Be patient: Remember learning to read doesn't happen all at once. Like learning to walk begins by crawling and then gradually pulling up and finally taking that first step, reading is also a gradual process. It will involve a series of stages that, over time, lead to independent reading and to fluency. Give your child time.

Model reading: Remember you are a role model. You can also help your child be motivated to read by reading books yourself. If your child sees you reading the newspaper and enjoying books and magazines, he will want to model your behavior.

Tell family stories: Tell your children stories about your family and experiences you had growing up. Tell them about their grandparents, relatives and family traditions. Encourage your child to tell you stories as well.

Read everything: Read all kinds of things: cereal boxes, street signs, poems, comics, recipes, newspaper articles, maps, greeting cards, and email messages. Give your child a subscription to a magazine for children and encourage your friends to give him books for gifts. Keep reading to your child even after he or she has learned to read. This will keep alive the magic of shared reading.

Talk to your child's teacher: Use your child's teacher as a resource to find out about your child's reading level and books and authors that she would recommend. Ask about reading strategies she uses.

Selected Readings

The material in this book has been developed from a group of outstanding researchers who have carefully analyzed and described the process of family, parent and child interactions and processes of behavior change over the past 30 years. Their work and theories have formed the foundation for the writing of this book. It is impossible to site all the researchers who have contributed to our understanding of competent parenting. The following selected readings may be of interest to those who wish to read further.

Theories and Research Reviews Underlying the Incredible Years Parent Program

Bandura, A. (1986). *Social foundations of thought and action.* Englewood Cliffs, NJ, Prentice-Hall.

Baumrind, D. (1978). Parental disciplinary patterns and social competence in children. *Youth and Society,* 9, 239-276.

Bernhardt, A. J., & Forehand, R. L. (1975). The effects of labeled and unlabeled praise upon lower and middle class children. *Journal of Experimental Child Psychology,* 19, 536-543.

Brestan, E. V. and S. M. Eyberg (1998). "Effective psychosocial treatments of conduct-disordered children and adolescents: 29 years, 82 studies, and 5,272 kids." *Journal of Clinical Child Psychology* 27: 180-189.

Brunner, J. S., Jolly, A. L. & Sylvia, K. (Eds.). (1976). *Play: Its role in development and evolution.* New York: Penguin.

Camp, B. W., Bloom, G., Herbert, F., & Van Doorninck, W. (1977). Think aloud: A program for developing self-control in your aggressive boys. *Journal of Abnormal Child Psychology.* 157-168.

Farmer, E. M. Z., S. N. Compton, et al. (2002). "Review of the evidence base for treatment for childhood psychopathology: Externalizing disorders." *Journal of Consulting and Clinical Psychology* 70(6): 1267-1302.

Gardner, H. L., Forehand, R., & Roberts, M. (1976). Time-out with children: Effects of an explanation and brief parent training on child and parent behaviors. *Journal of Abnormal Child Psychology,* 4, 277-288.

Jones Harden, B., M. B. Winslow, et al. (2000). "Externalizing problems in Head Start children: An ecological exploration." *Early Education and Development* 11(3): 357-385.

Henderson, A. and N. Berla (1994). *A new generation of evidence: The Family is critica to student achievement.* Columbia, MD, National Committee for Citizens in Education.

Jouriles, E. N., W. D. Norwood, et al. (1996). "Physical violence and other forms of marital aggression: Links with children's behavior problems." *Journal of Family Psychology* 10(2): 223-234.

Kazdin, A. E. and J. R. Weisz (2003). *Evidence-Based Psychotherapies for Children and Adolescents*. NY, Guilford Press.

Kazdin, A. E. (2002). Psychosocial treatments for conduct disorder in children and adolescents. *A guide to treatments that work*. P. E. Nathan and J. M. Gorman. New York, Oxford University Press: 57-85.

Kendall, P. C., & Braswell, L. (1985). *Cognitive-behavioral therapy for impulsive children*. New York: Guilford Press.

McEvoy, A. and R. Welker (2000). "Antisocial behavior, academic failure and school climate: A critical review." *Journal of Emotional and Behavioral Disorders* 8: 130-140.

Meichenbaum, D. (1979). Teaching children self-control. In B. B. Lahey & A. E. Kazdin, (Eds.), *Advances in clinical child psychology*, (Volume 2). New York: Plenum.

Novaco, R. W. (1978). Anger and coping with stress: Cognitive behavioral intervention. In J. P. Foreyt & D. P. Rathsen (Eds.), *Cognitive behavioral therapy: Research and applications*. New York: Plenum.

Patterson, G. R. (1982). Coercive family process. In *A social learning approach*. 3. Eugene, OR: Castalia.

Raver, C. C. and J. Knitzer (2002). *Ready to enter: What research tells policy makers about strategies to promote social and emotional school readiness among three and four year old children*. Mailman School of Public Health, Columbia University, National Center for Children in Poverty.

Rimm-Kaufman, S. E., R. C. Pianta, et al. (2000). "Teachers' judgements of problems in the transition to kindergarten." *Early Childhood Research Quarterly* 15: 147-166.

Roberts, M. W. McMahon, R. J., Forehand, R., & Humphreys, L. (1978). The effect of parental instruction giving on child compliance. *Behavior Therapy*, 9, 793-798.

Rubin, K. H. (1980). Fantasy play: Its role in the development of social skills and social cognition. In K.H. Rubin (Ed.), *Children and play*. San Francisco: Jossey-Bass.

Schneider, R., & Robin, A. (1976). The turtle technique: A method for the self- control of compulsive behavior. In J. Krumboltz & C. Thoresen (Eds.), *Counseling methods*. New York: Holt, Rhinehart and Winston.

Shure, M. (1994). *I Can Problem Solve (ICPS): An interpersonal cognitive problem- solving program for children*. Champaign, IL, Research Press.

Shure, M. B. (1997). Interpersonal cognitive problem solving: Primary prevention of early high-risk behaviors in the preschool and primary years. *Primary Prevention Works*. G. W. Albee and T. P. Gullotta. Thousand Oaks, CA, Sage: 167-188.

Research by Dr. Webster-Stratton Using Incredible Years Parenting Program

Webster-Stratton, C. (1988). Self administered videotape therapy for families with conduct-problem children: Comparison with two cost-effective treatments and control group. *Journal of Consulting and Clinical Psychology*, 56 (4), 558-566.

Webster-Stratton, C. (1989). The long-term effectiveness and clinical significance of three cost-effective training programs for families with conduct-problem children. *Journal of Consulting and Clinical Psychology*, 57 (4), 550-553.

Webster-Stratton, C. (1990). Stress: A potential disruptor of parent perceptions and family interactions. *Journal of Clinical Child Psychology*, 19 (4), 302-312.

Webster-Stratton, C. (1990). Long-term follow-up of families with young conduct problem children: From preschool to grade school. *Journal of Clinical Child Psychology* 19(2): 144-149.

Webster-Stratton, C. and M. Herbert (1994). *Troubled families—problem children: Working with parents: A collaborative process*. Chichester, Wiley & Sons.

Webster-Stratton, C. and M. Hammond (1997). "Treating children with early-onset conduct problems: A comparison of child and parent training interventions." *Journal of Consulting and Clinical Psychology* 65(1): 93-109.

Webster-Stratton, C. (1998). "Preventing conduct problems in Head Start children: Strengthening parenting competencies." *Journal of Consulting and Clinical Psychology* 66(5): 715-730.

Webster-Stratton, C. (2000). *How to promote social and academic competence in young children*. London, England, Sage Publications.

Webster-Stratton, C. (1991). Coping with conduct-problem children: Parents gaining knowledge and control. *Journal of Clinical Child Psychology*, 20 (4), 413-427.

Webster-Stratton, C., M. J. Reid, et al. (2001). Preventing conduct problems, promoting social competence: A parent and teacher training partnership in Head Start. *Journal of Clinical Child Psychology* 30(3): 283-302.

Webster-Stratton, C., M. J. Reid, et al. (2001). Social skills and problem solving training for children with early-onset conduct problems: Who benefits? *Journal of Child Psychology and Psychiatry* 42(7): 943-952.

Reid, M. J., C. Webster-Stratton, et al. (2001). "Parent training in Head Start: A comparison of program response among African American, Asian American, Caucasian, and Hispanic mothers." *Prevention Science* 2(4): 209-227.

Webster-Stratton, C. and M. J. Reid (2002). An integrated approach to prevention and management of aggressive behavior problems in preschool and elementary students: School-Parent Collaboration. *Interventions for students with emotional and behavioral disorders*. K. Lane, F. Gresham and T. O'Shaughnessy. Needham Heights, MA, Allyn &Bacon: 261-272.

Webster-Stratton, C. and M. J. Reid (2003). "Treating conduct problems and strengthening social emotional competence in young children (ages 4-8 years): The Dina Dinosaur treatment program." *Journal of Emotional and Behavioral Disorders* 11(3): 130-143.

Hartman, R. R., S. Stage, & Webster-Stratton, C. (2003). "A growth curve analysis of parent training outcomes: Examining the influence of child factors (inattention, impulsivity, and hyperactivity problems), parental and family risk factors." *The Child Psychology and Psychiatry Journal* 44(3): 388-398.

Webster-Stratton, C., M. J. Reid, et al. (2004). "Treating children with early-onset conduct problems: Intervention outcomes for parent, child, and teacher training." *Journal of Clinical Child and Adolescent Psychology* 33(1): 105-124.

Webster-Stratton, C. and M. J. Reid (2004). "Strengthening social and emotional competence in young children—The foundation for early school readiness and success: Incredible Years Classroom Social Skills and Problem-Solving Curriculum." *Journal of Infants and Young Children* 17(2).

Webster-Stratton, C. and M. J. Reid (2005). Treatment and Prevention of Conduct Problems: Parent Training Interventions for Young Children (2-7 Years Old). *Blackwell Handbook on Early Childhood Development*. K. McCartney and D. A. Phillips. Malden, MA, Blackwell.

Beauchaine, T. P., C. Webster-Stratton, & Reid, M. J. (2005). "Mediators, moderators, and predictors of one-year outcomes among children treated for early-onset conduct problems: A latent growth curve analysis." *Journal of Consulting and Clinical Psychology.* 73 (3) 371-388.

Other Books for Parents

Barkley, R. A. (2000) *Taking Charge of ADHD – A Complete, Authoritative Guide for Parents.*

Dunn, J. (1984). *Sisters and brothers,* London: Fontana.

Elkind, D. (1987). *Miseducation.* New York: Alfred A. Knopf.

Ferber, R. (1985). *Solve your child's sleep problems.* New York: Simon & Schuster, Inc.

Forehand, R. L., & McMahon, R. J. (1981). *Helping the non-compliant child.* New York: Guilford Press.

Lewinsohn, P. S., & Munuz, R. F., Yongren, M. A., & Zeiss, A. M. (1986). *Control your depression.* Englewood Cliffs, NJ: Prentice-Hall.

Mayle, P. (1979). *Divorce: What shall we tell the children?* London: W.H. Allen.

Patterson, G. R., & Forgatch, M. S., (1987). *Parents and adolescents living together, Part 1: The basics.* Eugene, OR: Castalia Publishing Company.

Patterson, G. R., & Forgatch, M. S. (1989). *Parent and adolescents living together, Part 2: Family problem solving.* Eugene, OR: Castalia Publishing Company.

Satter, E. (1987). *How to get your child to eat...but not too much.* Palo Alto, CA: Bull Publishing Company.

Sutton-Smith, B., & Sutton-Smith, S. (1974). *How to play with your children.* New York: Hawthorn Books, Inc.

Webster-Stratton, C. (1986). Playing with your child. In Fischoff, A. (Ed.), *Birth to three: A self-help program for new parents.* Eugene, OR: Castalia Publishing Company.

Webster-Stratton, C. (1990). *Wally's Detective Book for Solving Problems at School.* Incredible Years, Seattle. (book to be read to children to promote problem solving)

Webster-Stratton, C. (1990). *Wally's Detective Book for Solving Problem at Home* Incredible Years, Seattle. (book to be read to children to promote problem solving)

Index

Abandonment, 87–88, 296–297
Academic coaching, 35–36
Active children, temperament and, 19–20
Active listening, 182–185, 221
ADHD, 285–292
Adolescents and divorce, 294–295
Advocating for your child, 223
Age. See Developmental level
Aggression, 119, 144, 147–148, 153, 178–180, 224, 232–234
Anger
  controlling upsetting thoughts, 162–164, 172–173
  coping strategies, 176–181
  feeling-talk, 187–189
  friendship skills, 154–155
  over divorce, 294
  parental response to, 97–99
  undermining consequences, 116
Apologies after Time Out, 99
Attention, 34, 84–85, 87, 100, 102–103, 164, 244–245, 285–292
Attention rule, 18

Bedtime routines, 261–267
Bedwetting, 115, 281–284
Blaming, 192–193, 195, 200, 203, 222–223
Board games, 32
Bonding, 24
Bribes and rewards, 63

Calming, 138, 165, 173–174, 194–195, 242. See also Time Out; Turtle technique
CARE building blocks, 309–312
Chill bottle, 94
Choices, 277–278
Cognitive development, 233
Commands, 70–77, 79–80, 103–105, 197–198, 257–258
Communication, 30–31
  about divorce, 296–297
  descriptive commenting, 34–35

friendship skills, 147–148, 150
between parents, 173–174, 195–196
parent-teacher communication, 214–221
problem solving using, 199
screen time and, 234, 238
during Time Out, 103
Competition, 32
Complaints, communicating, 189–192, 196, 222
Compliments, 197
Computers, 232–233
Conflict resolution, 104, 153. See also Problem solving
Consequences, 111–117
  of dawdling, 245–246
  following through on commands, 78
  good eating habits and, 279
  overcoming bedwetting, 283
  overcoming sibling rivalry, 251
  problem-solving and, 122, 127–128, 209
  of stealing, 269–270
  "when-then" commands, 77
  See also Time Out
Consistency, 99, 105–107, 136, 197, 289, 298
Cooperative interaction, 32, 151, 155–157, 185–187
Coping thoughts, 169–170, 174
Creativity, 30–33, 207
Criticism, 73–75, 97–98, 125–126, 161–162, 182–187, 192
Crying, 99

Dangerous and abusive behaviors, 85–86
Dawdling, 244–247
Delayed praise, 49
Democracy, 101–102
Depression, 162, 187–189, 294–296, 304
Descriptive commenting, 34–35, 73–74
Discipline, 19, 24, 67–68, 84, 110, 241–242. See also Time Out
Disobedience/noncompliance, 93–96, 102, 256–260
Distraction, 83–84
Divorce, 293–299

Eating habits, 235, 275–280
Emotional health and regulation, 33–34, 133–145, 154–155, 161–175, 199, 309. See also Feelings
Emotional literacy, 36–37
Emotion coaching, 36–37, 150–152
Empathy, 147, 157, 254
Encouragement, 34–35, 46, 101, 129–130, 311
Enthusiasm, 47, 148
Expectations, 18–29, 42, 56–57, 67, 112–113, 201, 206, 233–234, 240, 243, 247
External rewards, 42
Eye contact, 82–83, 87

Fantasy, 33–34, 293–294
Fears, 265–267, 300–307
Feelings, 126, 143, 163, 167–168, 187–189, 204–205, 220, 293–307. See also Emotional health
Filters, communication, 195–196
Fortune-telling, 168–169
Friendship skills, 146–157, 217
Frustration, 72–73, 126

Hitting, 90–91, 93, 95–96, 129–130, 249–250
Honesty, 273
Humor, 167, 201–202

Ignoring, 81–89, 98–99, 245, 262–263, 267, 289
Imaginary friends, 34
Imaginative play, 33–34
"I" messages, 173–174, 185–189, 198, 220–221
Impulse control, 147, 285–292
Incentives. See Rewards
Independent thinking, 30, 32–33, 37–38
Intentions, 168

Labeled praise, 47
Learning, 233–234
Limitations, accepting, 290
Limit-setting, 60–61, 68–80, 85, 101–102, 236–237, 240–241, 288–289. See also Time Out

Logical consequences, 111–112
Loneliness, 146–147
Lying, 91, 271–274

Make-believe play, 33–34
Manipulative behavior, 39, 42–43
Mealtime problems, 275–280
Medication for ADHD, 291
Medication for bedwetting, 284
Modeling behavior
    for ADHD children, 292
    bedtime routines, 264
    compliance, 259–260
    controlling upsetting thoughts, 163, 167
    coping self-talk, 174
    eating habits, 279
    emotional regulation, 135–138, 141
    feeling-talk, 187–189
    friendship skills, 148–150
    honesty, 273
    nonfearful behavior, 304
    problem-solving skills, 119–124, 128
    public behavior, 243
    reading, 312
    screen time, 236–237, 239
    self-praise, 45
    teacher-parent partnerships, 215–216

Nagging, 102
Natural consequences, 111
Night lights, 263, 266
Nighttime wakening, 265–267, 284
Noncompliance/disobedience, 93–96, 102, 256–260
Nonviolent discipline, 19

Overuse of Time Out, 100–101

Parental behavior. See Modeling behavior
Parenting pyramid, 23–25
"Pass the hat" game, 153
Perfection, 170–171
Personality, 19–20
Physical restraint, 103
Planned rewards, 52–53
Play
    academic and emotion coaching, 35–37
    avoiding power struggles, 31–32

benefits of, 40
creative play/fantasy, 32–34
descriptive commenting, 34–35
following the child's lead, 30–31
friendship skills, 146–157
interactive reading, 308–312
misbehavior during, 39
overcoming dawdling, 245
parent-teacher collaborations, 225
problem-solving skills, 37–38
screen time, 232–234, 236–239
sibling rivalry, 255
Polite commands, 75
Politeness in communication, 189–191
Positive behaviors, 86–87, 189–190, 196
Positive response cycle, 162
Positive thoughts, 163, 165, 168–169, 191
Power, responsible use of, 20
Power struggles, 31–32, 104, 197–198,
    256–260, 275–276
Praise
    building up the 'good feelings'
        account, 108–109
    children rejecting, 44
    commands and, 80
    for compliant behavior, 258
    coping with ADHD, 288
    descriptive commenting, 34–35
    developing friendship skills, 149–150,
        152
    effective communication of, 191–192
    emotional regulation, 144–145
    encouraging creative play, 32–33
    encouraging self-praise, 44–45
    following through on commands, 78
    as followup to ignoring, 87
    for good television viewing habits, 238
    honesty, 274
    ignoring positive behaviors, 86–87
    linking to behavior, 44
    manipulative nature of, 42–43
    maximizing the effectiveness of, 46–50
    overcoming dawdling, 245
    overcoming fears, 302
    overcoming stealing, 270
    parent-teacher communication, 214, 220
    for problem solving efforts, 210
    problem solving skills, 131

public behavior, 241
replacing tangible rewards with, 56,
    64–65
self-praise, 50, 166–167, 173
setting expectations through, 43
spoiling children through, 42
Pretend play, 33–34
Privileges, 61, 95–96, 104, 116, 252
Problem solving, 37–38, 118–132
    between adults, 199–211
    aggression as strategy for, 233
    brainstorming, 207–208
    children with ADHD, 289–290, 292
    developing friendship skills, 153
    emotional regulation, 139–140, 142
    goals and expectations, 206–207
    interactive reading to explore, 309
    overcoming fears, 306
    parent-teacher partnerships, 219–223
    planning strategies, 208–210
    sibling rivalry, 249–251
    steps towards effective, 200–203
Public behavior, 106, 240–243
Punishment, 48–49, 115
Put-downs, 48–49

Question commands, 74–75

Reading, 214–215, 217–218, 308–312
Reinforcement, 84, 86–87, 91, 124,
    242–243, 249, 258, 263–264, 267,
    287–288, 301–302, 305. See also
    Praise; Rewards
Rejection, 146–148
Relaxation, 177–181, 276, 306
Remorse over Time Out, 99
Repetitive play, 31
Requests, 197–198
Research methodology, 22–23
Responsibility, 114–115, 255, 283
Rewards and incentives, 52–69
    choosing appropriate rewards, 60–69
    coping with ADHD, 288
    developing friendship skills, 152,
        156–157
    examples of tangible rewards, 54–55
    external, 42
    good eating habits, 278–279

objectives of, 56–60
overcoming bedwetting, 282
overcoming dawdling, 245
overcoming fears, 303
overcoming sibling rivalry, 251
parent-teacher collaborations, 223–225
spontaneous and planned, 52–53
versus Time Out, 90–91
Role playing, 34, 148–150, 311
Routines, establishing, 246–247, 261–264
Rules, 71–74, 241

Scheduling anger time, 163–164
School programs for ADHD, 291–292
School readiness skills, 35–36, 233–234,
   308–312
Screen time, 151, 214–215, 232–239
Self-control, 84, 99, 176–181, 199, 289
Self-criticism, 192
Self-esteem, 39, 42, 44, 146–148
Self-image, 145
Self-management, 128–129
Self-praise, 50, 166–167, 173
Self-talk, 138–139, 154, 165, 167, 170–171,
   176–177, 180, 247, 305–306
Separation anxiety, 261, 303–304
Sharing, 124–125
Sibling rivalry, 248–255
Skill building through academic
   coaching, 35–36
Sleep. See Bedtime routines; Nighttime
   wakening
Social skills, 30–31, 64–65, 135–136,
   224, 240–241, 292, 306. See also
   Friendship skills; Problem solving
Spankings, 103, 162, 208–209
Spoiling children, 42
Start commands, 75–76
Stealing, 168–169, 268–270
Sticker dependence, 64–65
Stop action, 189, 194–195
Stress, 162, 172–173, 176–181, 281–283,
   293
Study schedules, 214–215
Support. See Praise

Talking. See Communication
Tangible rewards. See Rewards

Tantrums, 32, 82–83, 85–86, 240–242,
   301–303
Targeted praise, 50
Tattling, 249
Teachers, 69, 155–157, 209, 212–227,
   287, 312
Teasing, 146
Television. See Screen time
Temperament, 19–20, 44, 119, 135–136,
   147–148, 260
Testing limits, 82–83, 96–97, 259
Thought interruption, 163
Thought-stop, 169–170
Threats, 87–88
Three Strikes Rule, 98–99
Time Out, 78, 90–110
   calming after, 94, 100
   consequences and, 116
   for dawdling, 246
   emotional regulation, 142–143
   noncompliance, 258–259
   problem solving skills, 123
   public behavior, 242
   refusal to go, 95–96
   sibling rivalry, 251
   strategies for, 91–97
   stress, anger, and negative thoughts,
      171, 176–181
   table behavior and, 279
Time projection for controlling stress, 166
Toddlers, Time Out for, 93
Truce, 189
Turtle technique, 140–142, 154–155, 164

Validating problems, 193
Video games, 232–233, 236–239
Viewpoint, child's, 124–125, 129–131
Violence, 19, 178–180, 232–234

Whining, 83, 85–86, 101

Yes-butting, 196